# ON THE POETRY OF GALWAY KINNELL

UNDER DISCUSSION
Donald Hall, General Editor

# On the Poetry of Galway Kinnell:

*The Wages of Dying*

Edited by Howard Nelson

*Ann Arbor*
THE UNIVERSITY OF MICHIGAN PRESS

1990   1989   1988   1987   4   3   2   1


Library of Congress Cataloging-in-Publication Data

On the poetry of Galway Kinnell.

   (Under discussion)
   Bibliography: p.
   1. Kinnell, Galway, 1927–      —Criticism and
interpretation.   I. Nelson, Howard, 1947–      .
II. Series.
PS3521.I582Z8   1987      811'.54      87-19226
ISBN 0-472-09376-2 (alk. paper)
ISBN 0-472-06376-6 (pbk. : alk. paper)

*To the memory of Henry O. Nelson and Thomas I. Myers*

The mind may sort it out and give it names—
When a man dies he dies trying to say without slurring
The abruptly decaying sounds. It is true
That only flesh dies, and spirit flowers without stop
For men, cows, dung, for all dead things; and it is good,
   yes—

But an incarnation is in particular flesh
And the dust that is swirled into a shape
And crumbles and is swirled again had but one shape
That was this man. When he is dead the grass
Heals what he suffered, but he remains dead,
And those who loved him know this until they die.
             —from "Freedom, New Hampshire" (adapted)

# Editor's Note

I realize that books of this kind are likely to be read piecemeal, as the reader picks and chooses according to names and topics that interest him or her most. Still, I hope the organization gives a useful shape to the welter of opinion and analysis Kinnell's poetry has elicited, just as I hope to have fairly represented the full spectrum of response.

There are people I want to thank. I am grateful to Donald Hall for giving me the opportunity to assemble the book, and for his correspondence, criticism, and advice throughout the project. I am grateful to Galway Kinnell for his help with the chronology and for sharing some of his worksheets with me; and to the writers who wrote essays especially for this book: Robert Bly, Joseph Bruchac, Paul Mariani, William Matthews, John Unterecker, Marsha Peterson White, and Anne Wright. Cayuga Community College granted me aid in the form of some release time from teaching. The Cayuga Community College Library has been an excellent base of operations for research, and I am indebted to the staff there—Doug Michael, Kathy McCullough, Kathy Long, Judy Campanella, Nagulinie Singanayagam, and especially Martha Lollis, who deserves a line on the title page. I appreciate very much the help of Linda Howe—her sharp eyes and copyediting expertise. Finally, I thank my family—Stephanie, Sarah, Zack, Tess, and my mother, Dorothy Nelson—for their support, which comes in many forms.

# Contents

## Part Three   Appraisals—Notes and Essays

## Part Four   Focus on Poems

# Introduction

*The Weight of Words, the Road between Here and There*

Reading the poems of Galway Kinnell, I feel a distinctive weight in his words. I don't mean just that he writes the opposite of light verse—witty, ironic, sprightly in thought and rhythm—though that would be true enough; nor that he writes on large themes in a serious or even solemn manner, though that too would be a fair generalization. I mean something else, both more specific and mysterious: that through the resources of Kinnell's art and spirit, words in his poems take on exceptional gravity; that whatever "uplift" they may offer, they also pull us down. Intelligence becomes less cerebral and involves the heart and other old caves of the body, and poetry resists becoming what someone has called "upper-brain-roof-chatter" and dwells among earthly things, and consciousness deepens, running in the deeper passages of life. I want to elaborate a little on my metaphor of weight, as a way of setting what I see as the crucial characteristics of Kinnell's work in the foreground before the discussion and debate of this collection begin.

The first element that contributes to the weight is imagery. The early long poem, "The Avenue Bearing the Initial of Christ into the New World," prophesied the abundance of vibrant, sharply observed images Kinnell's poetry would continue to contain. He has said, "Part of poetry's usefulness in the world is that it pays some of our huge unpaid tribute to the things and creatures that share the earth with us." He has paid that tribute steadily, and the things and creatures, in turn, have lent their palpable weight to the poems.

But it is a matter of more than abundance. There are poets

whose poems have many images, and yet the final effect is only an elegant play of sensibility. With Kinnell, it is not the number of images that is remarkable, but a strange, shining density he instills in them. This quality requires skill in description, but it derives also from a way of seeing things. He says, "If the things and creatures that live on earth don't possess mystery, there isn't any." He is stubborn in his commitment to the earthly and in his experience of finding the spiritual in physical things. For him, porcupines and dogs can rightly be understood as angels. He appears at times as a kind of evangelist of the physical world; and his images have the capacity to make us believe.

There is a moment in "Flower Herding on Mount Monadnock" when Kinnell walks out in the early morning and hears a bird's call; then, "The song of the whippoorwill stops / And the dimension of depth seizes everything." It is like that frequently in his poems: the dimension of depth takes hold of the images, and things take on clarity and weight in the pressures of that depth. The images exist in the poems as certain sights and sounds exist forever in memory.

> I think I want to go back now and live again in the present
>     time, back there
> where someone milks a cow and jets of intensest nourishment
>     go squawking into a pail,
> where someone is hammering, a bit of steel at the end of a
>     stick hitting a bit of steel, in the archaic stillness of an
>     afternoon . . .

> ("First Day of the Future")

What Kinnell describes is not always beautiful, of course; far from it, as "The Bear" and other of his best-known poems illustrate. (And "The Bear," whatever else it may be about, is about deeply inhabiting the physical, the mammal body, with its senses and strange hair and scents.) Any number of poems or passages might be chosen, but I will let "Saint Francis and the Sow" stand for the physical brilliance and weight in Kinnell's poetry: words of blessing for a heavy creature, a mother on the earth, almost the earth herself in the person of the pig. If it begins to sound as if I use "earth" as a magical word, I mean to; for Kinnell it is.

as Saint Francis
put his hand on the creased forehead
of the sow, and told her in words and in touch
blessings of earth on the sow, and the sow
began remembering all down her thick length,
from the earthen snout all the way
through the fodder and slops to the spiritual curl of the tail,
from the hard spininess spiked out from the spine
down through the great broken heart
to the sheer blue milken dreaminess spurting and shuddering
from the fourteen teats into the fourteen mouths sucking and
    blowing beneath them:
the long, perfect loveliness of sow.

Not just the concrete nouns, like "snout" and "spine," but also the adjectives, "creased" and "blue milken," and perhaps especially the pungent verbs like "shudder" and "spurt," "suck" and "blow"—all contribute to the poem's sensuous life, until even words like "spiritual" and "dreaminess" seem embodied.

Kinnell has not written much criticism, but what he has written is worth the attention of anyone interested in contemporary poetry and is essential for anyone wanting a full sense of Kinnell. The collection of revised interviews, *Walking Down the Stairs* (1978), is not criticism exactly, but it describes his basic intentions and poetic values well. Among the essays, two are especially important: "Poetry, Personality, and Death," and "The Poetics of the Physical World." These essays, written in the early seventies, are original, didactic, and eloquent. Here is a passage, as much prose-poem as criticism, from "The Poetics of the Physical World," in which Kinnell comments on the place of the image in modern poetry:

Why does it seem, in the modern poem, that the less formal beauty there is, the more possible it is to discover the glory of the ordinary? I think of Donatello's statue in wood of Magdalen: her body ravaged, her face drawn with suffering, her hair running down her body indistinguishable from her rags. She is in ruins. Yet her feet remain beautiful. The reason they are beautiful is that they have touched the earth all their life. In the same way, in the bedraggled poem of the modern, it is the images, those lowly touchers of physical reality, which remain shining.

Then there is his music. A good deal of contemporary poetry does not lose much when read only with the eye and the brain, but Kinnell's requires the tongue, throat, and chest as well. It must be spoken, even if very quietly, to be truly appreciated. Once again, intelligence becomes sensuous.

Like many of his contemporaries, Kinnell began writing in meter and rhyme but grew restless and adopted freer forms. For some poets, for contemporary poetry in general, including now the work of those brought up in open form, the shift entailed a considerable muting of musical effects. In Kinnell's case, however, the move to free verse brought him into a new and richer music.

In a poem that I discuss later, "The Road Between Here and There," Kinnell says, "Here I forgot how to sing in the old way and listened to frogs at dusk make their more angelic croaking." An earlier version of that line read, "Here I forgot to sing in the old way, permanently, and learned from the frogs at dusk, as well as from Smart and Whitman[,] my peculiar croaking." Neither Walt Whitman nor Christopher Smart (we are speaking here of the Smart of *Jubilate Agno,* not "A Song to David") sing in what suffices for music in much recent work: colloquial speech rhythms, the minor music of talk. Both of them, and the frogs in their own way too, sing with elaborate repetitions and variations, and rhythms that are entrancing, in the strong sense of that word. Their singing is at once free, instinctual, and artful. They also have amplitude. Their musics have not forgotten the chant, the croon, the background drone, the sound of waves. The same is true of Kinnell's. He lacks the sense of abandon we find in Whitman and Smart, and he only now and then achieves cadences that one might want to call biblical, but he does flow out on a generous, sonorous flow of language.

When he referred in an interview (speaking of Whitman) to "the rhythm of what's being said," Kinnell did not mean that whatever is said has sufficient rhythm for poetry, but that there are rhythms "so expressive that one could take away the words and still almost convey the whole meaning." A tall order. Yet it is the case that through involved syntax, enjambments, parallelism, and variations in line length, Kinnell creates lagging, varied rhythms that function as a bass line, an underpinning, for the other music of meaning. Particularly from his third book *Body Rags* onward, he writes a raggedly yet richly cadenced poetry that cannot be either scanned or skimmed; its gradual, sinuous uncoiling prohibits both. His poems generally look unlike Whitman's on the page, and his rhythmic phrasings rarely come in such large sweeps—but in spite of the differences, at times when I read Kinnell and notice the undermusic, a line from "Song of Myself" comes into my mind: "Only the lull I like, the hum of your valvèd voice."

Here I may be influenced by having heard Kinnell read his poems, for he is a great reader—or reciter rather: he usually speaks his poems from memory, book or manuscript held in his hand but rarely looked at. Once having heard him, I cannot easily separate the written voice in the poems from the spoken voice. Probably most readers of this book will share this problem—if we want to call it that—for Kinnell has read as often and as widely as any contemporary poet.

Just as his poems have a strong rhetoric while eschewing the exclamatory, so his way of speaking poems is both passionate and soft-spoken. He has a commanding presence, solid and dark, reticent and self-possessed. His voice has good timbre. But what is most memorable about his readings are the cadences, the flow and eddies of the language—the rhythmic hum of the voice.

That, and his care for the individual words, their shape and weight on the tongue. There is a beauty in his enunciation—a subtle thing, each word firmly and delicately grasped for its instant as it is sent out onto the air. This care in speaking words is an expression of the love of words one sees in the poems themselves. It is clear that for him words are alive. He thinks of them, for example, not as becoming obsolete, but extinct: "When I encounter an old word on the verge of extinction, which seems expressive, I feel excited. I can't help entertaining the possibility of rescuing it. . . ." Dylan Thomas described his first step in becoming a writer as falling in love with words, the finite, tactile, aural creatures themselves, almost detached from meaning: "The first thing was to feel and know their sound and substance." Reading Kinnell's poems, or listening to him speak them, one hears another poet who has not lost that kind of appreciation. It may seem odd to compare these poets, their moods being generally so far apart, but the point of connection is that they both have a rich language, a sensual joy in words: Kinnell is like a soberer, more restrained Thomas, just as in his inspired passages of description, where he taps into the in-stress of a thing, he resembles a Hopkins without the springing rhythms, a Hopkins with heavier bones.

The handiest touchstone for Kinnell's love for words themselves would be "Blackberries" (quoted in Donald Hall's essay in this collection), a perfectly realized lyric, in which he pays equal and intertwining homage to both the things of the world and the words by which we name them. In it, eating ripe berries becomes a "silent, startled, icy, black language," and words like "strengths" and "squinched" become "many-lettered, one-syl-labled lumps" that "fall almost unbidden to my tongue," like the berries—"which I squeeze, squinch open, and splurge well." Very few contemporary poets care or dare or are able to com-municate the peculiar pleasure of words on the tongue as vividly as Kinnell.

The love of words leads at times to a certain exoticism, as when Kinnell occasionally brings in archaisms or words from other languages—"the violinist effleurages out of the chanterelle / the C three octaves above middle C"—or when he works and packs a line very elaborately, as when he describes a piece of driftwood and notes that "a plane's long, misericording shhhhhhhhh's long ago soothed away the halo fragments the sawmill's circular saw had tormented across its planes." Both of these examples are from recent work, where his handling of language tends to be most lavish. In generalizing across his ca-reer as I am doing, they are not unprecedented but neither are they representative, for Kinnell's savoring and weighing of words includes simple and common ones as well. At the begin-ning of *The Book of Nightmares* the poet sits in the rain and speaks a few words into the fire he has made: "*stone    saint    smooth stone.*" It is a ritual moment, but instead of invoking the muse he invokes words, with their particular sounds, contours, textures,

and weights; he is like a man pausing and holding in his hands the material with which he is about to build.

As a last example of this aural, almost tactile attentiveness to language, I will cite not one of the grander passages, which some readers call purple and others glorious, but rather stanzas from a short-lined love poem from Kinnell's second book, *Flower Herding on Mount Monadnock*—"Poem of Night":

> I move my hand over
> Slopes, falls, lumps of sight,
> Lashes barely able to be touched,
> Lips that give way so easily
> It's a shock to feel under them
> The hard smile of bones.
>
> Muffled a little, barely cloaked,
> Zygoma, maxillary, turbinate.

The anatomical names for the bones of the face are as strange and hard as the bones they stand for, and clearly Kinnell wants us to note them with care and curiosity, just as the man in the poem touches the face of his lover. More important, however, than the inclusion of these unusual words is the work with the simpler words that precede them. The poem is hushed. For the first four lines it is all smoothness, quiet, gentle touching, and this is expressed through the sounds—liquids, sibilants, and open vowels, *l*'s, *s*'s, and *o*'s, with only a delicate presence of harder consonant sounds, *p*'s and *b*'s: a delicate touching in the darkness. The speaker's sudden consciousness of the bones—and of what they must remind us, at one level or another—enters at just the moment of the first truly hard sound, "shock." "Hard smile" has little sound value, and it occurs where the speaker's reverie has been interrupted by the thought of death. Now that both the beauty of the face and the awareness of the bones beneath it are fully in mind, the two are held together in a line that blends liquid *l*'s and hard *c*'s and *k*'s; the latter are, precisely, "barely cloaked." Then, the less lyrical affection, or perhaps I should say the odder lyricism, of "Zygoma, maxillary, turbinate." Then,

> I put my hand
> On the side of your face,
> You lean your head a little
> Into my hand—and so,
> I know you're a dormouse
> Taken up in winter sleep,
> A lonely, stunned weight.

In these stanzas one can see—or rather hear—a man holding not only the delicate weight of a woman's face, but that of words as well.

Kinnell has a way of concentrating on a subject until it seems that he has brought the poem down to a level of essential saying—as if he had found the true specific gravity of the subject, as if he had seen the shape behind the shape, the elemental behind the particular. One can look, for example, at the fire-lighting scene at the beginning of *The Book of Nightmares* and see an experience deliberately distilled to an archetypal form, but one can look also at other, more particularized fires, such as the earlier one in "Middle of the Way" or the later one in "Break of Day," and still sense behind the poem's details the fundamental timeless act carried out at its center.

This quality in his work can be related to various statements Kinnell has made. For example, "I know it's the dream of every poem to be a myth," and later, "When I said that, I don't know if I meant myth in the usual sense. Perhaps I meant that the poem is a kind of paradigm of what the human being wants to say to the cosmos." Or,

> Often a poem at least starts out being about oneself, about one's experiences, a fragment of autobiography. But then, if it's really a poem, it goes deeper than personality. It takes on that strange voice, intensely personal yet common to everyone, in which all rituals are spoken. A poem expresses one's most private feelings; and these turn out to be the feelings of everyone else as well. . . . The poem becomes simply the voice of a creature on earth speaking.

Perhaps it is related also to the comment made in conversation to Donald Hall: "I have no interest in any poem to which the poet does not bring everything he knows." As Hall notes in his essay included in this book, it is easy to exaggerate or oversimplify the high seriousness implied by such a remark, for it seems to rule out small lyrics on modest subjects—of which Kinnell has written a good many. Hall cites "Blackberry Eating" and says, "Certainly Galway Kinnell has not brought everything he knows to this poem." He is right—partly. In another way, though, Kinnell did say everything he knew when he wrote the poem. Everything he knew about blackberry eating, or at least the essence of the experience: the true, sweet juice; a man savoring among the thorny stalks the fruit of this world and of language, like a grateful Adam.

This quality of "essential saying" is evidenced, I think, by another series of comments—certain kinds of comments that crop up repeatedly in criticism of Kinnell's work. For example, when the Australian poet Andrew Taylor speaks of Kinnell's poems' "extraordinary totality, their air of having said all there is to say," or when Alan Williamson notes "those frequent moments of stunned sensation in which human beings turn into force and object, and nature into embodied metaphysics, before our eyes." Or, from different angles, when Marsha Peterson White says of a poem against suicide, "Among the major sequences, the memorable lyrics, and other often-anthologized pieces of Galway Kinnell, 'Wait' is an inconspicuous poem— until you are suffering the desolation that stems from bereavement, abandonment, betrayal, or loss. When you are in need of counsel that is wise, calm, and painfully honest, then you will count the poem among Kinnell's masterpieces." Or when Ted Solotaroff, in his essay on "The Ultimate Project of Technology," Kinnell's poem on nuclear destruction, speaks of "the deep circuitry of the collective mind into which the poem has now tapped." Or when Richard Tillinghast says of "Little Sleep's-Head Sprouting Hair in the Moonlight," "I can think of no more moving statement of a parent's heart-breakingly illogical hope of shielding a child from the death he accepts for himself." The motif would include Harold Bloom's complaint

about "a certain overambition that makes of each separate poem too crucial an event," and also his comment elsewhere in the same review that "'Flying Home' will convey an authentic shock of recognition to anyone who has shared recently in that experience."

This is argument by collage, but the point is that Kinnell attempts and is often able, more often and more surely than all but a very few, to render the essence of experiences; to drive, as Thoreau would say, his spikes into beams and not lathe and plaster; to pronounce the words that lie at the bottom of an experience like stones in a stream.

There are moments of sudden joy and awakening in Kinnell's poems, when "a lark bursts up all dew" or a crow cries "from a branch nothing cried from ever in my life." But never too far off is "the cow, the cow / of nothingness, mooing / down the bones." Or emptiness, the word he more often employs. When his daughter is born he sees her "slow, / beating, featherless arms / already clutching at the emptiness." "Poem of Night," with its beautiful intimacy in the dark, concludes with these lines:

> I think of a few bones
> Floating on a river at night,
> The starlight blowing in place on the water,
> The river leaning like a wave toward the emptiness.

As he approaches the end of his most ambitious work, *The Book of Nightmares,* he writes:

> This is the tenth poem
> and it is the last. It is right
> at the last, that one
> and zero
> walk off together,
> walk off the end of these pages together,
> one creature
> walking away side by side with the emptiness.

Examples could be multiplied. Like "earth," "emptiness" is one of Kinnell's crucial words.

Possibly this recognition of emptiness is an insight into the nature of things. Without doubt, it is a description of a spiritual condition, highly and variously developed in modern people, though by no means original with them. From early on in his poetry Kinnell struggles with this emptiness—this gnawing loneliness, this self-consciousness, this sense of incompleteness or separation so persistent that it sometimes seems that only the loss of consciousness itself could finally cure it. He does not overcome the problem; but he has brooded, thought, and felt his way to an understanding of it, and it turns out that while the emptiness diminishes life it can also intensify it. Paradoxes. The emptiness is a weight like lead in Kinnell's poetry. It is also the agent that can turn lead to gold. As he summarizes the equation at the end of one poem, "Goodbye," "It is written in our hearts, the emptiness is all. / That is how we have learned, the embrace is all." Among other things, this understanding enhances the beauty and importance of poetry. Its crosscurrents can be felt in the absolutes and qualifications that press against one another in the final lines of his poem to Etheridge Knight: "sing to us / here, in this place that loses its brothers, / in this emptiness only the singing sometimes almost fills."

This sort of paradoxical understanding does not make Kinnell a unique figure. Rather, it places him within a major tradition in modern poetry—the line that asks "what to make of a diminished thing," and includes in their various ways Eliot's negative path to revelation, Stevens's insight that "death is the mother of beauty," and Yeats's knowledge that "all the ladders start, / in the foul rag-and-bone shop of the heart."

The emptiness Kinnell speaks of cannot really be separated from two other factors; ultimately they may be three aspects of the same situation. The second is the sense of the world's brokenness: the full awareness of how bedraggled, vulnerable, and hacked a thing life tends to be. This awareness may cause a man to hold his child tighter in middle of the night, and it may lead him into political work and protest: field work in the civil rights movement, poetry readings against the Vietnam War, poems such as "The Last River" and "The Ultimate Project of Technology." The third factor is time and mortality, Kinnell's obsessive theme.

In "The Poetics of the Physical World" he recasts his understanding of the emptiness in terms of time and eternity:

> It is through something radiant in our lives that we have been able to dream of paradise, that we have been able to invent the realm of eternity. But there is another kind of glory in our lives which derives precisely from our inability to enter that paradise or to experience eternity. That we last only for a time, that we know this, radiates a thrilling, tragic light on all our loves, all our relationships, even on those moments when the world, through its poetry, becomes almost capable of spurning time and death.

Kinnell's poetry represents in large part an extraordinary four-decades-long and still ongoing meditation on time and mortality. It runs from the early poem "Meditation Among the Tombs," through "Freedom, New Hampshire," Kinnell's great elegy to his brother, whose death at thirty-two no doubt embedded the elegiac impulse all the deeper inside him, down through many memorable poems, such as "Spindrift" and the title piece in *Flower Herding on Mount Monadnock,* and the more ragged, almost runic lyrics of *Body Rags,* such as "Last Songs," "The Falls," and "The Poem." It runs through the heart of *The Book of Nightmares,* which contains the lines that many critics have pointed out as a key formulation of Kinnell's vision of death: "*the wages / of dying is love.*" It continues in *Mortal Acts, Mortal Words,* the title taken from lines by Petrarch that return us to the metaphor of weight: ". . . mortal beauty, acts, and words have put all their burden on my soul."

In the opening poem of that book, "Fergus Falling," the poet's young son climbs a pine tree, and when he reaches the top he catches sight of the pond in the valley—or rather sees "its oldness," for the pond has already been thoroughly associated in the father's mind and in the poem with lives that have touched it and now are gone. Kinnell says that when the boy glimpsed the pond he "became heavier suddenly / in his bones . . . / and the soft pine cracked." Thus the fall into time is gracefully captured in the poem's small narrative. Kinnell has gazed at "the oldness" intently throughout his life as a poet, and the heaviness in his bones can be felt in his poems—in the vibrant etching of their images, in their sensuous, earthbound music, in the intentness and seriousness with which they hold their subjects within them.

The meditation on time and mortality continues in Kinnell's most recent collection, as its title, *The Past,* indicates. Though he can make fun of his persistence in this theme—" . . . even though I squandered all my talents composing my emigration papers"—he nonetheless persists. Approaching sixty, his children grown, some of his close friends and contemporaries dead, gone already "back to the end," he looks at transience and mortality now, not with greater emotional intensity, but with a new complexity. There is an awareness in many of the poems of having arrived in a new world, "the future." He wishes it were the present, the eternal now of *what is.* Sometimes this future he inhabits is almost transfigured by the dual knowledge of all that has come before it and of time running out. At other times it seems disappointing. Notes of calm, bemusement, gratitude, and desperation are all sounded, sometimes in the same chord:

> The rails may never meet, O fellow Euclideans,
> for you, for me. So what if we groan?
> That's our noise. Laughter is our stuttering
> in a language we can't speak yet. Behind,
> the world made of wishes goes dark. Ahead,
> if not tomorrow then never, shines only what is.

One of the most beautiful poems in *The Past* is "The Road Between Here and There." I would like to end by quoting and commenting on this poem, not only because it represents recent work but also because it recapitulates the points I have tried to highlight in this introduction, and some of Kinnell's fundamental images and loves as well.

Here I heard the terrible chaste snorting of hogs trying to re-
enter the underearth.

Here I came into the curve too fast, on ice, and being new to
these winters, touched the brake and sailed into the
pasture.

Here I stopped the car and snoozed while two small children
crawled all over me.

Here I reread *Moby Dick* (skimming big chunks, even though
to me it is the greatest of all novels) in a single day, while
Fergus fished.

Here I abandoned the car because of a clonk in the motor and
hitchhiked (which in those days in Vermont meant
walking the whole way with a limp) all the way to a
garage where I passed the afternoon with ex-loggers who
had stopped by to oil the joints of their artificial limbs.

Here a barn burned down to the snow. "Friction," one of the
ex-loggers said. "Friction?" "Yup, the mortgage rubbing
against the insurance policy."

Here I went eighty but was in no danger of arrest, for I was
"blessed speeding"—trying to get home in time to see my
children before they slept.

Here I bought speckled brown eggs with bits of straw shitted
to them.

Here I brought home in the back seat two piglets who
rummaged inside the burlap sack like pregnancy itself.

Here I heard on the car radio Handel's concerto for harp and
lute for the second time in my life, which Inés played to
me the first time, making me want to drive after it and
hear it forever.

Here I hurt with mortal thoughts and almost recovered.

Here I sat on a boulder by the winter-streaming river and put
my head in my hands and considered time—which is next
to nothing, merely what vanishes, and yet can make one's
elbows nearly pierce one's thighs.

Here I forgot how to sing in the old way and listened to frogs
at dusk make their more angelic croaking.

Here the local fortune teller took my hand and said, "What is

still possible is inspired work, faithfulness to a few, and a
last love, which, being last, will be like looking up and
seeing the parachute dissolving in a shower of gold."
Here is the chimney standing up by itself and falling down,
which tells you you approach the end of the road between
here and there.
Here I arrive there.
Here I must turn around and go back and on the way back
look carefully to left and to right.
For here, the moment all the spaces along the road between
here and there—which the young know are infinite and all
others know are not—get used up, that's it.

In a postscript to Paul Zweig's posthumous collection *Eternity's Woods,* Kinnell speaks of Zweig's poems' freedom, intensity, and "idolatrous attachments." In his elegy for James Wright in *The Past,* "Last Holy Fragrance," he writes,

It will be a long time before anyone comes
who can lull the words he will not now ever use
—words which, now he has left, turn this way and that—
hum and coax them to press up against,
shape themselves by, know, true-love, and idolize.

"The Road Between Here and There" is a generous, at times whimsical poem, a pleasure in its catalogue of vivid particulars, but beneath these qualities lies, as always in Kinnell, a seriousness, for the poem is also a catalogue of idolatrous attachments. The words "idolize" and "idolatrous," as his use of them in reference to these two men whose work and lives he deeply admires suggests, are for Kinnell positive ones—though they have also an edge that acknowledges the desperation or anxiety or sadness of a man who accepts that his faith is one that offers no transcendent reassurances. To call an attachment idolatrous is to say that it is important and passionate and that its object is finite and will perish.

Included in the poem's catalogue is much that dwells at the center of Kinnell's imagination and attachment to the world. There is the love of children, whom we love not merely because

The Road Between Here and There
==============================

Here I heard the terrible chaste snorting of hogs trying to
    re-enter the underearth.

Here I came into the curve too fast, on ice, and touched the ~~being new to Vermont~~ [*being new to Vermont*]
    brake pedal and ~~ended up in~~ *slid into* the pasture.

Here I stopped the car and ~~snoozed~~ *slept deeply* while two small children
    crawled all over me.

Here I re-read <u>Moby Dick</u> (skimming large chunks, even though
    to me it is the greatest of all novels) in a single day,
    while Fergus fished.

Here I abandoned the car because of an odd clonk in the motor
    and hitchhiked (which in those days in Vermont meant walking
    the whole way with a limp) the whole way to a garage where
    ·I passed the afternoon with ex-loggers who *had* dropped by to
    oil the joints of their artificial limbs and tell lies.

Here a barn burned down to the snow. "Friction," one of the
    ex-loggers said. "Friction?" ~~I said~~. "Yup, ~~friction,~~"
    he said, "the mortgage rubbing against the insurance policy".

Here I went eighty but was not arrested for I was "blessed-
    speeding"--trying to get home in time to see my children
    before they slept.

Here I bought speckled brown eggs with bits of straw shitted
    to them.

Here I brought home in the back seat two piglets who rummaged
    inside the burlap sack like pregnancy itself.

Here I hurt with mortal thoughts and yet / almost recovered.
    insert ( )

Galway Kinnell is an assiduous and continuous reviser. This
worksheet of "The Road Between Here and There" shows the poem
in process and is one of several earlier versions that he kindly made
available to me. — ED.

~~Here I~~ sat on a boulder by the steaming river ~~while~~ *and* the weight
~~of my head made my elbows~~ nearly pierce my thighs.

Here I thought more about time than one should -- ~~for it is~~
nothing -- but what vanished out from under during thought.
Here I found a man my age doing the crossword puzzle in front
of the TV, either not knowing, or knowing too keenly, all
that's left ~~is~~ love like throwing oneself out of an airplane
~~and visionary work.~~

Here I heard on the car radio Handel's concerto for harp and
flute for the second time in my life, which Inés had played
to me for the first time, making me want to drive after
it and hear it forever.

Here I forgot how to sing in the old way, permanently, and learned
from the frogs at dusk~~, as well as from Smart and Whitman~~
my ~~peculiar~~ *new life's* croaking.

Here is the chimney standing up by itself and falling down, which
tells one one approaches the end of the road between here
and there.

Here I arrive there.

Here I must turn around and go back and on the way back look
carefully to left and to right.

For here, the moment *all* the spaces along the road between here and
there, which the young know are infinite ~~and~~ *but* the rest ~~of~~
~~us~~ know are not, ~~all~~ get used up, the road ~~disappears into~~
~~the grave.~~ *ends.*

they are ours but also because they manifest our deepest connections with life itself: intimacy, vulnerability, continuity. The brokenness of human beings is here, both in the loggers with their lost limbs, and in the poet who "hurt with mortal thoughts and almost recovered." Love for a woman. The passion of great art. The insistence, wry but real, that the spiritual be met among earthly creatures, human and nonhuman: "blessed speeding" to see his children, the frogs' "angelic croaking." Animals, for their own sakes and for their closeness to the fundamental cycles: the pigs associated with death in the opening line, and later with birth. The image of falling to earth. The weight of the knowledge of time, "which is next to nothing, merely what vanishes, and yet can make one's elbows nearly pierce one's thighs."

In "The Road Between Here and There" we find images drawn with firm, bold, relaxed strokes, expressing great affection and loyalty to the world of physical things. The poem has the incantatory music of long, full-breathed lines and parallelisms, but also the pleasure of the shape and vividness of individual words and phrases—"chaste snorting," "snooze," "clonk," "piglets," "concerto for harp and lute"—and of the sounds within them clicking and reverberating against one another—"Here I bought speckled brown eggs with bits of straw shitted to them." It is a seemingly random and personal list, yet many of the pieces will seem familiar to most readers, as will the way in which a life is in memory strangely made up of such fragments. And perhaps it is the awareness of time and mortality that stands behind it all, defining and anchoring everything in clarity and gravity.

Kinnell brings the long last sentence, and the fullness of the poem, to an abrupt end with the five almost stutterlike monosyllables, "get used up, that's it." That's how it is with our lives: whatever they may contain, finally, more or less suddenly, we are cut off, that's it. But along the way, there are these indelible things—places, happenings, creatures, relationships—and this ability, not just to stutter or groan, but to name, know, and sing them in the weighted song of true poems.

# Chronology

Galway Kinnell has earned his living for the most part through teaching and giving poetry readings. In both activities he has been extremely peripatetic, with New York City and Sheffield, Vermont, as his primary home bases. I haven't included in this chronology all of the many colleges and universities at which he has taught. As for the readings, I mention only a few that are notable for some special reason.

1927   Born February 1, 1927, Providence, Rhode Island, fourth of four children of Elizabeth Mills and James Scott Kinnell. Parents are both immigrants to the United States, mother from Ireland and father from Scotland. Father earns living as carpenter and teacher of woodworking.

1932–43   Grows up in Pawtucket; attends public schools until final year of high school, when he is awarded a scholarship to attend Wilbraham Academy in Massachusetts. At Wilbraham he meets Roger Nye Lincoln, an English teacher who encourages him in writing.

1944   Enters Princeton; meets W. S. Merwin.

1944–46   Serves in U.S. Navy. Is sent back to Princeton for officer training program; meets and studies with Charles G. Bell.

1947   Spends summer at Black Mountain College.

1948   Graduates from Princeton, *summa cum laude.*

1949   Receives M.A. from University of Rochester.

1951–55   Lives in Chicago.

1955   Goes to France on a Fulbright grant. Stays two years.

1956   Translation of Rene Hardy's *Bitter Victory* published.

1957   Brother, Derry, dies in car crash.

1957–59   Lives on the Lower East Side in New York City.

| 1959 | Travels in Far East. |
|---|---|
| 1959–60 | Fulbright lecturer and journalist in Iran. |
| 1960 | *What a Kingdom It Was* is published. |
| 1961 | Buys abandoned farm in northern Vermont. |
| 1963 | Works in voter registration campaign for the Congress of Racial Equality in Louisiana. These activities lead to a week in jail and the poem "The Last River." |
| 1964 | *Flower Herding on Mount Monadnock* is published. |
| 1965 | Marries Inés Delgado de Torres. Translation of *Poems of François Villon* is published. Participates in Poets for Peace reading at Town Hall, New York City, the first of many anti–Vietnam War readings in which he will take part. |
| 1966 | Birth of daughter, Maud. *Black Light* is published. |
| 1968 | Birth of son, Finn Fergus. (He is referred to in *The Book of Nightmares* as "Sancho Fergus." Queried on this, Kinnell replied, "His actual name is Finn Fergus; but at the time I wrote of his birth it was still possible to be Sancho—") *Body Rags* and translation of Yves Bonnefoy's *On the Motion and Immobility of Douve* are published. |
| 1969 | Lives in Spain. |
| 1970 | *First Poems* (early work) and translation of Yvan Goll's *Lackawanna Elegy* are published. |
| 1971 | *The Book of Nightmares* is published. |
| 1974 | *The Avenue Bearing the Initial of Christ into the New World* (reprinting together *First Poems, What a Kingdom It Was,* and *Flower Hearding on Mount Monadnock*) is published. Receives the Shelley Prize from the Poetry Society of America. |
| 1975 | Receives the Medal of Merit from the National Institute of Arts and Letters. Organizes reading of Christopher Smart's *Jubilate Agno* by James Wright, Allen Ginsberg, Muriel Rukeyser, Philip Levine, and others. |
| 1977 | Revised *Poems of François Villon* is published. |
| 1978 | *Walking Down the Stairs* is published. Fulbright professor at the University of Nice. Receives Harold L. Landon Translation Prize. |

| 1979 | Visiting writer at MacQuarrie University, Sydney, Australia. |
|---|---|
| 1979–81 | Lives in Hawaii. |
| 1980 | *Mortal Acts, Mortal Words* is published. |
| 1981 | With Robert Bly, gives memorial reading for James Wright in New York. |
| 1982 | *Selected Poems* is published. Organizes antinuclear reading, Poets Against the End of the World, at Town Hall, New York City. |
| 1983 | Receives Pulitzer Prize for *Selected Poems;* cowinner of American Book Award. |
| 1983–84 | Serves as president of P.E.N. |
| 1984 | Awarded MacArthur Foundation grant. |
| 1985 | Divorce from Inés de Torres Kinnell. Gives reading of Whitman's "Song of Myself" at Ninety-second Street YMCA. Becomes Samuel F. B. Morse Professor of Fine Arts, New York University—his first tenured position. *The Past* is published. |

PART ONE  *Three Overviews*

(*through* The Book of Nightmares)

CHARLES G. BELL

# Galway Kinnell

In the winter of 1946–47, when I was teaching at Princeton University, a dark-shocked student, looking more like a prize fighter than a literary man, showed me a poem, maybe his first. I remember it as a Wordsworthian sonnet, not what the avant-garde of Princeton, Blackmur or Berryman, would have taken to—old diction, no modern flair. But the last couplet had a romantic fierceness that amazed me. The man who had done that could go beyond any poetic limits to be assigned. I was reckless enough to tell him so.

I was to lecture at Black Mountain that summer. He took a bit of his G.I. money and came along. Apart from some works of mine which seemed to move him, it was to Yeats that he gave himself with the totality that has always characterized him. By the fall he had written the first form of a four-page poem, "A Morning Wake Among the Dead" (later called "Among the Tombs"), which foreshadowed in volcanic latency all his later long poems. The death-haunted, tragic Kinnell had already spoken, though it would take years for the fact to be recognized.

In form, Kinnell was still using a romantic and Miltonic pentameter almost totally remade under impacts from Donne and the moderns—meter purposely broken up, rhymes concealed—a demonic wrestling with traditional measures. His matter was the reaffirmation of the Promethean and pioneer daring of America, to which I also, after the neo-Augustinian resignations of the war, was committed. He wrote a whole volume of Western poems which did not find a publisher, though some of them, revised, appear in the first sections of *What a Kingdom It Was*.

About 1956 Kinnell was able to get abroad. It was not too late

From *Contemporary Poets,* Third Edition, edited by James Vinson. © The Macmillan Press Ltd., 1980, and reprinted by permission of St. Martin's Press Inc.

for his "Prairie" style to be infused with French modernism, though without losing its passionate immediacy. The most remarkable fruit of this is "The Supper After the Last," in *What a Kingdom,* a symbolist vision and statement, at one time Promethean-romantic and mysteriously avant-garde.

Kinnell's break with traditional form has continued, leading to his espousal of free verse as the only possible medium for an American poet. It is significantly to Whitman that he has returned, with some inspiration from William Carlos Williams. But anyone who will take the twisted rhymes of the earlier Kinnell and set them beside the free verse of recent works—that staggering diptych of animal poems, "The Porcupine" and "The Bear" in *Body Rags*—will sense how far everything that has occurred, both in content and form, was within the province of the original Apocalyptic vision of "A Morning Wake Among the Dead."

What distinguishes that vision from anything else on the contemporary scene is its continuation of the titanism of the last century—whatever flamed from Goethe's *Faust* through Melville, Nietzsche, Rimbaud, to Rilke, Yeats, Jeffers. There is a sense in which Galway Kinnell has remained faithful to this heritage, though for a long time it handicapped him among those of a more oblique and verbal trend, poets who grew up as it were after Pound. Thus a review of *Body Rags* (in the *New York Review of Books*) spent most of its time complaining that Kinnell didn't write like Berryman—as if he hadn't had his chance at that and decided early against it.

Within Kinnell's passionate and personal vein, two drifts have revealed themselves, that of the longer poem prefigured in "A Morning Wake," "The Avenue Bearing the Initial of Christ," and "The Last River," and that of clarified small lyrics aimed at an ultimate transparency. The lyrical tendency reaches its earliest perfection in "First Song" ("Then it was dusk in Illinois") as in the other tender pieces ("Island of Night," "A Walk in the Country") published in Rolfe Humphries' *New Poems* though not included by Kinnell in any of his volumes. So too with "Spring Oak," a poem that illustrates Kinnell's critical pronouncement in his Beloit "Self-Study": "Only meaning is truly interesting." Even in *Body Rags* there are such distillates, "The Falls" and "How Many Nights." Reading them, as the "Self-Study" had also said, is "like opening a window on the thing the poem is talking about":

> How many nights
> have I lain in terror,
> O Creator Spirit, Maker of night and day,
>
> only to walk out
> the next morning over the frozen world
> hearing under the creaking of snow
> faint, peaceful breaths . . .
> snake,
> bear, earthworm, ant . . .
>
> and above me
> a wild crow crying "*yaw yaw yaw*"
> from a branch nothing cried from ever in my life.

Against such poems, the underworld involvement of "The Last River" goes another road, groping through caves and antres of "the flinty, night-smelling depths," "waiting by the grief-tree of the last river."

Kinnell's second book, *Flower Herding on Mount Monadnock,* as the title suggests (strange the Indian name for that solitary mountain on a peneplane should hold the Greek root of the One), is largely in the lyrical mode. Even the Wagnerian love-death has wonderfully refined itself in "Poems of Night": "A cheekbone, / A curved piece of brow, / A pale eyelid / Float in the dark, / And now I make out / An eye, dark, / Wormed with the far-off, unaccountable lights." While the title poem and "Spindrift"— "Sit down / By the clanking shore / Of this bitter, beloved sea"—stand at the pinnacle of the poignantly pure and deeply transparent.

At the moment I have before me various sketches of *The Book of Nightmares*. For oceanic participation, the section on childbirth ("Maud Moon") goes beyond anything Kinnell has done before:

It is all over, little one,
the flipping
and overleaping,
the watery
somersaulting alone in the oneness
under the hill, under
the old, lonely bellybutton pushing forth again
in remembrance, all over,
the drifting there furled like a flower, pressing
a knee down the slippery
walls, sculpting the whole world, hearing
a few cries from without not even as promises, the stream
of omphalos blood humming all over you.

What distinguishes this from the work of any other poet (though parallels can be found: Roethke, Rilke, even Whitman) is the intuitive immediacy of its entrance into prebirth and subhuman organic nature.

Of all the poets born in the twenties and thirties, Galway Kinnell is the only one who has taken up the passionate symbolic search of the great American tradition.

ANDREW TAYLOR

# The Poetry of Galway Kinnell

> *Where the track vanishes the first land begins.*
> *It goes out everywhere obliterating the horizons.*
> *We must have been walking through it all our lives.*
> — "Where the Track Vanishes," from
> *What a Kingdom It Was*

Born in 1927, Galway Kinnell belongs to that generation of American poets, now in their forties, who are old enough to have achieved full poetic maturity while still young enough to be displaying vigorous growth and development. He is less well known in Australia than contemporaries of his such as Allen Ginsberg, Gary Snyder, and Robert Bly, which is a pity. While in no way decrying the work of these other poets, in my opinion Kinnell's poetry is more substantial, more solid, than Snyder's, more accessible than Bly's and, unlike Ginsberg's later work, it continues to develop and deepen, building coherently on what he has written before.

A short poem from his third book, *Body Rags,* demonstrates with convenient simplicity what I see as a characteristic central to Kinnell's whole poetic endeavor:

LOST LOVES

I
On ashes of old volcanoes
I lie dreaming,
baking
the deathward flesh in the sun,

and dream I can hear
a door, far away,
banging softly in the wind:

---

From *Meanjin* 36 (July 1977). Reprinted by permission of Andrew Taylor.

Mole Street. Quai-aux-Fleurs. Françoise.
Greta. "After Lunch" by Po Chu-I.
"The Sunflower" by Blake.


2
And yet I can rejoice
that everything changes, that
we go from life
into life,

and enter ourselves
quaking
like the tadpole, his time come, tumbling toward the slime.

Despite the nostalgic elegiac first section, the poem is an affirmation. In its first stanza the poet is in the grip of mortality, "baking / the deathward flesh in the sun." This "deathward" tendency leads logically to the memories of the previous death-like experiences, the death of loves, imaged gently by the "door . . . banging softly in the wind." Nobody is there, or cares, to shut the door firmly. But the poet is doing his dreaming, and sunbaking, "On ashes of old volcanoes," and a volcano, even an extinct one, is a powerful example of how a massive upsurge of energy, frequently destructive but always awe inspiring, can emerge from underground.

Thus the poem changes from nostalgia to an affirmation of the vitality of change. For Kinnell, one's life is—or can be—a process of rebirth. Just as the tadpole dies as a tadpole, "tumbling toward the slime," in order to be born anew as a frog, so can the poet "go from life / into life." This is not quite the same thing as going from one life to another life, of merely changing identity. Rather, it is a matter of quitting life, in order to reenter it or, as the poem says, to "enter ourselves."

"Lost Loves" is structured on, and expresses, a transformational process which is basic to almost all the best of Kinnell's poetry. As I interpret it, it has three essential components. First, through suffering of some kind the poet undergoes a death of the self, of a conscious self. He goes "from life." However, this does not involve death as we usually think of it. Rather, it is a withdrawal to a prehuman or preconscious state, an "animal" state, consistently represented by animal imagery, in this case a tadpole. This animal image is the second component. The third is a rebirth, a moving back "into life," and is accompanied by a variety of emotions, the most characteristic being rejoicing, wonder, or awe.

This transformational process or pattern has a key place in many of Kinnell's poems. Something like it takes place in his novel, *Black Light,* also. It is the characteristic strategy of many of the poems in his third volume, *Body Rags,* in particular of the two most striking, "The Porcupine" and "The Bear." And it is the pattern of the whole development of his latest book, *The Book of Nightmares.* It has obvious similarities with Christ's death, descent into Hell, and resurrection, but the Christian story is a specialised, ethicalised version of the more basic myth which fires Kinnell's imagination. More accurately, Kinnell's imagination seizes powerfully on what seems to be a universal process and repeatedly works through it in a modern context. Furthermore, the Christian version of the myth tells of a transcendence of the spirit over mere matter, and of right over wrong; and the central event is an actual, bodily death; and the end result is not a transcendence of the physical, but a fuller involvement with it, and a fuller comprehension of it.

In an essay called "Poetry, Personality, and Death" Kinnell quotes with approval from Snyder's *Earth House Hold:* "The archaic and primitive ritual dramas, which acknowledge all sides of human nature, including the destructive, demonic, and am- bivalent, were liberating and harmonising." Kinnell goes on to state that "our deepest desire . . . is to be one with all creation." This was the aim of alchemy: ". . . it was a symbolic science, and its occult aim was to propitiate the sexual, creative forces in nature, and to transfigure the inner life." The triumph of chem- istry over alchemy in the seventeenth century was the "fatal moment . . . when the human mind learned the knack of de- taching itself from what it studied, even when what it studied was itself." Kinnell's article is an impressive plea for a life—and a literature which articulates it—in which the human is reunited with nonhuman, and the conscious mind with the unconscious. Rejecting the merely confessional in poetry, he quotes a prose

31

poem by Robert Bly, and then comments: "[This] poem is personal yet common, open yet mysterious. . . . We move toward a poetry in which the poet seeks an inner liberation by going so deeply into himself—into the worst of himself as well as the best—that he suddenly finds he is everyone."

Clearly, in his own poetry Kinnell wishes to articulate "the archaic and primitive ritual dramas" which liberate, harmonise and integrate. In doing this, his poetic voice will escape the merely personal and will speak for all men. One could put this another way: Kinnell wants his poetry to approach the condition of a myth. I believe that he succeeds.

Some of Kinnell's earliest mature poems in *What a Kingdom It Was,* his first volume, show him in the process of divesting these later preoccupations of their more habitual and more traditional Christian vestments. For example, in "To Christ Our Lord" the poet, as a boy, has shot a bird for "the Christmas meal" and now, as he is eating it, is conscience-stricken at the act:

> Now the grace praised his wicked act. At its end
> The bird on the plate
> Stared at his stricken appetite.
> There had been nothing to do but surrender,
> To kill and to eat; he ate as he killed, with wonder.

The boy is "stricken," and "surrenders," like the shot bird. They share the same fate. Finally, wandering alone in the snow after dinner, the boy witnesses an act of symbolic resurrection: "Then the Swan spread her wings, cross of the cold north, / The pattern and mirror of the acts of earth." Out of the boy's suffering and wonder, his spirits are in a mysterious way lifted by the nonhuman Swan. However, the hint of the supramundane is not Christian, but rather a chilly intimation of a life pattern figured in the stars which is yet "pattern and mirror of the acts on earth." Neither does anything else in *What a Kingdom It Was* conform to a Christian pattern, even though that pattern is clearly very much in the poet's mind. In fact, the longest, and the finest, poem in this volume pays no overt attention to Christ whatsoever, despite the fact that it is called "The Avenue Bearing the Initial of Christ into the New World." He refers, of course, to

Avenue C, in downtown Eastside Manhattan, a godforsaken place, as it appears from the poem, though teeming with life.

One must be careful not to construe the Avenue C poem too much in the light of what I want to say of Kinnell's other poems. It displays an excellence of another kind, intermittently apparent throughout his work, and which does not coalesce fully with his pattern of dramatic progression until *The Book of Nightmares*. This other excellence could be described as a Whitmanesque openness to experience, a ready flow of sympathy, of compassion, for "the drowned" who "suffer a C-change, / And remain the common poor," as the poem treats one day in the life of the denizens of Avenue C.

But its structure has some relation to the transformational progression I am discussing. In between the awakening "pcheek pcheek pcheek . . ." of the baby birds in the first line, and the whimsically humorous conclusion, Kinnell travels in the company of Whitman towards an appraisal of death:

> Maybe it is as the poet said,
> And the soul turns to thee
> O vast and well-veiled Death
> And the body nestles gratefully close to thee—
>
> I think of Isaac reading Whitman in Chicago,
> The week before he died, coming across
> Such a passage and muttering, Oi!
> What shit! And smiling, but not for you—I mean,
>
> For *thee,* Sane and Sacred Death!

This passage is followed by a description of a fire in Gold's junkhouse, where even the remnants of human failure are consumed: "It is cold suddenly, we feel chilled, / Nobody knows for sure what is left of him." This mood of dispossession is only dispelled—and then only partially—three sections later (13) with the noticing of spring rain, and a final, qualified acceptance of the common lot. The mood of the poem is best summed up by these lines from the final section:

It is night, and raining. You look down
Towards Houston in the rain, the living streets,
Where the instants of transcendence
Drift in oceans of loathing and fear, like lanternfishes,
Or phosphorus flashings in the sea, or the feverish light
Skin is said to give off when the swimmer drowns at night.

Significantly, although this is the only time in the poem in which this happens, these "instants of transcendence" are associated both with death and the animal, nonhuman world.

Significant though this is, one must be careful not to place too much stress on it. The whole tenor and structure of the Avenue C poem is closer to "Song of Myself" than it is to "The Porcupine" or "The Bear." The poem is a rich testament to the power of compassion, humour and fortitude to embrace the milling poverty of life and thus transcend it. This entails, of course, embracing the *not us* as well as what *is* us. This compassion is an essential qualification of Kinnell's journey towards myth.

Several other poems from *What a Kingdom It Was* need to be mentioned here. "Freedom, New Hampshire" is a moving elegy to the memory of the poet's brother. Here Kinnell confronts a physical death, a death which was to haunt him in much later poems than this. A man's death is mediated to the poet's deep sense of the continuity of life by the death and burial of a cow. Out of the cow's grave, as out of a filled-in dungheap, grows next season's lush grass. But next season's grass, when it comes to the physical loss of a brother, cannot bring that brother back:

When a man dies he dies trying to say without slurring
The abruptly decaying sounds. It is true
That only flesh dies, the spirit flowers without stop
For men, cows, dung, for all dead things; and it is good, yes—

But an incarnation is in particular flesh
And the dust that is swirled into a shape
And crumbles and is swirled again had but one shape
That was this man. When he is dead the grass

Heals what he suffered, but he remains dead,
And the few that loved him know this until they die.

Kinnell's belief in a continual feeding of life from death can-
not compensate for the death of one, a particular, brother: the
poet feels the helplessness of his compassion, even of his belief.
This is a crucial confession. In later poems, the poet internalises
his death, and that is where he starts making myths.

A prelude to this is a remarkably cheerful, and deceptively
playful, little poem, called "Duck-Chasing." Here it is in full:

> I spied a very small brown duck
> Riding the swells of the sea
> Like a rocking-chair. "Little duck!"
> I cried. It paddled away,
> I paddled after it. When it dived,
> Down I dived: too smoky was the sea,
> We were lost. It surfaced
> In the west, I torpedoed west
> And when it dived I dived,
> And we were lost and lost and lost
> In the slant smoke of the sea.
> When I came floating up on it
> From the side, like a deadman,
> And yelled suddenly, it took off,
> It skimmed the swells as it ascended,
> Brown wings burning and flashing
> In the sun as the sea it rose over
> Burned and flashed underneath it.
> I did not see the little duck again.
> Duck-chasing is a game like any game.
> When it is over it is all over.

The poem is so light, so cheerfully holiday, that one thinks
twice before commenting on it. But it would be doing Kinnell a
disservice not to take seriously what he says so directly. "Duck-
chasing is a game like any game." But "when it is over," when
we no longer play it, "it is all over." In other words, duck-
chasing becomes an image of life, which is a game of imitating

the duck to the point of identifying with it—becoming animal—even "floating . . . like a deadman." But the object of this duck-chase is not to catch the duck, but to set

> Brown wings burning and flashing
> In the sun as the sea it rose over
> Burned and flashed underneath it.

That is why the duck-chaser "yelled suddenly." The poem is an early and light-hearted illustration of Kinnell's later pronouncement, that "our deepest desire . . . is to be one with all creation."

Any full account of Kinnell's poetry must look much more carefully than I can here at his second volume, *Flower Herding on Mount Monadnock,* which demonstrates and dramatises his deep involvement with what he sees as an unremitting regenerative bias in the world. This is not plain optimism; it is an optimism bound to a wheel of fire. In fact, images of fire, or the aftermath of fire, are frequent in this book.

"Tillamook Journal," for example, is a Snyder-like trek through backcountry, in which Kinnell hikes back to "the Burn," "more black / Ashes than it was earth." Yet this barren ruin, "just one more of the / Plundered breasts of the world," comes exhilaratingly alive for him again as he hears

> a dark wind
> Blasting out of the darkness,
> Where before me the tempestuous ocean
> Falls with long triple crashes on the shore.

Kinnell is aligning himself with a clearly romantic poet. Wordsworth, on regaining his imaginative powers that momentous night on Mount Snowdon, was awakened by, or awakened to, "the roar of waters, torrents, streams, / Innumerable, roaring with one voice!"; Stevens, in *Esthetique du Mal IX,* "regains sensibility" when

> A large, loud water
> Bubbles up in the night and drowns the crickets' sound.

It is a declaration, a primitive ecstasy,
Truth's favours sonorously exhibited.

"Middle of The Way," another poem in this volume, concludes with what could be Kinnell's credo:

I know that I love the day,
The sun on the mountain, the Pacific
Shiny and accomplishing itself in breakers,
But I know I live half alive in the world,
I know half my life belongs to the wild darkness.

Kinnell's wild darkness with its tempestuous ocean is Wordsworth's "Torrents, streams, / Innumerable" and Stevens's "large, loud water." The darkness can appear in two aspects. In its negative aspect, it is a loss, loss of identity, death of consciousness, death of the Self; and it entails pain and fear. In its positive aspect, it is the nonself, the unconscious, the preconscious, the unpredictable source of vitality, the Mystery; and it elicits wonder and awe. It is the "inconceivable realm" for which "a man," Kinnell himself, "feels the dark / Homesickness" in "Ruins Under the Stars." Needless to say, if a man feels this homesickness, he needs a firm sense of *this* world to prevent him from toppling into the next.

*Body Rags,* Kinnell's third book, certainly has this firm sense of the world. The Blakean opening section of the first poem, "Another Night in the Ruins," shows that Kinnell is as attentive to detail as he was in the Avenue C poem:

In the evening
haze darkening on the hills,
purple
of the eternal, a last bird
crosses over, '*flop flop*',
adoring
only the instant.

The poem concludes that "we aren't, after all, made / from that bird which flies out of its ashes." A man only has one life, which he admitted in "Freedom, New Hampshire." ("Another Night in the Ruins" also concerns his brother's death.) In the absence of the phoenix's immortality, one must give oneself wholly to the act of living, even though the act is what finally destroys one:

HOW MANY NIGHTS

How many nights
have I lain in terror,
O Creator Spirit, Maker of night and day,

only to walk out
the next morning over the frozen world
hearing under the creaking of snow
faint, peaceful breaths . . .
snake,
bear, earthworm, ant . . .

and above me
a wild crow crying 'yaw yaw yaw'
from a branch nothing cried from ever in my life.

Here we have the transformational pattern clearly expressed. Something like a dark night of the soul (complete with a cry to the "Creator"), a death of self, gives way to a new life imaged in the cry of the crow where never before in the poet's life had there been anything. And this is accompanied by an awareness of, an intimacy with, the subworld of animal life. By going below the surface to the less than human, the poet emerges revitalised though isolated from other humans.

*Body Rags* is a powerful book, and it deserves far more attention than I can give it here. The poems in it are remarkable for the vitality of their language, their conciseness, the subtle finesse (in a physical sense) of their rhythms, and their extraordinary totality, their air of having said all there is to say. However, I must confine my comments to one poem only, the one which in my opinion is the book's finest.

"The Bear" is the clearest, and also the most startling enactment of the primordial drama in *Body Rags*. Its narrative structure follows Eskimo myths perhaps, but the extraordinary transformations that take place are entirely Kinnell's. The poem begins with the poet as hunter, scenting "in late winter" the "chilly, enduring odor of bear." Late winter awakens us to the arrival of spring, new life; and that is in fact what finally results. But contrary to our usual expectations, though not contrary to our deepest knowledge, we—the poet and the hunter—have first to go through a death.

This death is both the death of the bear, and the death of the poet/hunter's Self. The poet/hunter shares in the bear's death— he drags himself forward with bear knives in his fists just as the dying bear drags himself on with his claws. He eats the blood-soaked and frozen bear turds. He is *living off* the bear's death, for the bear's death is essential to him. Yet when the bear is actually dead, what the poet/hunter does is

> tear him down his whole length
> and open him and climb in
> and close him up after me, against the wind,
> and sleep.

"And dream," the poem continues. Inside the bear, in his sleep, the poet dreams the whole death over again, not living off it this time, but living through it himself.

Every time I read this poem to others, it brings a gasp of shock at its physical brutality. Yet the final section is in its context as tender, and as tentative, as anything in modern poetry in English:

> I awaken I think. Marshlights
> reappear, geese
> come trailing again up the flyway.
> In her ravine under old snow the dam-bear
> lies, licking
> lumps of smeared fur
> and drizzly eyes into shapes
> with her tongue. And one

hairy-soled trudge stuck out before me,
the next groaned out,
the next,
the next,
the rest of my days I spend
wandering; wondering
what, anyway,
was that sticky infusion, that rank flavor of blood, that poetry,
    by which I lived?

It is essential to recognize that this poem is not an allegory about "killing the animal in oneself." Quite the opposite. The bear is killed, but his body is eagerly inhabited by the spirit and the body of the poet/hunter, who is already half-bear. In other words, as the poet becomes bear we have a death of the specifically human. But while the bear, *qua* bear, dies, the bear/poet/hunter gives birth to humanity and awe, like the "dam-bear" who "lies, licking / lumps of smeared fur / and drizzly eyes into shapes / with her tongue." By entrusting himself to the animal, to the part of himself which "belongs to the wild darkness," Kinnell has regained contact with a regenerative vitality.

There is involved here a transformation of sex. The original bear was male, like the hunter. Having killed it, and climbed inside, symbolically transforming it into female, the poet's dream makes it *in fact* female. It bears cubs, one of which is the poet, reborn into wonder. But the poem does not reject the male any more than it rejects the animal; its whole process endorses it as one of the two essential elements of the creative process. One of the poem's great strengths is that it holds these two elements in creative poise.

In "The Bear," Kinnell goes through the death of his male identity—both bear and hunter—in order to be reborn by means of his "dream," by means of an imagination revitalised by its voluntary yet mandatory suicide.

The poem ends on a note of puzzlement, like that of a child relearning the universe. The poet asks "what, anyway, / was that sticky infusion, that rank flavor of blood, that poetry, by which I lived?" The frozen, blood-soaked bear turd? The excreta and the ebbing life-blood of mankind? Much of Kinnell's poetry does have "that rank flavor of blood," as though the poet were a self-immolating Christ, or Caesar, "stabbed twice from within," achieving his own death. But in "The Bear," Kinnell writes a different poetry. "The rank flavor of blood" becomes the sweet smell of spring. Abandoning the merely personal, his conscious, human Self, not just letting it die but actively killing it, Kinnell reaches to creative sources that bear him back into the world lonely, wandering, wondering. And unmistakably alive.

It should now be clear that the transformational pattern I have been examining is not only central to Kinnell's poetry, but also a means of realising his deepest concerns. It provides the basic structure, in fact, for the whole of his most recent book, *The Book of Nightmares*.

It is appropriate to consider this book as a single poem. It has ten parts, each consisting of seven sections, and it involves the poet in a descent into death in a number of different forms, out of which he is finally, as we would now expect of him, in some sense reborn. But this rebirth—if we can call it that—is a very tentative affair, and is evidenced not so much by any upturn in tone, as by the poem's overall vitality of language and rhythm.

The poem (and by that I mean the whole book) begins with a birth, with the poet lighting a twig fire in the rain to memorialise the birth of his daughter. Yet even this birth is as ambiguous as the poet's memorial fire, it is a death to her previous existence in the darkness:

> as they cut
>
> her tie to the darkness
> she dies
> a moment, turns blue as a coal,
> the limbs shaking
> as the memories rush out of them.

The poet confesses to his daughter that all his songs come from that ambivalent and animalistic darkness where beginnings happen:

> I had crept down
> to riverbanks, their long rustle
> of being and perishing, down to marshes
> where the earth oozes up
> in cold streaks, touching the world
> with the underglimmer
> of the beginning,
> and there learned my only song.

In order to revisit this darkness, the poet has to "let go" like the hen which can be hypnotised to lay its head "thrown back / on the chopping block, longing only / to die." Even in death the hen is a source and a storehouse of the future. The poet accomplishes this death in many ways. The animal agency is less prominent here. In its place, the poet adopts the shoes, the postures, the clothes of other men who have now died. Kinnell haunts the sagging beds in "the Hotel of Lost Light," to seek out and possess the shapes of previous occupants, in order to undergo their death:

> Flesh
> of his excavated flesh,
> fill of his emptiness,
> after-amanuensis of his after-life,
> I write out
> for him in this languished alphabet
> of worms, these last words
> of himself, post for him
> his final postcards to posterity.

In doing this, "the carnal / nightmare soars back to the beginning."

There is no doubt of the anguish which the poet suffers in these central sections of the poem. It is indeed a book of nightmares, even when the nightmares are as terribly real and wide awake as America's bombing of North Vietnam. In section 6, the poet shares in the anguish and guilt of a whole country which cannot obliterate the death of which it is guilty: *"Lieutenant! / This corpse will not stop burning!"* After this, the poem begins its tortuous way up. Yet to go up, the poet has to "go down / into the unbreathable goaf / of everything [he] ever craved and lost." It is only on doing this that the prehuman, the animal, in its rudimentary and most repulsive form, can start its regenerative activity:

> In clothes
> woven out of the blue spittle
> of snakes, I crawl up: I find myself alive
> in the whorled
> archway of the fingerprints of all things.

The last section of the poem contains another birth, this time his son's. The precarious resolution finally achieved is well summed up here:

> This is the tenth poem
> and it is the last. It is right
> at the last, that one
> and zero
> walk off together,
> walk off the end of these pages together,
> one creature
> walking away side by side with the emptiness.
>
> Lastness
> *is* brightness

and the poem ends with an image of a minimal assertion of life wedded inseparably to its opposite: the laughing flea on the corpse.

*The Book of Nightmares* is a survival poem rather than a triumph. At times it verges on morbidity, with the poet gnawing on the bitter flesh of his own heart. But anything more positive at the end would be either gratuitous or melodramatic. The whole poem culminates in integration and acceptance, rather than in a more spectacular victory. By accepting zero at the end, the poet can also experience entity.

The transformational pattern I have been tracing is naturally not unique to Kinnell. But Kinnell, more than any other poet I know of, has found it a fertile, even essential, dramatic form. What he has done with it establishes him as a major religious, or, if you object to that word, a major mythic poet.

I think it is Mircea Eliade who says that one function of a myth is to preserve the sense of the sacred life. If by sacred one means that mysterious, and apparently inexhaustible, fund of vitality below the specifically human consciousness, in the unconscious and in our interactions with the other forms of living creatures, then Kinnell's poetry does this. His poetry is the product of a soul deeply concerned with salvation, i.e., of a psyche or imagination deeply concerned with psychic health and regeneration. It deliberately and courageously involves the unconscious, all that is "wild darkness," in an age-old integrative, re-novating process.

The imagination for Kinnell takes on the role of apprehending a sense in life which escapes the rational and mundane, a sense of the wholeness of life, and the wonder it wakens in us. The transformational drama I have analysed is both a way of attaining this sense, and an expression of it. It has its distinct dangers: once one enters the "wild darkness" there is a chance one may not get out again. In *The Book of Nightmares* it was a close thing. But overall I think Kinnell's own words (in "Poetry, Personality, and Death") fitly describe not only his intention, but also his achievement.

> The death of the self I seek, in poetry and out of poetry, is not a drying up or withering. It is a death, yes, but a death out of which one might hope to be reborn more giving, more alive, more open, more related to the natural life. I have never felt the appeal of that death of the self certain kinds of Buddhism describe—that death which purges us of desire, which removes us from our loves. For myself, I would like a death that would give me more loves, not fewer. And greater desire, not less.

CHARLES MOLESWORTH

# The Rank Flavor of Blood
## *The Poetry of Galway Kinnell*

When Ezra Pound called for the "direct, objective treatment of the thing itself," he was in some sense echoing the historicism of late nineteenth-century thought. Historicism implicitly rejects systems, whether of an ideological or a theological sort; and, in attempting to understand historical events without the benefit of any transcendent framework, it tacitly accepts the end of absolute value and absolutist authority as signalled by the French Revolution. Though Pound's polemic addressed itself to eradicating the "emotional slither" he identified with late Victorian poetry, it inadvertently limited the poet almost exclusively to the ironic mode. Since mythical statements, and expressions of direct sentiment, would be curtailed by any rigorous adoption of "direct, objective treatment," the lyric poem might well lose the chief sources of its resonance. One way for the poet to render some justice to the complexity of experience is by turning to his own divided consciousness as his chief subject and presenting the consciousness directly while ironically qualifying the mind that observes it. Or the poet might take different, fragmentary, but conflicting values inherent in an experiential situation, relate them one to another, dampening his own intentions and judgments, and energize the poem through an ironic interplay of multiple but partial "truths." Poets, especially ironic poets, became in some sense historicists of imagination.

From such impulses we can trace the development of the typical American poem of the two decades that span the Second

Reprinted from *The Fierce Embrace* by Charles Molesworth by permission of the University of Missouri Press. Copyright 1979 by the Curators of the University of Missouri.

World War: Eberhart's "The Groundhog," Nemerov's "The Goose Fish," and Shapiro's "Auto Wreck." Few poets produced much work outside this dominant mode, marked as it was by logical structure, "tension," and ironic verbal surfaces. The two major exceptions are Randall Jarrell and Theodore Roethke, though both of these, with poems like "Death of the Ball-Turret Gunner" and "Elegy for Jane," respectively, showed they had mastered the ironic idiom. But changes began to occur: Olson's "Projective Verse" and Allen Ginsberg's "Howl" were clear signs, at least with the comfort of retrospection, that a new poetics was developing. It might be instructive to trace some of the lineaments of this new idiom by focusing on one poet's career for a certain period, namely that of Galway Kinnell in the 1960s.

Kinnell's poetry of this period involves itself with a virtual rediscovery of how to view objects intensely, while continuing to avoid any prescribed system. Even as early as his long poem "The Avenue Bearing the Initial of Christ into the New World," which falls outside the scope of the present study, though it deserves an essay of its own, Kinnell's poetry has been celebratory and in-clusive in its characteristic attitude toward the world of objects. "There are more to things than things," says one modern French philosopher, and the contemporary poet instinctively agrees; but how to discover that "more" without falling into mere at-titudinizing remains problematic. Pound taught his successors, who include most American poets, that no authority could re-place personal testament, especially when such testament in-volved accurate perception and attentive apperception. But poets could still remain estranged from things; they might fall into a glorified listing of the mundane, or make the operations of the mind so dominant that the poems would lose their subjects in a welter of "impressions." Pound's influence dominated develop-ments in American poetry so completely that poets as diverse as, say, Robert Creeley and William Meredith could easily refuse to yield to each other in their admiration for Pound's accomplish-ments. Kinnell took from Pound, however, only so much as could fruitfully be grafted onto the traditions of Blake and Whit-man; and, though for some Pound's concern with "technique" might seem inimical to inspiration, such need not be the case.

Pound's concern with objective "vision" on the physiological level corrects rather than replaces the concern with the "visionary." But Kinnell was still faced with the problem of how to bring his poetry out of the modernist cul-de-sac of irony into a postmodernist aesthetic. He did this in large measure by two actions, which may appear contradictory but are in fact complementary: self-discovery and self-destruction, the heuristic and the incendiary actions of poetry.[1] Kinnell became a shamanist, rather than a historicist, of the imagination.

The first volume to contain poems Kinnell wrote in the sixties was *Flower Herding on Mount Monadnock* (1964), a book divided into two parts, the first heavily concerned with cityscapes and urban consciousness, and the second almost totally rural in its subjects and locales. The last poem of the first section, "For Robert Frost," offers a convenient transition into the second section, a transition important for the next volume, *Body Rags* (1968), filled as it is with a poetry of nature rather than of history. Such a reductive distinction can be misleading, of course, and it may help to look briefly at the poem for Frost to see in part how Kinnell views America's most famous "nature poet." The pastoralism of Frost both echoes and disjoins Kinnell's sensibility:

> When we think of a man who was cursed
> Neither with the mystical all-lovingness of Walt Whitman
> Nor with Melville's anguish to know and to suffer,
> And yet cursed . . . A man, what shall I say,
> Vain, not fully convinced he was dying, whose calling
> Was to set up in the wilderness of his country,
> At whatever cost, a man, who would be his own man,
> We think of you.

The qualified praise here may well bring to mind Auden's elegy for Yeats, a typically modern poem in the way it refuses to follow the ordinary "rules" for elegiac praise and insists on an honesty that threatens to dislocate the very discourse of the poem and move down to the level of verse epistle or even satire. Still, Kinnell sees Frost as "cursed," not perhaps as the same sort of *poète maudit* as Melville, but as someone tied to, perhaps

47

bound down by, his bourgeois virtues of self-reliance and rugged individualism. The obverse of those virtues reflects the loneliness, the alienation, in Frost's life, the "desert places," against which confusion the poems offer only a "momentary stay." This surely is the side of Frost that most attracts Kinnell (as the third section of the poem makes clear), and he almost appears to be exorcising those other, civilized virtues of Frost that made him such a master ironist. When we look back on this poem from the perspective of Kinnell's two latest books, the most stringent criticism of Frost he proposes may be when he says that the older poet was "not fully convinced he was dying." Such an affirmation of life *against* death will become for Kinnell a weakness, a mark of the weak self-love, an unwillingness to accept the "last moment of increased life." As he says in "The Poetics of the Physical World,"[2] "The poetics of heaven agrees to the denigration of pain and death; the poetics of the physical world builds on these stones."

Along with death, Kinnell places pain at the base of his poetics, and pain plays a large part in the poems of *Flower Herding*. The first section of the book is concerned with pain as a subject, or at least as a surrounding condition of other subjects. Chief among these subjects, Kinnell places an awareness of time's on-goingness, an intense awareness that this particular moment, this *now* is isolate, thrown up by itself to baffle and defeat human expectations. Here is a passage from "The River That Is East," the first poem of the book:

> We stand on the shore, which is mist beneath us,
> And regard the onflowing river. Sometimes
> It seems the river stops and the shore
> Flows into the past. Nevertheless, its leaked promises
> Hopping in the bloodstream, we strain for the future,
> Sometimes even glimpse it, a vague, scummed thing
> We dare not recognize, and peer again
> At the cabled shroud out of which it came,
> We who have no roots but the shifts of our pain,
> No flowering but our own strange lives.

All New York poems with bridges in them, such as this one, must recall Hart Crane, though part of the success of this poem lies in how effectively it uses its poetic forebears without being strangled by them. This is true of much of Kinnell's poetry and is one of the several ways in which he resembles Theodore Roethke. The images here of mists, scum, and shrouds should remind us of how early Kinnell was involved in a poetry obsessed with death and pain, a product of a consciousness in which sharp juxtapositions and sudden changes of perspective appear endemic. The root and the flower of his experience exist without any system except what they may discover for themselves in an existential framework.

It is in section II of *Flower Herding* that we find the first seeds of Kinnell's "poetics of the physical world," as the poet concentrates on natural, as opposed to urban, objects, moments, and landscapes. Here, too, pain and death are present, almost omnipresent. But the isolate moments, the "leaked promises" of continuity, or of wholeness, become, in the rural setting, moments of ecstasy. The perspective of the future as "a vague, scummed thing / we dare not recognize" fades into a more empty perspective, perhaps; but it is that very emptiness that constitutes such promise for Kinnell. As Kinnell suggests in "The Poetics of the Physical World," death represents the last, absolute perspective; its very finality makes it a magnificent possibility, or rather, the source of magnificent possibilities.

We may note that the desire to *be* some other thing is itself suicidal; it involves a willingness to cease to be a man. But this is not a simple wish for extinction so much as it is a desire for union with what is loved. And so it is a desire for more, not less, life.

Reading *Flower Herding* as part of a putative spiritual autobiography, the reader will decide that it is only when Kinnell escapes the city for the country that the possibilities of mortality become positive rather than negative. When we regard *Flower Herding* as the barometer of other, larger currents at work in American poetry in the sixties, it clearly stands with Bly's *Silence in the Snowy Fields* (1962) and Wright's *The Branch Will Not Break* (1963). These three books can be seen as developments away from the ironic mode practiced and perfected by, among others, Ransom, Tate, Nemerov, and Wilbur, and toward a poetic mode first announced by Theodore Roethke as early as 1950, but largely unheeded until ten years later. Here is Roethke characterizing the lyric poet in "Open Letter," from *On the Poet and His Craft:*

> He must scorn being "mysterious" or loosely oracular, but be willing to face up to a genuine mystery. His language must be compelling and immediate: he must create an actuality. He must be able to telescope image and symbol, if necessary, without relying on the obvious connectives: to speak in a kind of psychic shorthand . . . He works intuitively, and the final form of his poem must be imaginatively right.

Such phrases as "psychic shorthand" and "telescop[ing] image and symbol" illuminate the shifts in perspective and the imagistic density that make the typical Kinnell poem. Here are the final lines of the title poem of *Flower Herding:*

> It burns up. Its drift is to be nothing.
>
> In its covertness it has a way
> Of uttering itself in place of itself,
> Its blossoms claim to float in the Empyrean,
>
> A wrathful presence on the blur of the ground.
>
> The appeal to heaven breaks off.
> The petals begin to fall, in self-forgiveness.
> It is a flower. On this mountainside it is dying.

Heaven and the void vie with each other to be the flower's proper domain; the flower makes claims it cannot demonstrate, and yet it forgives itself; it needs its covertness in order to survive, and yet it must utter itself, make known and articulate its "invisible life." All of these contradictory impulses suggest that we can "interpret" the flower as an image from the processes of nature and as a symbol for the act of writing the poem, or even for the psychic paradoxes of the poet himself.

Nowhere are such leaps from the imagistic to the symbolic

made clear; in fact, the tone of the poem occasionally works against such leaps, especially in the last line. But the pain and the ecstasy of the consciousness that employs such telescopings tell us that aspiration and acceptance are two aspects of the same intentionality. We might even say that the dialectic between aspiration and acceptance provides the central energy of the poem and that that dialectic reveals its terms most clearly in the tone of a line such as "A wrathful presence on the blur of the ground," where overtones of an almost biblical phrasing terminate in the flatness of the final five words. But the flatness of such a termination, along with phrases like "breaks off," can't be called ironic, at least not if we use irony to mean a kind of qualifying defensiveness. If anything, the variations in texture in these lines reflect quite openly the actuality of the circumscribed transcendence in the poem, circumscribed because it sustains itself only through an acceptance of death. And the persistence of fire and death imagery throughout Kinnell's poetry forces us to disregard, or at least to minimize, the habitual expectation of ironic distance that we bring to much modern poetry. His obviously attempts to be a poetry of immersion into experience rather than a suspension above it.

Kinnell's next book after *Flower Herding* presents several difficulties; these result in part simply because several of the single poems in *Body Rags* are difficult ("The Last River" and "Testament of the Thief"), but also because the mode of expression throughout can seem half-formed, occasionally alternating between the densely remote and the flatly commonplace. At least seventeen (out of twenty-three) of the poems are constructed in "sections," and the section becomes the organizing principle of *The Book of Nightmares* as well as of the best poems in *Body Rags:* "The Poem," "The Porcupine," and "The Bear." But eight of the poems in *Body Rags* contain only two sections each, and these represent, I think, some of Kinnell's least successful poems. At the same time, the concentration of imagery and attention that they contain, along with the multiple and shifting perspectives, eventually culminates in what remains Kinnell's typical strength. Here is one poem that has some strength but finally fails to be as powerful as several others in the same format:

I

A woman
sleeps next to me on the earth. A strand
of hair flows
from her cocoon sleeping bag, touching
the ground hesitantly, as if thinking
to take root.

2

I can hear
a mountain brook
and somewhere blood winding
down its ancient labyrinths. And
a few feet away
charred stick-ends surround
a bit of ashes, where burnt-out, vanished flames
absently
waver, absently leap.

Postmodernist poetry insofar as it rejects or moves beyond
irony, runs the risk of sentimentality on the one hand and of
being "loosely oracular" on the other. Here, the "blood wind-
ing / down its ancient labyrinths" is susceptible to either charge,
though perhaps especially the latter. Such resonance as the poem
does have originates in the subtly controlled tone and syntax of
the last few lines. But, considering the total statement of the
poem as a dialectic between its two "sections" doesn't particu-
larly increase our appreciation of it. The poem goes beyond
descriptive prettiness only by hinting at emotions that would
probably be mawkish if further explored.

But it is ungracious to consider at too great a length any
failings in *Body Rags* when that volume contains at least three
poems that have already come to enjoy a wide and deep esteem:
"The Poem," "The Porcupine," and "The Bear." These are the
three poems in which Kinnell moves most clearly beyond the
suspension of irony toward the immersion of empathy, and they
are, I believe, sure indicators of a new postmodern aesthetic in

contemporary American poetry. By empathy I mean something other than Keats's "negative capability," though that concept forms part of Kinnell's poetics. Empathy in Kinnell's poetry, however, results in an important way at the edges of experience, that boundary along which the organism and the environment become interdefinitional. Irony occurs at the center of opposing vectors, at the point of greatest cumulative tension. On the other hand, empathy results from a systemic consciousness, an awareness of the field on which and through which the forces of experience act and make themselves visible. In some ways this accounts for Kinnell's feelings that the self, the ego, hinders true poetry, since the ego so often defends itself rather than adapt to new experience, thus effectively delimiting the consciousness instead of surrendering it to new forms. Such a poetics of empathy, however, stops short of aesthetic anarchy by insisting that reality itself has forms inherent in it, or at least that the mind will instinctively develop such forms for itself, out of its own powers, its own thirst for order. Robert Creeley quotes Allen Ginsberg as saying "Mind is shapely." And Denise Levertov gives the following definition of organic poetry:

It is a method of apperception, i.e., of recognizing what we perceive, and based on an intuition of an order, a form beyond forms, in which forms partake, and of which man's creative works are analogies, resemblances, natural allegories. Such poetry is exploratory.[3]

In order to complete its explorations, such a poetry must avoid an entrapping irony and make maximum use of empathy.

Each poet's method of exploring will be different, and the various forms of control he exercises will be based on his own method of apperception. For Kinnell, this reflexive act of sensory consciousness often takes shape, as I have suggested, along the edges, the margins of perception. Such consciousness need not be purely spatial in form, either; and Kinnell often uses a temporal marginality, a sense of the "just occurred" or imminent event as crucial in the discovery of the "form beyond forms, in which forms partake." As he says in "The Poem":

> On this hill crossed
> by the last birds, a sprinkling
> of soil covers up the rocks
> with green, as
> the face
> drifts on a skull scratched with glaciers.
>
> The poem too
> is a palimpsest, streaked
> with erasures, smelling
> of departure and burnt stone.

Along with the images of burning, "build-soil," and painful scars that occur frequently in Kinnell's work, this poem has two other images: the human face and a written text. Both of these latter figures recur with increasing frequency in *Body Rags* and *The Book of Nightmares,* and their resonances are indicative of Kinnell's attempts to "register" experience with the most sensible recorders available. In his essay "Poetry, Personality, and Death,"[4] Kinnell offers the following observations on the American face, a face he thinks has literally been marked and transfigured by the technological age:

> Contrast the ancestral faces one still sees in Europe, contrast the faces in old paintings and photographs. Is it just my imagination that the American chin has thickened, its very bones swollen, as if to repel what lies ahead? And those broad, smooth, curving, translucent eyelids, that gave such mystery to the eyes—is it my private delusion that they have disappeared, permanently rolled themselves up, turning the eyes into windows without curtains, not to be taken by surprise again? And that the nose, the feature unique to man, the part of him which moves first into the unknown, has become on our faces a small neat bump?

Concern with the face in large part springs from a concern with sensuous experience, with receiving the primary data of our environment, with exploratively moving "into the unknown." The face offers a force field of sensitively registered changes and dispositions; it also provides a collection of "edges" that take shape according to our willingness to immerse ourselves in our experience. Speaking in "The Porcupine" of the "clothespins that have / grabbed our body-rags by underarm and crotch," Kinnell describes the animal in these terms:

> Unimpressed—bored—
> by the whirl of stars, by *these*
> he's astonished, ultra-
> Rilkean angel!
>
> for whom the true
> portion of the sweetness of earth
> is one of those bottom-heavy, glittering, saccadic
> bits
> of salt water that splash down
> the haunted ravines of a human face.

Physiognomy takes on the scope of geography, and again, in proper Rilkean fashion, the transcendence of the poem's desires springs from contact with the earth, as the human face becomes the source of the porcupine's intensely craved salt and becomes of more interest than "the whirl of the stars." The larger systems of signification are replaced by pain.

Kinnell had begun *Body Rags* with a poem called "Another Night in the Ruins," which has the following terminal section:

> How many nights must it take
> one such as me to learn
> that we aren't, after all, made
> from that bird which flies out of its ashes,
> that for a man
> as he goes up in flames, his own work
> is
> to open himself, to *be*
> the flames?

The volume ends with "The Bear," a shamanistic immersion in the unknown, a "dance of solitude" that describes in great detail the hunting of the animal with "the chilly, enduring odor of bear." I think one phrase that might adequately hint at how the poem achieves its power over us is Denise Levertov's *natural allegory*. Pursued so intensely, the bear must end up "meaning something else," but only the briefest of analogical touchstones appears at the end of the poem, after the speaker has killed the bear and is watching a dam bear give birth to her cubs, "lumps of smeared fur":

> the rest of my days I spend
> wandering: wondering
> what, anyway,
> was that sticky infusion, that rank flavor of blood, that poetry,
>     by which I lived?

Exploration and attentiveness provide the grounds of existence for the hunter of bear, for the poet; and those grounds are both the occasion and the subject of his most insistent questionings.

The hunter kills the bear by coiling a bone and freezing it in blubber; when the bear ingests it, the bone uncoils and pierces his inner organs. The resultant internal bleeding dominates the images of the poem, and the speaker eventually tracks down the bear, hacks "a ravine in his thigh," tears him "down his whole length," and climbs inside. Once the hunter is inside, his empathetic identification with the bear becomes literal, and the poet recapitulates by dreaming the bear's death. The final death agony of the poet-shaman-dreamer can easily be read as the moment of greatest artistic risk, when the flux of experience yields to the stasis of form.

> and now the breeze
> blows over me, blows off
> the hideous belches of ill-digested bear blood
> and rotted stomach
> and the ordinary, wretched odor of bear,
>
> blows across
> my sore, lolled tongue a song
> or screech, until I think I must rise up
> and dance. And I lie still.

Only by digesting the blood that leaked into his stomach, that is, only by destroying himself, could the bear have lived; and such self-transcendence, Kinnell seems to be saying, can only be achieved by someone tracking down and recording the experience. Such evidence as becomes available for this act may only be a carcass, a remnant of what has "just occurred"; but, through empathetic dream-work, through poetry, such exploration and attentiveness can be the source of new life. Again, from "Poetry, Personality, and Death":

> The death of the self I seek, in poetry and out of poetry, is not a drying up or withering. It is a death, yes, but a death out of which one might hope to be reborn more giving, more alive, more open, more related to the natural life. . . . For myself, I would like a death that would give me more loves, not fewer. And greater desire, not less.

The song may be no more than a screech, but it still expresses the organism's need to come to terms with its environment, and for Kinnell such a coming to terms involves growth. Throughout his poetry there flows the awareness that growth involves a kind of dying, and *The Book of Nightmares* becomes the fullest statement of this theme. Though the theme itself might be expressed as a paradox, the mode of its expression in the poems remains that of empathetic immersion, rather than that of ironic suspension.

Empathy as Kinnell employs it in *The Book of Nightmares* makes most statements about his "themes" appear reductive. In a poem that uses ironic tension suspended throughout a logical structure, the thematic argument still constitutes a weakened paraphrase of what the poem "really says," but this difficulty of determining what the poem "says" is geometrically increased when the poem uses an affective structure, articulated more by associative links than by a deductive sequence. When Susan Sontag called for an "erotics rather than a hermeneutics" of art, she was asking for a method much more suited for a postmodernist, nonironic literature. Such an approach might best lead us into this book of Kinnell's, a book densely palpable in its concern with the suffering flesh and peaked with frequently climactic longings. As Robert Bly says, "in poems ideas lie curled under tree roots, only a strong odor of fur indicating anything is there," though we should add that this is certainly truer for the poems of which Bly approves than for other, more "thematically consistent" poetry. It might be possible to indicate the change from a thematic, "argued" poetry to an associative poetry, of which *The Book of Nightmares* represents such a brilliant example, by considering as symptomatic the change from a predominant use of visual imagery to a more and more frequent use of olfactory and gustatory images. "The rank flavor of blood" in "The Bear" controls the affective energies in that poem much more strongly than do any of the visual images it contains. But perhaps the best way to appreciate *The Book of Nightmares,* or rather our experience of it, is to plunge into it, gathering and sorting ideas only as they become dominant.

There are ten poems in *The Book of Nightmares,* each with seven sections. Like the Commandments with alchemical glosses, the poems are about holiness grossly apprehended in a world charred by ignorance and intensity. The titles of the individual poems— "The Dead Shall Be Raised Incorruptible," "The Call Across the Valley of Not-Knowing," "Lastness"—are like titles of religious tracts or gnostic testaments; yet enough narrative fragments and images recur and develop from poem to poem to make the book a considerable whole. Inside each of the ten poems, the sections vary in texture, pace, intensity, and mode. Some are exacting transcriptions of climactic moments; others are quiet, loving exempla, or mysterious, mystically symbolic constructs. The subtile syntax, often articulating the curve of a perception or the morphology of an emotion, echoes the sort of thing that we saw at the end of "Night in the Forest."

Complex and rich as all this is, the voice that sustains itself and discovers itself throughout the poems remains somehow straightforward. It's almost as if Kinnell constantly and innocently surprises himself, finding, "as he obeys the necessity and falls," that "the dead lie, / empty, filled, at the beginning, / and the first / voice comes craving again out of their mouths." The young daughter who "puts / her hand / into her father's mouth, to take hold of / his song" is the initial addressee of the book (if such a spirit can be described by that rhetorical term), and her innocent grasping after the human voice stands for the central mystery that is both the cause and the occasion of Kinnell's book. Again, the human face and the work of art are the key traces of emotion.

In Kinnell's poetry, deeply human utterances are like animals. They are best witnessed as expressive gestures. The bear that concluded *Body Rags* makes several reappearances in this book, in several guises. Nowhere does he speak, but he is witness to human speech whether he "sits alone / on his hillside, nodding from side / to side" or is "floundering through chaos / in his starry blubber" as Ursa Major. Notice too the shifting perspective, the sudden awareness of infinite extension for the bear, something that happens frequently in these poems. Other images besides the bear recur, each equally part of the failed flesh of the world as well as of its fulfillment. A decapitated hen becomes a hen-flower, filled with a "mass of tiny / unborn eggs, each getting / tinier and yellower as it reaches back toward / the icy pulp / of what is." An unborn child can "rouse himself / with a huge, fishy thrash, and resettle in his darkness."

*The Book of Nightmares,* filled with obsessive images, carries back from the darkness a "languished alphabet." But this set of characters can spell more than objects; it speaks as well of people and events. The daughter who appears in the first and the son who hears the final reflections of the poem are just two, though the two most important, of the people with whom Kinnell converses. Indeed, if one were to formulate a thematic statement equivalent to the poem's energies, that statement would have to recognize the daughter's birth and the poet's own imagined death as the terminal points of the work. There is also a "stranger extant in the memory" though extinct from the palpable world, perhaps a suicide, but certainly a possessed individual who defines for the poet not only the limits of pain but also the body that suffers, "all bodies, one body, one light / made of everyone's darkness together."

Again, it should be pointed out that the book succeeds beautifully as a whole; but what makes the total more than the sum of the parts is the tough, but complexly responsive, sense of form that Kinnell has discovered for his own voice. Each of the ten poems is variously incendiary and heuristic. The poet's attention burns through level after level, each vision catching up sparks and flashes from other sightings. The fires of the world must be met with fire if the poet is to truly discover all the edges of his possibilities. "Somewhere / in the legends of blood sacrifice / the fatted calf / takes the bonfire into his arms, and *he* / burns *it*."

Destructive though the element of fire may be, Kinnell's forms are always instructive. There is an almost didactic tone in some parts of this book, a didacticism close to the evangelical. (That alone should make the book distinct from the dominant modern mode of irony.) But the poet draws back from priesthood because he continually rediscovers himself, and discovers in himself "the hunger to be new." Proposing new visions, like Adam he awakes to find them true: "The witness trees heal / their scars at the flesh fire." Nightmares are incendiary, but the book is heuristic. Or, to put it another way, what we see in our nightmares will surely char us unless we can transcribe it. The shaman-speaker of the last poem in *Body Rags* ends his days wondering; but in this later book, the shaman-speaker is closer to the answer to that question, "what . . . was the rank flavor of blood . . . by which I lived?" Again, it is through dream that the answer is formulated:

> a face materializes into your hands,
> on the absolute whiteness of pages
> a poem writes itself out: its title—the dream
> of all poems and the text
> of all loves—"Tenderness toward Existence."

Once more the human face and the poetic text coincide to register the vision. Learn, he tells his child, "to reach deeper / into the sorrows / to come," anticipate the "still undanced cadence of vanishing." Then, with the child soothed and put back to sleep, he adds a promise. The promise is to learn, even if the lesson is preceded by destruction, and the promise constitutes Kinnell's testament.

> Little sleep's-head sprouting hair in the moonlight,
> when I come back
> we will go out together,

we will walk out together among
the ten thousand things,
each scratched too late with such knowledge, *the wages
of dying is love.*

Kinnell has discovered his own way of looking at things here, and though irony may be weakened, certainly American poetry is the stronger for it.

NOTES

1. See Richard Howard's essay in *Alone with America: The Art of Poetry in the United States Since 1950* (New York: Atheneum, 1969), 258–71, where Kinnell's use of fire imagery is discussed.

2. The essay was originally presented as a lecture at Colorado State University in 1969.

3. In *Naked Poetry,* ed. Stephen Berg and Robert Mezey (Indianapolis: Bobbs-Merrill, 1969), 441.

4. In *Field* 4 (Spring 1971): 56–75. See also the interview with Kinnell in *Ohio Review* (Fall 1972): 25–36.

PART TWO   *Book Reviews*

JAMES DICKEY

# From "Five First Books"
*[What a Kingdom It Was]*

I liked Galway Kinnell's poems mainly for their wholehearted
commitment to themselves, and for what I can only call their
innocence. Mr. Kinnell cares quite openly and honestly about
almost everything he has ever seen, heard of, or read about, and
finds it rather easy to say so. There is nothing very tragic or
tearing about him, or nothing very intense, either. He seems to
me a natural poet: humanly likeable, gentle, ruminative. But he
is dishearteningly prolix. Prolixity is, of course, the foremost
and perhaps only natural enemy of the natural poet, and Mr.
Kinnell is going to have to do battle with it if he is to realize
himself. Some of these pieces are almost too trivial to be be-
lieved, and even the best of them keep blurring into each other,
since there is no real division, nothing to *individualize* them,
make them separately experienceable. They are just part of the
amiable weather of the book. Poetry can do better than this, and
so can Kinnell. The last long poem, "The Avenue Bearing the
Initial of Christ into the New World," has some beautiful lines
about such unbeautiful objects as carp in grocer's tanks and veg-
etable pushcarts. Here, you feel quite strongly a genuine pres-
ence, an integrated personal reality, powerful and *projected*. Kin-
nell realizes the difference between knowing something because
you have been told it is so and knowing it because you have
lived it. And this latter kind of knowing is what good poetry can
give, and what Kinnell in some of his work gives, too. His first
book is not as deep and abiding as we might like; I find myself

Reprinted by permission of Farrar, Straus and Giroux, Inc., from *Babel to Byzan-
tium*, by James Dickey. Copyright © 1961, 1968 by James Dickey. First appeared
in *Poetry* 97 (February 1961), copyright © 1961 by the Modern Poetry Associa-
tion. Reprinted by permission of the Editor of *Poetry*.

remembering his themes and a few scattered details, but not the way in which they are told, or, as happens with the very best poems, the *words* in which they are told. But Mr. Kinnell has made an authentic beginning, and many poets die without getting even this far. Perhaps to a degree more than is true of other poets, Kinnell's development will depend on the actual events of his life. And it is a life that I think we should watch. It is warm, generous, reflective, and friendly. And as poetry it holds out some promise, largely because of this necessary involvement with the author's life, of being in the end magnificent. It is not entirely impossible that the Wave of the Future may turn out to have begun at Avenue C, or some place within walking distance of it.

LOUISE BOGAN

# From "Verse"
## [*What a Kingdom It Was*]

[Galway Kinnell's] first book of poems, *What a Kingdom It Was,* is remarkably unburdened by this or that current influence. Kinnell is direct and occasionally harsh, and he keeps his syntax straight and his tone colloquial. His chief concern, we soon discover, is the enigmatic significance, more than the open appearance, of Nature and man. "Freedom, New Hampshire," an elegy for his brother—a full realization of country boyhood, with a boy's confrontation of cruelty and unreasonable happiness left intact— is also an affirmation of immortality. Kinnell's longest and most pretentiously titled poem, "The Avenue Bearing the Initial of Christ into the New World," deals with a most difficult subject— life in a city slum. Here pitfalls abound—sentimentality, insincerity, the possibility of mixed and unresolved feelings of pity and guilt. Kinnell bypasses all these. City streets are for a time his home; he feels the vitality of their people; he responds with extreme sensitiveness to multiple sights, sounds, smells; without any furtive condescension, he places Avenue C in the human context. Sympathy, identification, insight sustain this long poem in every detail, and Kinnell chooses his details with startling exactness.

From *A Poet's Alphabet,* edited by Robert Phelps and Ruth Limmer (New York: McGraw-Hill, 1970). First appeared in the *New Yorker,* 1 April 1961. Reprinted by permission of Ruth Limmer, as Trustee of the Estate of Louise Bogan.

DEWITT BELL

# From "Wonders of the Inner Eye"
## [*Flower Herding on Mount Monadnock*]

Galway Kinnell's second book, *Flower Herding on Mount Monadnock*, has the virtues of his first one—strength and surprising innovations of technique, but it brings with it a new subtlety, depth and simplicity. . . . The book is intensely rooted in the land, the city, the language of America. But the simplicity is the external simplicity of the *haiku*—the seemingly effortless utterance that probes so deeply. It is a memorable book.

The title itself is an example of Kinnell's adeptness at connoting many things in one statement. Monadnock is a mountain in New Hampshire—many of the poems are concerned with man's aloneness with nature. But "monad" is Leibnitz's term for an individual unit reflecting in itself the whole universe. Extracted from its philosophical system the word can be the Zen Buddhist principle of the One, or the Blakean "world in a grain of sand." It is just this kind of awareness Kinnell is out to reach.

The poems themselves are compositions in every sense of the word. The themes are simple, but the variations so woven that objects and ideas gain significance and relationship from their place in the pattern. For instance in "Spindrift," a poem in seven parts, the poet picks up a shell on a deserted beach in the first part, and sees it as "a fan of gold light." In the last part he cites an old man, looking out to sea at the sunset; and the old man and the shell unite:

> Nobody likes to die
> But an old man
> Can know

From the *New York Times Book Review*, 5 July 1964. Copyright © 1964 by The New York Times Company. Reprinted by permission.

A kind of gratefulness
Towards time that kills him,
Everything he loved was made of it.

In the end
What is he but the scallop shell
Shining with time like any pilgrim?

JOHN MALCOLM BRINNIN

# From "Plath, Jarrell, Kinnell, Smith"

## [*Flower Herding on Mount Monadnock*]

. . . In this grouping of poets Kinnell is the quiet one—deft, meditative, scrutinizing correspondences, hearkening to intimations. Like Jarrell, he is conscious of the penumbra of a "second" reality; but in his case the missing dimension is not a mythical projection but an impenetrable otherness. "I know I live half alive in the world," he says. "I know half my life belongs to the wild darkness." This is bold, and naïve, but Kinnell means what he says:

Sometimes I see them,
The south-going Canada geese,
At evening, coming down
In pink light, over the pond, in great,
Loose, always dissolving V's—
I go out into the field,
Amazed and moved, and listen
To the cold, lonely yelping
Of those tranced bodies in the sky,
Until I feel on the point
Of breaking into a sacred, bloodier speech.

The "wild darkness" sends out its emissaries, but most often nature is an unresponsive wall against revelation, a wall that won't give, a weeping wall. This immediate sense of the physical-cum-metaphysical extends to personal identity. "I could

From *Partisan Review* 34 (Winter 1967). Reprinted by permission of John Malcolm Brinnin.

make out a beggar," says Galway Kinnell, "Down the long street he was calling *Galway!* / I started towards him and began calling *Galway!*" The explicit figure of the *Doppelgänger* comes into the book just this once. But even without the dramatic intrusion his presence would be distinctly felt. The charm and force of many of Kinnell's poems lies in his ability to watch himself do what he does with a wise, untroubled stare. A mystical disposition suggests a vision blurred. But Kinnell's eye is exact and exacting: a Bleecker Street wino looks in upon the scene of a poetry reading from "the mowed cornfield of his gawk"; on a summer morning the poet sees "the old crane / Who holds out his drainpipe of a neck / And creaks along in the blue"; and watches "Milton Norway's sky-blue Ford / Dragging its ass down the dirt road / On the other side of the valley."

The quotient of "nature" poems in this volume is high, perhaps too high. While many poems in this vein are as economical as line drawings, a certain sameness of attitude dominates a run of them and threatens to fix the poet in the dead stance of man-against-the-sky. In the city, on the other hand, this man has things to say that are new. In "The River That Is East," a kind of postlude to *The Bridge,* he suggests in just five packed stanzas what has happened, in less than thirty years, to the epical pretensions of a visionary and, by implication, to the illusions of a culture.

MONA VAN DUYN

# From "The Poet as Novelist"
## [*Black Light*]

The conscious exoticism of Galway Kinnell's first novel (appear-
ing after two books of poems) enables it on the one hand to seem
a distanced parable, on the other hand to impress the reader, in
the Novel's old cocky way, with its command of realistic detail
about a hitherto-unexperienced world. Description and image
also flicker between daylit reality and moonlit symbol. Jamshid,
a virtuous Moslem rug-weaver of Iran, commits a murder in-
stantly, unthinkingly, on hearing his daughter insulted. Then
he, who lived always by patterns, who would close his shop
when a sun-patch crept "over the border of the geometrical and
turn[ed] into chaos," who worked with "nervous speed" when-
ever it was "a question of a gap through which darkness was
visible," finds that he has not healed the gap his daughter's
unchastity would make in his ordered life, but has instead cast
himself into an ever-widening world of darkness and chaos.

Into his exile he goes, across the dreamlike landscape of the
desert, finding at each near-encounter with death a new dimen-
sion and devotion to life, finding in torment an ecstasy, in filth
some purity or refinement. In the end, in the walled red-light
district of Teheran, among suppurating whores, he may or may
not have lain with his own daughter, figurative incest being a
deep part of all human love, literal incest being a dark human
sin.

The existential "idea" of this novel is a tired one, unassisted
by the easy paradox of the title. But the style is flawless, neither

From *Poetry* 109 (February 1967). Copyright © 1967 by The Modern Poetry
Association. Reprinted by permission of the Editor of *Poetry* and Mona Van
Duyn.

too rich nor too spare: ". . . as he lay there he felt the strange-ness of this material under his hands—an earth made of stones that had been grated, rained, blown, and burnt into a substance that was hardly earth at all, but a form of nothingness, a sub-stance from which nothing living would spring again. As if death had been ground up and strewn here in a thick layer. He saw the jagged, unburdened columns rising in the darkness and the great stones with their heavy, closed eyes. He fell asleep, and slept deeply."

The bird-of-paradise which Jamshid is literally reweaving in a rug on page one appears again, again, again, its feathers, its song, its natural, its symbolic, self, growing in meaning, collect-ing to itself more and more weight. It is in its images that this novel is really alive; *they* are its compelling action. A strange, haunting book.

GERALD BURNS

# From "Poets and Anthologies"
[*Body Rags*]

Galway Kinnell is notable for a kind of earthy spirituality no-
body else can match. His animal poems ("The Porcupine,"
"The Bear") are top-notch, Spanish as his insect poems are Ori-
ental. At a fast guess I would say that if anyone is setting himself
up to write the great American long poem (if only to contain
himself) it's he, making *Body Rags* a few more Notes Toward.
His short things are delicate—"Getting the Mail," "Night in the
Forest"—but unlike our watercolorists imply violence. And
"The Last River" (which has an original Charon, and Thoreau
for Virgil) is the canonical epic descent into hell, striking and
good. But much of it could have been written by Elizabeth
Bishop. Not really, but I'd like to think that his adjectives,
which he handles with evocative precision, are coming to be a
kind of prison for him and he knows it, senses it (the book is full
of chains, prison, and poison). Marianne Moore says "Wariness
is essential where an inaccurate word could give an impression
more exact than could be given by a verifiably accurate term,"
and heaven knows she's no obscurantist. This is a terrible thing
to say, but reading "The Last River" I kept wishing he'd read
Gary Snyder with attention, and rewrite it sans adjectives and
adverbs, as an exercise. If you do a thing too well why do it? and
as Miss Stein reminds us, poetry is a matter of nouns.

---

From *Southwest Review* 53 (Summer 1968). Reprinted by permission of Gerald
Burns.

HAYDEN CARRUTH

# From "Making It New"
## [Body Rags]

. . . Even today—this epoch of foundation grants, cushy teaching appointments, reading tours, etc.—most of us write our poems in the worst possible conditions. Galway Kinnell is a case in point. In his first two books Kinnell worked out a personal style of great promise, a clean, spare line that was never merely taut or hard, leading through small disparate statements of experience to the crowning statement, the poem itself, recapitulating and unifying the disparities. In his new book, *Body Rags,* he has brought this style to a kind of perfection, especially in two poems about the killing of animals, "The Porcupine" and "The Bear." These are the grisliest poems I have ever read. Yet from their shock and repulsion Kinnell draws his crowning unity of feeling, into which we are in turn assimilated, whether we like it or not. These two poems strike me as the sort that are born to be famous; they will be in our anthologies for many lives to come (assuming anthologies, assuming lives). Only a shade less successful is Kinnell's long poem called "The Last River," comprising the memories and dreams of an imprisoned civil-rights worker in the South. It ends with a vision of the modern Inferno no less powerful than [Robert] Duncan's, and with greater authenticity of detail. As far as I know it is the strongest single piece of writing the Movement has produced so far. Together with "The Porcupine" and "The Bear" it makes *Body Rags* a very fine book indeed; so fine that one is compelled to ask: how much richer and broader might Kinnell's work be if he had been permitted to write as steadily as Duncan has written in a comparable period of years?

Reprinted by permission from *The Hudson Review,* Vol. XXI, No. 2 (Summer 1968). Copyright © 1968 by The Hudson Review, Inc.

JOHN LOGAN

# The Bear in the Poet in the Bear
[*Body Rags*]

Each generation looks about to see who the great ones are in the
arts, and in our time we can single out Galway Kinnell as one of
the few consummate masters in poetry. His third book, *Body
Rags*, is uniformly strong beside *What a Kingdom It Was* (1960)
and *Flower Herding on Mount Monadnock* (1964), and it takes some
risks those books do not. In two of the three poems in the final
section of the new book, "The Porcupine" and "The Bear,"
there is some of the best poetry to be found any place today,
while the long, civil rights–concerned poem, "The Last River,"
which makes up the entire second section, is one of the most
pertinent and ambitious poems of the time.

The latter poem turns the situation of a jail in the deep South
into a Dantesque drama and reflection of considerable complex-
ity. One should know that Kinnell was in fact jailed for civil
rights activities in Selma. Although I admire it, I do not find the
poem entirely successful because the elements of formal repeti-
tion and of classical allusion sometime appear too heavy-handed.
For example this:

> He comes out of the mist,
> he tells me his name is Henry David,
> He takes my hand and leads me over the plain of crushed
>    asphodels.

However, if one is going to seek an analogue to Virgil as a
guide through the hell of Selma, it would be difficult to better

From *The Nation*, 16 September 1968. Reprinted by permission.

the choice of Henry David Thoreau who, in a planned act of civil disobedience during the Mexican War, refused to pay taxes to a government he considered abstract.

"The Last River" repeats many of the images of the nineteen (mainly short) poems which constitute the first section of the book. There is a good deal of specifically religious symbolism ("Let's go I say, a big / salty wafer of spit in my mouth") and there are wings, flowers and flames employed in connection with a Roethke-like motif of opening and/or being transformed. But the longer poem, understandably in a poem of the South, lacks the snow that frequently falls in the shorter ones—sometimes in a climate a bit like that of Robert Bly:

> Soon it will be spring,
> again the vanishing of the snows,
>
> and tonight
> I sit up late, mouthing
> the sounds that would be words
> in this flimsy jew's-harp of a farmhouse.

The farmhouse, by the way, is a real one near Sheffield, Vermont, red, windy, on top of a beautiful hill at the end of an isolated, unimproved road, and it has for some years been a site of inner and outer lookings and of labors which Galway Kinnell has turned into poetry.

"The Last River" also contains the title motif:

> a man of noble face
> sits on the iron bunk, wiping
> a pile of knifeblades clean
> in the rags of his body.

This is varied twice in the description of the horrid Charon-figure in the poem: "limbs tied on with knots and rags"; and once in "The Porcupine" where the title phrase "body-rags" occurs directly. The title is perhaps meant to echo the famous "aged man" passage from Yeats's "Sailing to Byzantium," possibly as prefigured by Pound (Yeats's secretary at the time) in a letter to Viola Baxter, October 24, 1907: "This body-rag thing tattered on my soul."

The two poems "The Porcupine" and "The Bear" I think the best in the book. They make up a pair on related subjects having finally to do with the poet and with poetry. There is a strong identification of the poet-speaker with the animal in each case, and the animals themselves share certain qualities—ponderousness, voraciousness and resilient, brute strength.

Kinnell details seven (highly ironic) points in which the porcupines resemble man in general and poets in particular. In his bear poem, the identification of the poet and the bear is made extraordinarily close—in the first place, through the starving speaker's subsistence on the blood-soaked turds of the bear he hunts, so that that which has passed through the bear passes also through the poet, and in the second place, through the fact that the poet cuts open the warm carcass of the bear and takes shelter there against the vicious wind and cold.

> . . . lumbering flatfooted
> over the tundra,
> stabbed twice from within
> splattering a trail behind me

He is born out of the body of the bear again, having thought in his dream that he "must rise up and dance"—and he writes his poem. But first he makes an agonized step, infantlike and bearlike as well (it is a "hairy-soled trudge"), and like the ancient mariner he wanders the rest of his days wondering "what anyway . . . was that sticky infusion, that rank flavor of blood, that poetry, by which I lived." The present poem is to be seen as the fruit of that wondering, and it is a remarkable one in its reenactment of the existential loneliness, the sense of abandonment before the elements and the dual role of hunter and hunted under which we all live out our lives.

The image of poetry itself as a "sticky infusion" of bloody bear shit must make us reflective when we find it in the work of one of our best poets. The figure of the poet-as-bear is familiar from the work of Theodore Roethke and Delmore Schwartz.

Roethke's bear, like Kinnell's, dances: "O watch his body sway! / This animal remembering to be gay." Schwartz, Roethke and Kinnell are all big men, and they have projected their size into an image whose emotional dynamics all poets share to a certain extent, beginning with their disbelief in the likelihood of a creature such as melancholy, flesh-heavy man bursting into song.

The element of bearlike ponderousness or awkwardness we are familiar with in the image of the poet, for it relates to his (no doubt justified) feeling of being "out of his element" like Baudelaire's albatross on the deck of a ship.

Voraciousness is another element in this image, for the poet gluts himself with reading and experience out of which to write, and it contributes to the concept of ponderousness, particularly in those constipated times when one produces nothing. Kinnell's porcupine is voracious as the bear—and on a diverse diet as if for making poems:

> Fatted
> on herbs, swollen on crabapples,
> puffed up on bast and phloem, ballooned
> on willow flowers, poplar catkins, first
> leafs of aspen and larch,
> the porcupine
> drags and bounces his last meal through ice,
> mud, roses and goldenrod, into the stubby high fields.

The last line reminds us of Eliot's line adapted from Mallarmé's description of poetry: "Garlic and sapphires in the mud."

The resilient strength of bear and porcupine is a quality the poet desperately needs in order to counterbalance his (killing) sensitivity and which, like them, he sometimes possesses sufficiently to survive.

But neither the bear nor the porcupine in Kinnell's poems *does* survive. They die slow, terrible deaths, the first from the inner stabbing of a sharpened stick coiled in his food and the other for being shot three times and falling to unwind his guts from a tree limb.

Seeing the poet as imaged by the bear returns one to the image of poetry itself as the excretion of the wounded animal:

"that sticky infusion, that rank flavor of blood, that poetry by which I lived." The visceral connotation is not of itself arresting, for again it is part of the general image of poetry which, when it is any good, comes certainly from the inner depths—and the sexual ring of "sticky infusion" is predictable and right. But there is an aura of violence (self-destructive, dying) to the visceral imagery of the poems and to the phrase "rank flavor of blood" which stops me, and I want to comment on it.

In the porcupine poem the self-pain is quite specific:

> In my time I have
> crouched, quills erected,
> Saint
> Sebastian of the
> sacred heart, and been
> beat dead with a locust club
> on the bare snout.

And in the bear poem the figure of the poet's dream (himself) is "stabbed twice from within" (compare the "self-stabbing coil / of bristles reversing" in the porcupine poem) while the trail of generative blood behind the dying bear is related to the umbilical cord or life line of the producing poet. This figure of the agonized generative trail is repeated in "The Porcupine" and in the third poem which makes up this final section of the book, "Testament of the Thief." In the latter poem it takes the form of a pewk-worm whose path as it is drawn out of the body "by winding him up on a matchstick / a quarter turn a day for the rest of your days" creates a "map of my innards," that is, a poem of the interior life. In the former poem it is figured in the strung-out intestines of the shot porcupine who "paying out gut heaved / and spartled through a hundred feet of goldenrod" before dying.

Poetry is a wandering trail of blood and bear shit. It is a pewk-worm wound through a hole in the buttocks or cheeks of a man. It is the tree-hooked entrails of a porcupine. The images are all repulsive and they are all figures of the slow destruction of the self. They remind specifically of George Barker's description of poetry: "I give you the image of the captive of the Gaels whose torture was to . . . unwind his intestines around a tree, for this is the poet . . . whose bowels are wound around Eden tree in coils at once agonizing and glorious. I mean each turn is a poem." Kinnell writes very similarly. "I have come to myself empty, the rope / strung out behind me / in the fall sun / suddenly glorified with all my blood."

The idea of the poet as masochist emerges. Sartre levels the accusation tellingly in *Literature and Existentialism*. But I would insist that poetry is not a record of self-destructive experiences. Rather, it is often a record of recovery from them. It is not the blood-soaked shit of a dying bear. Rather, it is the gold into which that stuff is turned by the magus gift of the poet. Thus the horse droppings in a poem of James Wright's "blaze into golden stones." But perhaps this is basically what Kinnell means by putting his poetics inside a poem, like a hunter inside a bear which shelters and transforms him into something fecund, dreaming.

On the other hand, if the content of Kinnell's bear poem does really have a masochistic bias to it, then this emphasis is (quite brilliantly and purposefully) weakened by the choice of a form in which the material is repeated from a dream inside the poem. For the meaning of the dream-within-the-dream Freud has said is often to put down the significance of the content so displayed, to say in effect "it was only a dream."

These two poems are very rich and mind-seizing and might be seen in other ways. I want finally to mention two other angles of vision: One might look at the images of porcupine gut, pewk-worm and bear trail simply as derivative from or extensions of the figure of the poet into something quite real (the poem). And one might look at the immersion of the hunter in the warm, colorful vitals of the bear as a figure of the contemporary poet who, withdrawn at last from libraries and from psychoanalysis (the book of himself), steeps himself instead in the pied field of human experience, partly revolting, partly serene and beautiful—like the porcupine amid the mud and the goldenrod.

THOMAS LASK

# From "The Makers and Their Works"

[*The Book of Nightmares*]

As we realize now, Galway Kinnell has been preparing us for some time for *The Book of Nightmares*. The language and the forms of the earlier work, the material and his treatment of it anticipate what has been done here. *The Book of Nightmares* is his most integrated book, a work of one mood, one subject really, a tormented cry of what the poet is and feels at this moment.

He has not lost the imagistic touch, noted earlier in such poems as "Night in the Forest" or in some of the stanzas of "The Poem," as these lines from his current book testify:

> and that wafer-stone
> which skipped ten times across
> the water, suddenly starting to run as it went under,
> and the zeroes it left,
> that met
> and passed into each other, they themselves
> smoothing themselves from the water . . .

The powerful nature poems, "The Porcupine" and "The Bear," in *Body Rags,* anticipate the handling of the hen in the second section of the current book. There is the same clinical, microscopic vision, which gives intense reality to the animal without sacrificing its symbolic value. The ending of "The Bear," unexpected as it is, is less a surprise than a fulfillment. And Mr. Kinnell's willingness to look at the underside of soci-

From the *New York Times,* 1 September 1971. Copyright © 1971 by The New York Times Company. Reprinted by permission.

ety, to poke in the scummy pot of our culture, where, he feels, so much that is rotten floats to the top, is not new either. We had more than a taste of it in "The Last River" and in that long poem with the burdensome title in *What a Kingdom It Was:* "The Avenue Bearing the Initial of Christ into the New World."

The nightmares of Mr. Kinnell's title are not nocturnal happenings or hallucinatory experiences of the mind but those constrictions of the heart that are a function of living. If any one thought broods over this book, it is the realization of our mortality—not for the poet but for all he loves. The burden of fatherhood, or his daring to bring anyone into the world to bear once again the weight of life, imparts to his lines an unending anguish. There is no more moving love letter to a young daughter than the lines Mr. Kinnell has written that begin, "I would blow the flame out of your silver cup." One line in that passage sums up all the rest: "I would alchemize the ashes of your cradle back into wood." Our lives begin a retrograde motion as soon as we are born, and men poison the time between the poles of life and death. One section, the sixth in the book, with its refrain, *"Lieutenant! / This corpse will not stop burning,"* stands for all the acts of cruelty to which the innocent are exposed. There is more than enough violence in the book, but it is somehow dissolved into the overall mood of the work. His treatment of animals, of the animals dead, eviscerated, or stumblingly alive, has the delicacy and lightness of a magician.

The violence of the jailer, the rough companionship of the imprisoned, a chance meeting with a woman on a plane, a musician's playing Bach all reinforce his consciousness of the worm in the bud, of the skull beneath the flesh. Put this way, his book may appear as no more than the echo of a theme going back at least to Ecclesiastes. The last chapter of that book has, perhaps, said it all. Even so, Mr. Kinnell has given fresh voice to the idea in terms that are close, immediate, contemporary. The book is all of a piece, no more to be broken off than a piece of one's heart. After reading it, one turns without plan or forethought to the beginning and starts anew.

M. L. ROSENTHAL

# Under the Freeway, in the Hotel of Lost Light
## [*The Book of Nightmares*]

Galway Kinnell's title for his new book of poems suggests its preoccupation: the world of terror raging beneath the sill of daylight consciousness. It is the world of Eliot's "Rhapsody on a Windy Night," where destructive reality invades the naked psyche. *The Book of Nightmares* is a sequence of ten poems, each in seven sections, that takes us on an extended inward journey toward the state of the speaker's soul at a specified moment—

> in March, of the year Seventy,
> on my sixteen-thousandth night of war and madness,
> in the Hotel of Lost Light, under the freeway
> which roams out into the dark
> of the moon, in the absolute spell
> of departure, and by the light
> from the joined hemispheres of the spider's eyes.

This key passage shows how much of a piece the book is with the whole post-Romantic tradition. The first pair of lines links social and private horror with the contemporary instant. The next two extend the horror to a meaningless cosmos; man is in the dark whether he seeks refuge or risks the unknown. The final lines charge the desolate scene with a malign spell. The ten poems of the sequence accept the implications of such a universe while holding on to lines of human meaning.

Each of the elementary motifs around which the work is built

From the *New York Times Book Review*, 24 November 1971. Copyright © 1971 by The New York Times Company. Reprinted by permission.

is conceived in this double light, as a reaching toward glimmers of transcendence beyond the acutely depressed vision of existence. They include the births of a son and daughter, the speaker's love for his wife, his abortive affair with another woman, his life-communion with other animals (brilliantly and morbidly explored in a poem about the killing of a hen), his identification with a drunk found dead in a hotel room, the gross violence (culminating in Vietnam) done by Christian man to himself and to others, and the spider-fly principle in human life. These basic motifs are interwoven in subtle ways, and all contribute to a dominant sense of mystical self-orientation in circumstances beyond control; the yearning implicit in the living flesh is the only shadow of hope in this interim dominion of death.

The surrender, the despair, that gives these poems their very pitch and melody is all the more striking because the natural symbols of affirmation—the wife's happy pregnancy, the birth of their children, and the couple's sexual harmony—come through with such tenderness and, sometimes, humor. Some readers might well consider Kinnell's description of the birth process as grimly realistic, but the net effect of the reconstructed experience is rather glorious and buoyant:

> and she skids out on her face into light,
> this peck
> of stunned flesh
> clotted with celestial cheesiness, glowing
> with the astral violet
> of the underlife. . . .

Indeed, the closer one looks at the sequence, the more clearly one sees that the real triumph, which is considerable, lies in just such moments of concrete realization, when the language exults at and transforms literal reality. The music of Kinnell's projections of reality is quite extraordinary. What is more dubious is his further projection of some unclarified personal complex of sufferings onto the same materials. Naturally, the unresolved sexual guilts and the broodings over war and death that saturate the poems are irrefutable sources of depression. But they are, if in varying proportions, our common lot, and there is nothing in the way Kinnell handles these themes that makes them particularly his.

To reinforce the psychological state he is trying to evoke, of a condition of visionary awareness heightened by private disorientation, Kinnell deploys a good deal of zodiacal, occult and religious symbolism. This aspect gives the volume much of its feeling of being heavily structured, with the sequence—and each poem within it—seeming to progress from a kind of despair to a kind of affirmation with many ups and downs and swirlings on the way. A "system" like that of Yeats's "A Vision" may be implied. The atmosphere is rich, sometimes thick, with allusions to the mysteries of augury and of the Crucifixion, and to such emblems and traditions as "the Archer," "the Bear," "the Crone" and "the sothic year."

Although some exciting effects of cosmic imperviousness to human affairs, heartbreaking and beautiful, are achieved, the structure is overloaded. Like that of Ted Hughes's "Crow," it proliferates its symbolism to cast a net over a superhuman range of reference. In both works, repeated readings do open up much of the wider meaning the poets seek to mobilize, but the problem remains. And at the end of *The Book of Nightmares,* we are after all back to the original lonely sensibility of the speaker. He is still on his isolated "path among the stones," yet passionately a part of the common life of all "who live out our plain lives," locating the sources of possibility however minimal:

> On the body,
> on the blued flesh, when it is
> laid out, see if you can find
> the one flea which is laughing.

Thus the sequence ends. Intellectually, the program isn't much, is it? Kinnell has echoed all the great, sad questions of the past concerning our destiny, and he has summoned up the famous masks of the poet, especially the crucified, freely confessing sinner-saint and the sufferer beyond all telling. Something like an astrologically oriented prophetic role attracts him too, and so we have a renewal of the poet as seer. But the real power of his book comes from its pressure of feeling, its remarkable empathy and keenness of observation, and its qualities of phrasing—far more than from its structural thoroughness or philosophical implications. It needs stripping down. But no matter. Whatever its weaknesses, *The Book of Nightmares* grapples mightily with its depressive view of reality and with essential issues of love, and it leaves us with something splendid: a true voice, a true song, memorably human.

ROBERT PETERS

# On Climbing the Matterhorn:
# Monadnock
[*The Book of Nightmares*]

Finding flaws in a poet as impressive as Galway Kinnell is about as presumptuous as fussing about the Matterhorn—the fact of a magnificent presence should be enough to satisfy all confronters. Few poets have been as well-dined and admired on the Poetry and Visiting Writer Circuits as Kinnell—the fact of his craggy presence and his memorized recitals of his work provide the chemistry of unforgettable appearances. He is so impressive that one is carried away, as if in the preliminary soundings of a Föhn wind, by his excellence. His books sell, and fresh young poets, particularly those attached to the more prestigious writing programs around the country, carry his books with the covers exposed to passersby, garnering Brownie points for their intelligence and perspicacity, and, meanwhile, inspiring the uncritical reverence one reserves for natural wonders.

My sense of Kinnell's work, after several years of reading it with admiration, is that it has become repetitious and flawed; his self-critical sense seems diminished—or, perhaps the truth is that since he has become a star, no editor dares give him the criticism he needs. He overstates, here, is sentimental there, overuses certain words until they become tags—Kinnell-words setting off easy Existentialisms. (The fact that Kinnell apparently knew Albert Camus is not entirely beside the point.) *The Book of Nightmares* has been almost universally praised since its appearance; and I make the complaints I am about to, realizing that

From *The Great American Poetry Bake-Off* (Metuchen, N.J.: Scarecrow Press, 1979). First appeared in *Northeast Rising Sun* 1 (January 1976). Reprinted by permission of Robert Peters.

there is still the energy, originality, and power in Kinnell to nurture several lesser poets.

Nevertheless, Kinnell seems to have reached the bottom of his bag of tricks. He presents too many of the same old devices. They don't explode the way they used to. Consider his diction, for example: certain words appear with the inevitability of Cher Bono's navel. Here is a sampling of Kinnell's navel-words: *darkness, light, bone/bones, haunted, existence, dying, graves, scars, rot.* The most cursory reading of *Nightmares* reveals these overworked tags. Consider *darkness.* Not only is the word sentimental; its vagueness belies precise meaning. The reader is lulled. A flag with *darkness* written on it goes up, and we are excused from any potent engagement with the poem. We experience a general gloom, a hissing bleakness. The poet spreads soft black butter (tar?) over our minds.

As a philosophical concept, of course, *darkness* had meaning in the forties and fifties when French Existentialism was in vogue at the better American colleges and universities. *Darkness* then was what *roses* were to the 1890s, and what *fuck* became to the sixties. A dark world, void and black, with God absent. . . . There's no use rerunning the Sisyphean tape. Kinnell lays his black slabs out there much as he laid them out during his earlier books.

Obviously, it is pigheaded to fault a poet for maintaining a life/world view throughout his career. Why should we expect a poet to change as he ages, to transmogrify his wisdom, so to speak, as living accumulates around him, as the barnacles and weeds adhere to his toughening hide? Thomas Hardy kept a knucklehold on similar views all his life, and barely changed them. Hardy called his stance meliorism—a sort of cop-out. And Hardy was frequently bad—repetitious, obvious, self-pitying. Most of the time, though, Hardy employed humor and irony to make his grim view somewhat more palatable. And he was, of course, a superb craftsman.

Kinnell generally lacks Hardy's saving irony. He wears a choirboy's seriousness. His interior bleeding is exactly that— unadulterated interior bleeding. The ease of his thinking, and the predictability, maintain a bright undergraduate's addiction to fairly slick philosophical concepts. His pain appears with an undergraduate's pride that he hurts so deeply. Passive and predictable, his sufferings now maintain themselves without a real, communicating pain.

But, to return to Hardy. I accept Hardy because of his irony, lyric skill, and wit, and I begin now to laugh *at* Kinnell as he presents me with further duplicate-images of himself as Existential Ur-*mensch* standing there facing me, holding his guts in his hands, his underwear sweat-fetid, seedy, his body scarred in various stages of healing, as he prepares to tuck his guts back into the cavity so as to free his hands for pushing that rock back up that interminable Monadnockian mountain.

Perhaps Kinnell is growing tired. Perhaps he is too famous, and merely repeats what fawning readers expect. His suffering is supposed to give us strength. His pain-postures make our own somehow easier to undergo. Or, they used to. I once thought his poems the nearest modern equivalents for those defiant Oedipean moments in Greek tragedy. I still respect his early work— and his personal courage on his trips to the South with freedom riders. There are original moments in *Nightmares*. The central sections of "Under the Maud Moon" are the best passages on birth I have read; the early portions of "The Hen Flower" exude much of Kinnell's earlier brilliance; and "Dear Stranger" is tellingly inventive.

Too often, however, Kinnell seems increasingly to lack what the nineteenth-century poets called *tact*—that poetic sense allowing the poet to know when he has violated formal demands of a work by pushing emotion too far (sentimentality), or by settling for mannered, dull writing when the poem requires his best work, or by his overwriting and straining. Obviously, the problems Kinnell has with his diction, already discussed, are failures of tact.

To be more specific: his fancy writing frequently assumes the delayed periodicity of old-fashioned poeticized writing. Here is a so-so, elaborate, periodic slab reminiscent of the Homeric delay Matthew Arnold loved so well. I guess that by using it Kinnell means to add to the momentousness of his theme—a momentousness he has already earned via the superb birth passage. But he doesn't sense that he might have intensified his power if he had been willing to edit out the excessive and the pretentious. Kinnell learns his "only song" during those first glimmerings of "the Maud Moon," when the Archer lay "sucking the icy biestings of the cosmos, / in his crib of stars." The poet creeps down to riverbanks, with "their long rustle / of being and perishing," reaches the marshes and the oozing earth, touches "the underglimmer" of the world's beginning.

Here is another of his devices—incorporating prepositional phrases into a line, seeking a portentousness which strikes me as simple pomposity: "he who crushed with his heel the brain out of the snake. . . ." This is hokey Swinburne or William Morris. "In the Hotel of Lost Light," periodicity winds down to a facile moment of almost absurd writing. Listen to the *post, postcards, posterity* word-play worthy of that lesser Victorian Stephen Phillips: Using "this languished alphabet of worms," he writes for *him* his final words, and posts for him "his final postcards to posterity."

More egregious than these lapses of tact within small areas of specific poems (a fine perfectly-shaped blue Santa Rosa plum with rot festering beneath the skin) is Kinnell's sentimentality. I realize that his poems to his children are much praised—and they are telling whenever Kinnell recites them. It is difficult to fault a man who writes of his kids. Who he is comes through, usually in the identifications of his own fate with his children's fate. "Little Sleep's-Head Sprouting Hair in the Moonlight," with its mythic overtones (the name sounds like a papoose-name), coming fairly well on in the book, will illustrate. The experience of the poet's taking his child out of her bed during one of her nightmares (after a few lines) turns sentimental. Kinnell hasn't earned, at least so far in this poem, the right to his pity. How does he know that little Maud feels lost? Isn't this merely a version of that old pathetic fallacy . . . a poet's imposing human gut-feelings on inanimate things in nature? A child, in a sense, especially a sleeping one, is an inanimate man (Wordsworth notwithstanding). It's as if Kinnell stains his child's veins with needles full of his own spleen. The image of his "broken arms" doesn't work for me. He forces the image into the broken shape of Existentialist suffering: Maud screams, waking from her nightmare. Kinnell sleepwalks to her, takes her up, holds her in the moonlight. The child clings to him, hard "as if clinging could save us." He says that she thinks he "will never die." He seems to "exude" to her "the permanence of smoke or stars"—all the while his "broken arms" are healing themselves around her. In section 3, the clever "*caca, caca*" section, Kinnell moves through the cuteness of indulgent parenthood to some slick writing, comparing his own eventual trip into oblivion as going with his daughter down

> the path of vanished alphabets,
> the roadlessness
> to the other side of the darkness. . . .

I imagine Dylan Thomas's ghost standing somewhere in the shade examining the contents of his nose. *Momentosity* is the word I invent for this writing . . . and it is an affliction that has also hit W. S. Merwin, who similarly strains after monumentalities he apparently no longer feels, but which his readers have come to expect. *Momentosity*. I invite the reader to compare also the various passages in *Nightmares* where Kinnell rides on the fame (back) of his Bear—the magnificent figure lifted from the earlier *Body Rags*.

Kinnell, to me, seems mired midway. I sincerely hope that his new work will indicate fresh turnings free of self-pity, stale romantic writing, and a stifling Existentialism. There is a principle of art that the more you struggle for momentousness the less likely you are to bring it off. There's an ease to the rising of every biscuit (poem); there's a leavening somewhere in most nightmares.

CHRISTOPHER RICKS

# From "In the Direct Line of Whitman, the Indirect Line of Eliot"

*[The Avenue Bearing the Initial of Christ into the New World]*

In the old days, when T. S. Eliot was an American poet, he saw the point of English humor: "Humor is distinctly English. No one can be so aware of the environment of Stupidity as the Englishman. . . . Wit is public, it is in the object; humor (I am speaking only of real humor) is the instinctive attempt of a sensitive mind to protect beauty against stupidity" (1918). Yet American humor has burgeoned since then. (Did America get helpfully stupider?) In films, plays, novels, poems, songs, the visual arts, jokes, and in the daily give-and-take, American humor has been a glory. And, of course, a challenge. The American artist who cuts himself off from humor, or is no good at it, may be cut off, not just from some valuable ways of looking at life but from a national source of energy, the hiding-places of the best American power. . . .

Kinnell began with a keen gratitude to William Carlos Williams, about whom he wrote a bad poem (its humor curdles to sarcasm), and likewise with a gratitude to Frost (ditto), and so to the most enduring of his gratitudes, to "the mystical all-lovingness of Walt Whitman." For Richard Howard's recent anthology, *Preferences,* Kinnell chose to pair with one of his own poems some of "Song of Myself." Whenever Kinnell is doing the hushed bated-breath thing, all portentous self-attentive first-personry ("I wake in the night," or "I sit listening / to the

From the *New York Times Book Review,* 12 January 1975. Copyright © 1975 by The New York Times Company. Reprinted by permission.

surf"), the importance comes on as winsome self-importance, or "Song of My Self-Importance." The cosmic browbeats the comic. Yet from the start—"Two Seasons," the very first poem in the book—there were fine poems in which self-importance, the intelligent *exclusion* of humor, was dramatically right because the poems were about rapt young lovers and how they manage temporarily to exclude so much and are fearful of humor. And from the start again (the second poem, "A Walk in the Country"), there was the glint of apt humor, delicate, wistful but wiry, in the two kinds of touchingness:

> And I thought, is it only me such
> Beauty refuses to touch?

The best of Kinnell, which is very good, comes when he resists the expected humorlessness of rural-piety poetry (which often disguises its humorlessness behind wisps of whimsy), and when he is not claiming to be either a sensitive plant or a sarcastic cactus. There are such penetratingly humorous poems as the parable, half-town and half-country, "Indian Bread"; or the gruff aggrievedness of "Duck-Chasing"; or the teeming townscape, humane, fascinated and therefore fascinating, of "The Avenue Bearing the Initial . . ."; or the miniature country vignette, "Spring Oak":

> Above the quiet valley and unrippled lake
> Where woodchucks burrowed new holes, and birds sang,
> And radicles began downward and shoots
> Committed themselves to the spring
> And entered with tiny industrious earthquakes,
> A dry-rooted, winter-twisted oak
> Revealed itself slowly. And one morning
> While the valley underneath was still sleeping
> It shook itself and it was all green.

The poem is itself a tiny industrious earthquake, committing itself to the spring and revealing itself, all with affectionate banter and without any of the pomposity which the American Mother Earth sometimes gets from her poetic children. The

concluding poem, "Flower Herding on Mount Monadnock,"
gets up, having wised up:

> I can support it no longer.
> Laughing ruefully at myself
> For all I claim to have suffered
> I get up. Damned nightmarer!

JAMES ATLAS

# From "Autobiography of the Present"

## [*The Avenue Bearing the Initial of Christ into the New World*]

It is good to have Galway Kinnell's early poems collected into a single volume, not only so that we can have before us the lineaments of his development, but because so many of these poems are brilliant in themselves. The present collection takes its title from a long poem that has been much anthologized in recent years, the extraordinary range and energy of which became apparent to me on reading it over after nearly a decade's lapse. *The Avenue Bearing the Initial of Christ into the New World* is one of the most vivid legacies of *The Waste Land* in English, building its immense rhetorical power from the materials of several dialects, litanies of place, and a profound sense of the spiritual disintegration that Eliot divined in modern urban life. And like Eliot's, Kinnell's is a religious poem, in which the chaotic forces of survival (in this instance, the turbulent, jumbled life of New York's Lower East Side, along Avenue C) ultimately preside over the terror latent in our late stage of civilization. Since it is impossible to isolate any single passage from the magnificent sprawl of this poem, I can only suggest its importance by stressing that my comparison of it to *The Waste Land* was intended to be less an arbitrary reference than an effort to estimate the poem's durable achievement.

The very early poems of his apprenticeship distinguish themselves from most such offerings in the quality of their feeling, their naturalness and depth of insight. Kinnell is in possession of

From *Poetry* 125 (February 1975). Copyright © 1975 by The Modern Poetry Association. Reprinted by permission of the Editor of *Poetry* and James Atlas.

a gift that so few poets have now, with their emphasis on subdued, laconic diction. Almost any stanza from his first two books yields the fierce vision refined later on:

> The sunlight streams through the afternoon
> Another parable over the sloughs
> And yellowing grass of the prairies.
> Cold wind stirs, and the last green
> Climbs to all the tips of the season, like
> The last flame brightening on a wick.

He is so close to his subject, the natural world in all its tyranny and splendor, that his sympathies are readily translated into the richness of cadence and language that poetry should always have. He echoes Wordsworth's inclination for the sublime, the generalizing of emotion from nature, combined with the passionate eye of Hopkins; and in the later poems, an awareness of the American landscape in both its political and pastoral dimension:

> Under
> The rain the continent wheeled, his own land
> Electric and blind, farmlights and cities'
> Blazes—points, clusters and chains—
> Each light a memory and the whole of darkness
> Memory.

There is a wonderful variety in these poems; reading through them all at once, one becomes aware of how much he has struggled to exercise his imagination, writing out of the deepest sources of contemplation, sketching in the temper of an afternoon with a few fine strokes, recording his immense love of the texture of experience, awaking in a forest "half alive in the world," and knowing "half my life belongs to the wild darkness." As a companion to the diffuse and dreamlike experiments of *The Book of Nightmares* and *Body Rags,* the publication of a Selected Poems is well-deserved; what is so remarkable is that these earlier poems should constitute in themselves such a major work.

SUSAN B. WESTON

# Galway Kinnell's *Walking Down the Stairs*

In the recently published *Walking Down the Stairs,* selections from interviews with Galway Kinnell published by the University of Michigan Press, one of the interviewers asks Kinnell: "That loneliness you say you wrote out of—do you think that young poets today are less rich because they lack that?" Kinnell replies, "I never thought of it as richness." One of the charming things about these interviews is the way Kinnell changes a question by butting his head through the interviewer's premises. This particular question meant "richness for poetry," of course, but Kinnell refuses to distinguish lonely poets from lonely people: no one is richer for being lonely.

Questions like this one are generated by the notion that poets are a special breed who welcome suffering, madness, and poverty for the sake of their poetry. If art is to provide our alternate medium of transcendence, as Matthew Arnold predicted, then we assume sacrifices of our poet-priests. From the *poètes maudits,* who cultivated the image, to the desperate poets Sylvia Plath and John Berryman, poets' lives have encouraged us to think that some kind of dementia is a prerequisite to creativity. Yeats, who lived a complex and full life, didn't help by speaking so often of his own "choice" between life and art. Many of us, at any rate, presume not only that the poet converts experience into poetry, but that he has the experiences in order to convert them into poetry. It is refreshing, then, to watch Galway Kinnell sidestep such notions. Does political activity enrich your poetry, he is asked. "Any involvement that brings you to a sense of

---

From *Iowa Review* 10, no. 1 (1979). Reprinted by permission of Susan B. Weston.

loving community," he replies, "is bound to be enriching—for a writer or for anyone." Similarly, when asked how he copes with "dry periods," Kinnell shows how much the question implies by answering that he regards "dry periods" as "complications of life."

This integration of poetry with life informs all of Kinnell's more interesting responses in *Walking Down the Stairs.* Sensitive to "either/or" thinking, he is quick to give "both . . . and" answers that are in the same inclusive spirit as his poetry. He balks, for example, at the distinction between "nature" poems and "urban" poems: "The idea that we and our creations don't belong to 'nature' comes from the notion that the human is a special being created in God's image to have dominion over all else. We are becoming aware again of our connection with other beings." Asked about surrealism, he makes a similar leap: "The use of the term 'inner life' means that one is not quite whole, that one has an inner life and an outer life, and they don't quite come together." In a culture that tends to separate the artist from his audience and art from life, these remarks make Kinnell an important spokesman for poetry. His commitment to relation—between poetry and everything else, between the poet and everyone else—makes this collection of interviews crucial reading for anyone interested in the survival of healthy literature.

Just this probing for relations, for coherent wholeness, characterizes Kinnell's best poems, and *Walking Down the Stairs* should send his readers back to the poetry with enhanced understanding. It strikes me that Kinnell's is an utterly healthy poetry, with none of the suppression of self that characterizes Eliot or Stevens and none of the perfecting of psychic wounds that characterizes much contemporary poetry. It is healthy precisely because it confronts horrors—drunks dying of cirrhosis; war and destruction; the communal nightmare of a failing culture; the individual nightmare of the failure of love—along with all that is lovely and loving. These facets of the single gem, the human condition, are examined with a jeweler's sense not only of their beauty but also of their dimension. "We're a race living for a while on a little planet that will die," Kinnell says in one interview. Kinnell's gift is a cursed awareness of time—not just of individual mortality but of geological time that lends special poignance to even the most hostile of human encounters. Thus when he concludes *The Book of Nightmares* with the message to his son, "the wages of dying is love," the moment is more than individual, more than parental; it looks back at all the nightmares recorded in the book and transforms them.

Less satisfying than Kinnell's general remarks in the interviews are his interpretations of specific lines in the poetry. The best reading in the book is his interpretation of the famous conclusion to "How Many Nights." The crow calling "from a branch nothing cried from ever in my life" elicits either-or questions: is the crow benign or evil? welcome or awful? Kinnell sweeps them all together in his answer that "whether or not the crow's cry is beautiful mattered less to me than that this hitherto mute region comes into consciousness." That's a wonderful reading, far superior to his comments about lines in *The Book of Nightmares*. Taken altogether, *The Book of Nightmares* affirms rather than horrifies, and Kinnell is insistent about the book's optimism. The conclusion, for example, is this vision of his dead body:

> On the body,
> on the blued flesh, when it is
> laid out, see if you can find
> the one flea which is laughing.

"Fleas on the body of a happy person would be a bit happier than other fleas," Kinnell explains in an interview, significantly changing the possible single flea to a definite swarm of happy fleas. This image, part of Kinnell's attempt to depict the happy continuity of symbiotic animal life in which we participate, recalls the worms and maggots that are the actual price of our being, at the end, decaying meat. A horrifying image only when taken out of the context of the entire poem, it is not particularly happy either. The interviewers, intent on probing Kinnell's "dark side" and his fatalism, tend to choose the book's most horrifying details to query, prompting him to respond with insistent optimism.

Kinnell's title, *Walking Down the Stairs,* is a confession of the interviews' fictional quality. He has tinkered with the actual

conversations the way one does one's evening repartee after it's delivered—while walking down the stairs, that is. In fact, the difference between these and the original interviews is not as great as the title would suggest (*l'esprit d'escalier,* after all, refers to the difference between the committed banality and the intended brilliance), and is worth noting only because the unedited versions confirm what one suspects from *Walking:* the public man—good-natured, eager to help the interviewer, optimistic—has few of the acerbic, ironic, or horror-stricken moments that possess the hugely floundering, hugely loving, hugely possessed speakers of Kinnell's poetry. If there is a fiction here, it is less that the poet has revised his conversations than that he himself has been revised by the occasion, the circumstance of being interviewed. The occasion creates a "public" figure whose views of the poetry cannot be those of the "private" man who created it.

What the interviews obscure by eliciting this polite public figure is Kinnell's essentially sexual vision. Though he says much the same thing in the interviews—that what we fear from death is extinction, what we welcome is absorption—the sexual basis of this idea is presented more explicitly in his two essays, "Poetry, Personality, and Death" and "The Poetics of the Physical World." These essays are useful for a glimpse of Kinnell seen neither in the privacy of creation nor in the publicity of exchange, for they show how Laurentian is Kinnell's desire for union with the "other." In "Poetry, Personality, and Death," for example, Kinnell analogizes: "As with poetry, so with love: it is necessary to go through the personality to reach beyond it." It is significant, then, given the vision explicitly expressed by the essays and the poetry ("The Call Across the Valley of Not-Knowing" is a beautiful expression of this Laurentian view of things) that Kinnell closes *Walking Down the Stairs* with the one thing barely mentioned in the other interviews, with the one thing that amounts to an abiding truth for him: "The body makes love possible." That phrase, Kinnell concludes, "*does* seem to have the ring of truth."

For some readers, perhaps the most interesting remarks in these interviews will be those about the poets most important to Kinnell. Yeats, Whitman, and Rilke are the three: Yeats for the associative linking device that Kinnell uses so brilliantly in "The Porcupine," "The Hen Flower," and other of his longer poems; Whitman for the inclusive "through the personality to the universal humanity" vision; and Rilke, Rilke, Rilke, like some angel who haunts this earthbound man. Much of Kinnell's poetry, especially that written after the birth of his children, is a meditation on Rilke's vision of the inseparability of life and death. *The Book of Nightmares* stands as a tribute to Rilke's *Duino Elegies,* particularly the ninth, which sparked the composition of Kinnell's book.

Kinnell's transformation of Rilke's vision into the terms of his own earthier temperament is recorded in his every comment about Rilke. Both poets accept mortality as the very condition for rejoicing; "the subject of the poem," Kinnell says in "The Poetics of the Physical World," "is the thing which dies." This echoes, as so much of Kinnell's work does, Rilke's ninth Elegy: ". . . The things that live on departure / are aware of your praising; transitory themselves, they count / on us to save them, us, the most transient of all." Kinnell's participation in the world of things and animals is, however, more visceral than Rilke's, less spiritual, less intellectual. For Rilke the poem is the means to the transformation of the world; for Kinnell it is a means to participation. When Kinnell comments in *Walking Down the Stairs* that "language itself comes from the deepest place, from sex," we get a glimpse of the fundamental difference between the two poets.

"Sometimes when I read one of his poems," Kinnell says of Rilke, "I feel it's exactly the poem a man would write while staying away from his daughter's wedding—very spiritual so as to transfigure what in lesser spirits might be taken for callousness." These interviews amply show that Kinnell is, by necessity and temperament, not that sort. They also show that his reluctance and inability to make the daily sacrifices to his art have taken their toll, if only in meager production. Creativity brought to fruition in the face of adverse circumstances bears the stamp of those circumstances, and it is no accident that Kinnell's finest achievement is *The Book of Nightmares.* Kinnell remarks, "It's easier for writers if they don't have children to raise . . . mouths to feed, tuitions to pay, bank loans to repay."

Easier, yes, but not necessarily better—at least for the poetry that manages to survive the circumstances. Kinnell is in his early fifties: with luck and the alchemy of energy, he might continue to live his busy, hard-pressed ordinary life and find the time to write what will certainly be the great poems of his maturity.

HAROLD BLOOM

# Straight Forth Out of Self
[*Mortal Acts, Mortal Words*]

It is twenty years now since Galway Kinnell published his first book of poems, *What a Kingdom It Was*. The glory of that volume was a long poem, "The Avenue Bearing the Initial of Christ into the New World," an overtly Whitmanian celebration and lament that remains one of the major American visions of New York City. Rereading it alongside Mr. Kinnell's new book confirms the sense I remember experiencing two decades ago, that here was another phantasmagoria of the city worthy of its ancestry, in that line that goes from Poe's "The City in the Sea" through Whitman on to its culmination in Hart Crane's *The Bridge*. Galway Kinnell had made a magnificent beginning and held a remarkable promise.

Whether his subsequent work as yet has vindicated that promise is problematic, though there have been very good poems in all of his books, including his new *Mortal Acts, Mortal Words*. His poetic virtues have remained constant enough, and have won him a deserved audience. Of his contemporaries, only the late James Wright and Philip Levine have been able to write with such emotional directness, without falling into mere pathos, the usual fate of American poets who speak straight forth out of the self. Mr. Kinnell is able to avoid the difficulties whose overcoming is necessary when we read John Ashbery, James Merrill and A. R. Ammons, among current poets, but whether his eloquent simplicities have the discipline of Mr. Levine's best poems is open to some question.

The poet and critic Richard Howard once characterized Gal-

From the *New York Times Book Review*, 22 June 1980. Copyright © 1980 by The New York Times Company. Reprinted by permission.

way Kinnell's poetry as being an Ordeal by Fire, which is to give him a generous accolade he may not have earned, or not fully as yet. The characterization points not only to Mr. Kinnell's most pervasive metaphor, the flame of Pentecost, but also to his largest poetic flaw, a certain overambition that makes of each separate poem too crucial an event. One must be Hart Crane to sustain a poetry in which each broken interval carries with it the open question of spiritual survival. Mr. Kinnell's gifts, whatever they will yet be, do not gracefully sustain such enormous tensions. Some of his best earlier poems, such as "The River That Is East" and "The Bear," had design and diction firm enough to outlast their own intensities, but most of the more recent verse does not. Much of *The Book of Nightmares* (1971) is devoted to a frontal assault on the American Sublime that only an American Rilke could now attain, and Mr. Kinnell, despite his formidable will and courage of sheer being, is not yet such a poet.

But I grow a little uneasy at my own ingratitude as a reader, when confronted by a lyric meditation as beautiful and gentle as "Wait" in this new volume. It is difficult not to be grateful for a poem as generous, honest, and open as "There Are Things I Tell to No One," or for a lyrical closure as precise as that in "The Gray Heron":

> It held its head still
> while its body and green
> legs wobbled in wide arcs
> from side to side. When
> it stalked out of sight,
> I went after it, but all
> I could find where I was
> expecting to see the bird
> was a three-foot-long lizard
> in ill-fitting skin
> and with linear mouth
> expressive of the even temper
> of the mineral kingdom.
> It stopped and tilted its head,
> which was much like
> a fieldstone with an eye

in it, which was watching me
to see if I would go
or change into something else.

Something also has to be said for Mr. Kinnell's descriptive powers, which are increasing to a Whitmanian amplitude. The last poem in the book, "Flying Home," will convey an authentic shock of recognition to anyone who has shared recently in that experience. But to sum up, this does seem to me the weakest volume so far by a poet who cannot be dismissed because he seems destined still to accomplish the auguries of his grand beginnings. Any just review of him could end by quoting Mr. Kinnell's version of a Fire Sermon from "The Avenue Bearing the Initial of Christ into the New World":

Children set fires in ashbarrels,
Cats prowl the fires, scraps of fishes burn.

A child lay in the flames.
It was not the plan. Abraham
Stood in terror at the duplicity.
Isaac whom he loved lay in the flames.
The Lord turned away washing
His hands without soap and water
Like a common housefly.

HANK LAZER

# That Backward-Spreading Brightness

[*Mortal Acts, Mortal Words*]

In "The Age of Criticism," Randall Jarrell writes that "most people understand that a poet is a good poet because he does well some of the time." That certainly is the case with Galway Kinnell's writing and with Kinnell's latest book. I'm sure that some readers will find it inferior to *The Book of Nightmares,* possibly because *Mortal Acts, Mortal Words* is lighter, less unified, and looser. But these two books are different. *Mortal Acts, Mortal Words* is a collection of poems, in fact, of several different kinds of poems. *The Book of Nightmares* is a book of poems, a single sequence of poems intended to be read as a unified whole.

At their finest, Kinnell's new poems, as with many of his earlier poems, are testaments of faith. The second section of "There Are Things I Tell to No One," one of the best poems in *Mortal Acts, Mortal Words,* is the heart of Kinnell's faith:

> I say "God"; I believe,
> rather, in a music of grace
> that we hear, sometimes, playing to us
> from the other side of happiness.
> When we hear it, when it flows
> through our bodies, it lets us live
> these days lighted by their vanity
> worshipping—as the other animals do,
> who live and die in the spirit
> of the end—that backward-spreading
> brightness. And it speaks in notes struck

---

From *Ironwood* 16 (Fall 1980). Reprinted by permission.

107

or caressed or blown or plucked
off our own bodies: *remember*
*existence already remembers*
*the flush upon it you will have been,*
*you who have reached out ahead*
*and taken up some of the black dust*
*we become, souvenir*
*which glitters already in the bones of your hand.*

It is fair to say that, like the previous passage, much of Kinnell's best poetry is Rilkean. It is *not* fair to say, therefore, that Kinnell is derivative. It just so happens that Rilke helped to stake out some rather elemental, crucial territory in the life/death interface. And Kinnell enters that territory too, but by his own vision or, as might be said, by his own lights.

There are, throughout this book, happy, glorious, celebratory lines. The poet takes a great and rich joy in this world: "no matter what fire we invent to destroy us, / ours will have been the brightest world ever existing." And there is still the death-hiss, still the world of dread and dissolution. But the advance that *Mortal Acts, Mortal Words* marks is in Kinnell's greater certainty of those impermanent but perfect moments of celebration. In this book the poet can say with conviction that "I have always felt / anointed by her love," and he can declare that "I am in the holy land."

But, again, to return to "There Are Things I Tell to No One," it is the earned sureness of this poetry that I admire: "In this spirit / and from this spirit, I have learned to speak / of these things, which once I brooded on in silence." Like Walt Whitman, Kinnell's great service is to show us that life, our life, is holy:

Yes, I want to live forever.
I am like everyone. But when I hear
that breath coming through the walls,
grace-notes blown
out of the wormed-out bones,
music that their memory of blood
plucks from the straitened arteries,

that the hard cock and soaked cunt
caressed from each other
in the holy days of their vanity,
that the two hearts drummed
out of their ribs together,
the hearts that know everything (and even
the little knowledge they can leave
stays, to be the light of this house),

then it is not so difficult
to go out, to turn and face
the spaces which gather into one sound, I know now, the
      singing
of mortal lives, waves of spent existence
which flow toward, and toward, and on which we flow
and grow drowsy and become fearless again.

I am proud to be corny and say that Kinnell, with such poetry, can deepen our appreciation of that great, brief gift: life. And he can also help us in that Rilkean task: to read the word "death" without negation.

The key fact for Kinnell is the uniqueness of each creature, life, moment, love. That is, as he writes in "52 Oswald Street," Kinnell draws his strength "from unrepeatable life." He writes with a great eye for the specific, particular beauty of this world:

the pelvic bones of a woman
lying on her back, which rise
smoothed by ten thousand years
on either side of the crater
we floated in, in the first life,
that last time we knew
more of happiness than of time.

For Kinnell, moments of epiphany and transcendence occur only by our becoming deeply familiar with the world. We transcend, that is, move to the realm of floating, first life, and that last time, only by being joined to the physical world.

That specific, intense union with the physical world must be accomplished by more than mere sight or vision. In his essay, "Poetry, Personality, and Death," which originally appeared in *Field* and is now available in *A Field Guide to Contemporary Poetry and Poetics,* Kinnell explains:

> Don't we go sightseeing in cars, thinking we can experience a landscape by looking at it through glass! A baby takes pleasure in seeing a thing, yes, but seeing is a first act. For fulfillment the baby must reach out, grasp it, put it in his mouth, suck it, savor it, taste it, manipulate it, smell it, physically be one with it. From here comes our notion of heaven itself. Every experience of happiness in later life is a stirring of that ineradicable memory of once belonging wholly to the life of the planet.

Yes, for Kinnell in his poetry too, seeing is but a first act, and no poem better illustrates that fact in his new book than "Saint Francis and the Sow," which, with its single, long, gorgeous sentence, requires quotation in its entirety:

> The bud
> stands for all things,
> even for those things that don't flower,
> for everything flowers, from within, of self-blessing;
> though sometimes it is necessary
> to reteach a thing its loveliness,
> to put a hand on its brow
> of the flower
> and retell it in words and in touch
> it is lovely
> until it flowers again from within, of self-blessing;
> as Saint Francis
> put his hand on the creased forehead
> of the sow, and told her in words and in touch
> blessings of earth on the sow, and the sow
> began remembering all down her thick length,
> from the earthen snout all the way
> through the fodder and slops to the spiritual curl of the tail,

from the hard spininess spiked out from the spine
down through the great broken heart
to the blue milken dreaminess spurting and shuddering
from the fourteen teats into the fourteen mouths sucking and
    blowing beneath them:
the long, perfect loveliness of sow.

"Saint Francis and the Sow" is a remarkable poem, fit to join company with Kinnell's finest animal poems of bear and porcupine. At the heart of Kinnell's work is the understanding that "sometimes it is necessary / to reteach a thing its loveliness." It is by way of hand and word, touch, snout, tail, spine, heart, and teat that the poet's, and our own, sacramental relationship to the world is achieved.

Aside from the perfect adjectives—creased forehead, thick length, earthen snout, spiritual curl, great broken heart, and blue milken dreaminess—there are several other features that intrigue me about this poem. The first is the long sentence and the adventurous, correct line breaks—both features of this entire volume. In other poems of the single long sentence, as in "The Rainbow," Kinnell is able to give us a compressed, united experience. If a moment can be said to have duration, Kinnell gives us a long moment. And in the musical elaboration of a single sentence, Kinnell allows the moment to labor, dance, and play toward its fit and powerful conclusion. When Kinnell's long sentences click, as in "Saint Francis and the Sow," "After Making Love We Hear Footsteps," "The Last Hiding Places of Snow," and "Flying Home," the long sentences convey the beauty of Kinnell's reading voice and the poems sound like rich, even-tempered blessings. An additional feature of the poem, and a feature worth noting in general about Kinnell's work, is the way, especially in the last line, Kinnell resists the impulse to create metaphors or similes out of the physical world.

I think that this resistance to metaphor and simile is one feature that sets Kinnell's work apart from some of the contemporaries—Robert Bly, especially—with whom Kinnell's work is often linked. In an interview with Wayne Dodd and Stanley Plumly, to be found in *Walking Down the Stairs,* a collection of interviews with Kinnell recently released from the University of Michigan Press's fine Poets on Poetry Series, Kinnell is asked what it is that he mistrusts about simile. His answer:

> I don't think things are often really like other things. At some level all things *are* each other, but before that point they are separate entities. Also, although they are common, as you say, in surrealist poetry, similes perhaps have the effect of keeping the irrational world under rational supervision. Perhaps the words "like" and "as if" draw a line through reality and say in effect, "Here we are no longer speaking of the real world—here we indulge our imaginations."

Kinnell, as in "Saint Francis and the Sow," insists on the perfection and uniqueness of the world that is. Thus, a difference between Kinnell and Bly, analogous to a difference between Whitman and Thoreau. Bly, like Thoreau, through metaphor and simile, or through what we now more loosely refer to as the image, creates symbols for the inner, spiritual world of man. Bly and Thoreau side more closely with Emerson's maxims in "Nature":

> Particular natural facts are symbols of particular spiritual facts. Nature is the symbol of spirit. . . . The use of natural history is to give us aid in supernatural history; the use of the outer creation, to give us language for the beings and changes of the inward creation.

Kinnell's sense of correspondence and symbolism in nature is closer to the side of Whitman when, at the end of section 13 of "Song of Myself," he cautions,

> And do not call the tortoise unworthy because she is not
>     something else,
> And the mocking bird in the swamp never studied the gamut
>     yet trills pretty well to me,
> And the look of the bay mare shames silliness out of me.

If anything, Kinnell is more rigorous than Whitman in respecting the integrity and otherness of the creature world.

Thus, at the end of "The Gray Heron," where Kinnell even allows himself to throw in a "like," our dominant impression is of the difference between the lizard world and the human world. The poet, where he expected to find the heron he had seen, instead finds

> . . . a three-foot-long lizard
> in ill-fitting skin
> and with linear mouth
> expressive of the even temper
> of the mineral kingdom.
> It stopped and tilted its head,
> which was much like
> a fieldstone with an eye
> in it, which was watching me
> to see if I would go
> or change into something else.

In the finest short poem in *Mortal Acts, Mortal Words*, "Daybreak," which I quote in its entirety, Kinnell does allow himself a very precise comparison:

> On the tidal mud, just before sunset,
> dozens of starfishes
> were creeping. It was
> as though the mud were a sky
> and enormous, imperfect stars
> moved across it as slowly
> as the actual stars cross heaven.
> All at once they stopped,
> and as if they had simply
> increased their receptivity
> to gravity they sank down
> into the mud; they faded down
> into it and lay still; and by the time
> pink of sunset broke across them
> they were as invisible
> as the true stars at daybreak.

But the more important analogy, between terrestrial and celestial heavens, is resisted. That correspondence (or contrast) remains outside the poem. Again, it is Kinnell's judicious adjectives—enormous, imperfect, actual, and true—that do so much in this poem, and that finally link together the opposite worlds of mud and sky, sunset and daybreak, imperfect starfish and true stars, our world and the other world. And the linking takes place so quickly, "all at once." It is just what Robert Frost says of the true poem in "A Figure a Poem Makes": "Like a piece of ice on a hot stove the poem must ride on its own melting." But what dominates Kinnell's poem, and Kinnell's poems throughout his career, is precision of description. The realm of correspondence is usually only implied.

Part of this wonderful particularity throughout Kinnell's career comes from his insistence on bringing to life old, nearly dead words. In *Mortal Acts, Mortal Words* Kinnell gives us the gritty substance of certain special verbs: wastreled, dismouthed, moil, and curvetting, among the most arresting in the text. Like his brother, Whitman, who in a key line in "Song of Myself" uses "athwart" ("You settled your head athwart my hips and gently turned over upon me") and later in the poem says, "My foothold is tenoned and mortised in granite," Kinnell too has a special fondness for the tangible but unusual verb.

The main weakness with *Mortal Acts, Mortal Words* is that there are a fairly large number of poems that feel like filler. Many of these weaker poems—poems with humor, or extensive word-play, or poems rooted in domestic life—add range to Kinnell's work, but they simply do not stand up to rereading. Though they add a necessary contrast or counterpoint to the overall collection, finally, poems such as "Angling, a Day," "In the Bamboo Hut," "Lava," "Crying," "Les Invalides," "On the Tennis Court at Night," and "Looking at Your Face," for this reader, don't make it.

In terms of the occasional failings in *Mortal Acts, Mortal Words* a pertinent poem to take a look at is "The Still Time." It is a poem weakened and blurred by its many plurals and vague, general terms: those summer nights, the steps of my life, everything that drove me crazy, and all the old voices. There are still beautiful moments in the poem, as when at the end of the next to the last stanza Kinnell writes,

> as though a prayer had ended
> and the changed
> air between the palms goes free
> to become the glitter
> on common things that inexplicably shine.

In this passage it is "*a* prayer," but even that release of air gets a bit blurred by the plural "things." Kinnell concludes the poem by saying,

> And all the old voices
> which once made broken-off, choked, parrot-incoherences,
> speak again,
> this time on the palatum cordis, all of them
> saying there is time, still time,
> for those who can groan
> to sing,
> for those who can sing to heal themselves.

It is the whole choir of old voices that weakens the specific, odd beauty of "broken-off, choked, parrot-incoherences." A voice singing to heal itself, *one* parrot-incoherence carefully listened to, would be much more effective.*

I belabor this point because such a weakness in the lesser poems casts into some doubt the strength of Kinnell's writing. That strength is his bold and beautiful endings. In the weaker poems the big endings feel more like rhetorical habit than the earned or urgent necessity of the poem itself. More often, though, in *Mortal Acts, Mortal Words,* the poem seems to rise naturally and easily to its strong ending. In already strong poems, such as "Saint Francis and the Sow," "There Are Things

---

*Apparently Kinnell accepted Lazer's point. When the poem was reprinted in *Selected Poems,* the change suggested here had been made.—ED.

I Tell to No One," "The Sadness of Brothers," or "The Rainbow," the ending simply takes the poem one notch higher.

At the end of "Fisherman," a poem consisting of words to a friend whose wife has died, obviously an inherently risky topic in terms of the subject's potential for sentimentality, Kinnell's last stanza is:

> I don't know how you loved
> or what marriage was and wasn't between you—
> not even close friends understand anything of that—
> but I know ordinary life was hard
> and worry joined your brains' faces in pure, baffled lines
> and therefore some deepest part of you has gone
> with her, imprinted into her—imprinted now
> into that world which only she doesn't fear any longer,
> which you too will have ceased fearing—
> and waits there to recognize you into it
> after you've lived, lived past the sorrow,
> if that happens, after all the time in the world.

This ending attains an eloquence as it labors upstream, battling all its qualifications, its obstacle course of buts, therefores, and whiches. But what rescues and exalts the ending is the qualification present in the last line: "if that happens." It is such a qualification that makes this ending feel at once moving and comforting, lofty and judicious.

So, too, in the marvelous poem "The Apple Tree." Kinnell speaks earlier in the poem about the moment

> When the fallen apple rolls
> into the grass, the apple worm
> stops, then goes
> all the way through and looks out
> at the creation unopposed, the world
> made entirely of lovers.

And Kinnell ends the poem by saying,

> The one who holds still and looks out,
> alone
> of all of us, that one may die mostly of happiness.

Again, I suggest that it is the double sense of "may" and the qualification implied by "mostly" that deepens this ending.

There is a more important point to be made about these endings than their employment of careful qualifications. Kinnell's strong endings are tied to a more comprehensive vision: his own special vision of death. As in "The Apple Tree," where the apples "fail into brightness" and where Kinnell explains that "we die / of the return-streaming of everything we have lived," Kinnell's own endings to poems are part of a backward-spreading brightness. As Kinnell points out in "There Are Things I Tell to No One," endings are a way of tying us to beginnings:

> Just as the supreme cry
> of joy, the cry of orgasm, also has a ghastliness to it,
> as though it touched forward
> into the chaos where we break apart, so the death-groan
> sounding into us from another direction carries us back
> to our first world.

By the very nature of endings we learn how inextricably and closely linked are those seeming opposites, life and death, which by our fear we mistakenly wish to keep apart. As in "The Choir," where "eyes, nostrils, mouth strain together in quintal harmony / to sing Joy and Death well," Kinnell's own endings present an analogy for Kinnell's vision of our own ending. The glorious, humane, fine-sounding conclusions to Kinnell's poems are, finally, to be linked to the "return-streaming" and to "that backward-spreading / brightness" that Kinnell has spent a career pointing out to us.

*Mortal Acts, Mortal Words* presents us with a passionately moral poetry, but it is not priggish nor self-righteous. In this book we get the sense of a man saying directly, eloquently, and emotionally the things he knows. He tells us the few repeated facts and conjectures that he believes matter. Toward the end of

"Flying Home," the last poem in the book, we land in an "imponderable world." And I believe that Kinnell's humility, the admission of a word such as "imponderable," is not the least bit phony. In the finest poems of *Mortal Acts, Mortal Words,* as in "Daybreak," we witness the perfect correctness of the slow starfish who moves through the mud and is suddenly receptive to gravity.

LIZ ROSENBERG

# A Poet with the Flame of Greatness
[*Selected Poems*]

Everyone—happy or unhappy, confirmed lover of poetry or despiser—should read Galway Kinnell. Kinnell is a great poet, not just a good one. He may be the only great poet still writing great poems in America today. No one else writes poetry so gorgeous or daring; no one is so flat-out emotional nor so beautifully and persistently philosophical.

His *Book of Nightmares* strikes me as the best single work of poetry to appear in the latter half of this century, and from that book the poem "Little Sleep's-Head Sprouting Hair in the Moonlight"—his most spectacular on his driven theme of love-and-death—will stand against any poem written at any time. This poem and, in fact, most of Galway Kinnell's best work is gathered under one cover in *Selected Poems,* and for that simple reason it is an important book.

For the most part the early poems have settled into place in light of the later work and are almost endearing because of the way they failed, the way that strict and iambic rhyme impose formality on the younger poet, like a prim tightening of the mouth that loosens into occasional beauty as if despite itself.

These early poems indicate influences that a poet is later smart enough to hide, or outgrow. So an early love for Yeats is most apparent in his first books—and this, I think, is where Kinnell found his lyricism and, most of all, his ambition; later, something drifts in from his contemporaries—riskiness and story-telling from James Dickey, humor from Allen Ginsberg, es-

From the *Philadelphia Inquirer,* 13 February 1983. Reprinted by permission of Liz Rosenberg.

pecially apparent in the Jewish list-making cadences of "The Avenue Bearing the Initial of Christ into the New World."

But Kinnell at his best is not just absorbed in the things of the world, but obsessed by them; his lists are less like catalogues than like powerfully built-up waves rolling in line after line, as when father cries out to daughter:

. . . Little Maud,

I would blow the flame out of your silver cup,
I would suck the rot from your fingernail,
I would brush your sprouting hair of the dying light,
I would scrape the rust off your ivory bones,
I would help death escape through the little ribs of your body,
I would alchemize the ashes of your cradle back into wood,
I would let nothing of you go, ever . . .

From this instant, the poet's voice softens, but loses none of its intensity:

until washerwomen
feel the clothes fall asleep in their hands,
and hens scratch their spells across hatchet blades,
and rats walk away from the cultures of the plague,
and iron twists weapons toward the true north,
and grease refuses to slide in the machinery of progress,
and men feel as free on earth as fleas on the bodies of men,
and lovers no longer whisper to the one beside them in the
        dark, O corpse-to-be . . .
        ("Little Sleep's-Head Sprouting Hair in the Moonlight")

(I am cheating by quoting the ending not from *Selected Poems* but the original in an earlier book. For some—to me mysterious and awful—reason, Kinnell has revised the above in this book to "*O you-who-will-no-longer-be.*")

*Selected Poems* contains a few poems almost as fierce as this, as well as others that are wonderfully and offhandedly funny, like "After Making Love We Hear Footsteps" and "The Correspondence School Instructor Says Goodbye to His Poetry Students"

("Goodbye, lady in Bangor, who sent me / snapshots of your-self, after definitely hinting / you were beautiful . . ."), and a few that are more simply, almost severely beautiful:

> Nine years ago,
> in a plane that rumbled all night
> above the Atlantic,
> I could see, lit up
> by lightning bolts jumping out of it,
> a thunderhead formed like the face
> of my brother, looking nostalgically down
> on blue,
> lightning-flashed moments of the Atlantic.
>
> ("Another Night in the Ruins")

Kinnell is not a poet who is easily reduced to review-size quotes. His power is immense, but cumulative. Those unfamiliar with his work really ought to buy each of his books, especially *The Avenue Bearing the Initial of Christ into the New World*, *Body Rags*, and *The Book of Nightmares*.

A cheaper and easier way is to buy these *Selected Poems*. Those who have read his other work will need no urging to buy this new one, too.

# RICHARD TILLINGHAST

## *Selected Poems*

Trying to define for myself the particular excellence of Galway Kinnell's poetry, I thought of something Robert Lowell once wrote about Allen Tate, in many ways Kinnell's opposite. Tate's poetry was, Lowell said, "burly" and written in a style that "would take a man's full weight and that would bear his complete intelligence, passion, and subtlety." Kinnell's poetry has that impressive, "burly" masculinity. He has done that most difficult thing for a writer—he has achieved a style that does not restrict his range but rather allows him to write on all sorts of subjects and to speak in many moods and tones of voice.

Kinnell's *Selected Poems* is the year's most important book of poetry, rivaled only by Charles Wright's *Country Music* (Selected Early Poems). There are very few living poets (James Merrill comes to mind) capable of lines whose music can compare to the great poetry of the past, lines such as "seed dazzled over the footbattered blaze of the earth" or "already in heaven, listen, the golden cobblestones have fallen still" or (of his daughter's birth):

> . . . she skids out on her face into light,
> this peck
> of stunned flesh
> clotted with celestial cheesiness, glowing
> with the astral violet
> of the underlife.

Prosiness is the damnation of many contemporary poets—no, *most* contemporary poets. (It is a flaw that Kinnell himself

---

From *Boston Review* 8 (February 1983). Reprinted by permission of Richard Tillinghast.

does not always avoid.) A great deal of nonsense is written about poetry these days, such as the claim of "language poets" that "grammar is prosody," but I still hold with Coleridge's assertion that " 'the man that hath not music in his soul' can indeed never be a genuine poet." Kinnell has music in his soul, and he is a genuine poet—one of the best.

Even more important than Kinnell's musical sense is the seriousness and the deep emotion of his work. In the poems to his children from *The Book of Nightmares,* looking ahead to a time when he will be dead and they will go on living, he projects this wish:

> may there come back to you
> a voice, spectral, calling you
> *sister!*
> from everything that dies.
>
> And then
> you shall open
> this book, even if it is the book of nightmares.

Poets from Wordsworth to Yeats to Lowell have infused their poetry with an awareness that, while it addresses itself most directly to that well-known stranger, the reader, it also functions as the poet's will and testament, the gift he bequeaths to his flesh and blood across time and death. *The Book of Nightmares,* especially, is Kinnell's gift to his children. I can think of no more moving statement of a parent's heart-breakingly illogical hope of shielding a child from the death he accepts for himself:

> I would suck the rot from your fingernail,
> I would brush your sprouting hair of the dying light,
> I would scrape the rust off your ivory bones,
> I would help death escape through the little ribs of your body,
> I would alchemize the ashes of your cradle back into wood,
> I would let nothing of you go, ever. . . .

The weight of these emotions is leavened by Kinnell's ability to laugh, to lighten occasionally the essential gravity of his vision. Here are his words to his son, projected into the time after his (Galway's) death:

> . . . Don't cry!
>
> Or else, cry.
>
> On the body, when it is
> laid out, see if you can find
> the one flea that is laughing.

There are lighter poems as well, such as "The Correspondence School Instructor Says Goodbye to His Poetry Students":

> . . . goodbye
> Miami Beach urologist, who enclosed plain
> brown envelopes for the return of your *very*
> "Clinical Sonnets"; goodbye, manufacturer
> of brassieres on the Coast, whose eclogues
> give the fullest treatment in literature yet
> to the sagging-breast motif; goodbye, you in San Quentin,
> who wrote, "Being German my hero is Hitler,"
> instead of "Sincerely yours". . .

This book is proof that poems can still be written, and written movingly and convincingly, on those subjects that in any age fascinate, quicken, disturb, confound, and sadden the hearts of men and women: eros, the family, mortality, the life of the spirit, war, the life of nations. I mention the last two because Kinnell has a vision of America in the tradition of Whitman, and is a visionary social critic in the tradition of Blake, as he shows in his justly renowned long poem, "The Avenue Bearing the Initial of Christ into the New World," and in the widely anthologized 1960s antiwar poem, "Vapor Trail Reflected in the Frog Pond," which employs, ironically, a phrase from Whitman:

> . . . I hear,
> coming over the hills, America singing,
> her varied carols I hear:

crack of deputies' rifles practicing their aim on stray dogs at
    night,
sput of cattleprod,
TV groaning at the smells of the human body . . .

One of his finest pieces is his poem to Robert Frost, which
captures both the silly and the sublime side of the old poet,
beginning "Why do you talk so much / Robert Frost?" charac-
terizing him as a man cursed "Neither with the mystical all-
lovingness of Walt Whitman / Nor with Melville's anguish to
know and to suffer, / And yet cursed," and ending with this
unforgettable image:

> . . . from the same doorway
> At which you lived, between the house and the woods,
> We see your old footprints going away across
> The great Republic, Frost, up memorized slopes,
> Down hills floating by heart on the bulldozed land.

Kinnell has his faults. He lapses into prosiness, as he at one
point admits, speaking of "this poem, or chopped prose." His
recent poetry, with striking exceptions, lacks the consistent
power of his two best collections, *Body Rags* and *The Book of
Nightmares*. But he always meets existence head-on, without
evasions or wishful thinking. When Kinnell is at the top of his
form, there is no better poet writing in America.

WILLIAM HARMON

# From "Kumin and Kinnell (and Kilmer)"

[*Selected Poems*]

Both Maxine Kumin (b. 1925) and Galway Kinnell (b. 1927) began as fabricators of regular iambic stanzas and then later relaxed. His *Selected Poems* ends with an airplane—"all its tires *know* the home ground"—much like that at the beginning of the title poem of her *Our Ground Time Here Will Be Brief*—"We gather speed for the last run / and lift off into the weather." His book goes from early to late and hers the other way, but the different arrangements do not obscure the many resemblances between these two bodies of poetry. His "Meditation Among the Tombs" is like her "Body and Soul: A Meditation"; his "Middle of the Way," her "Halfway"; his "song of a peabody bird," her sparrows' song *"Old Sam Peabody peabody pea"*; his *The Book of Nightmares,* her *The Nightmare Factory;* his "After Making Love We Hear Footsteps," her "After Love." For both, the anxieties of modern–urban–academic–commercial American life are opposed or subdued by persistent reliance on another sort of world (ancestral, rural, cruel but pure) experienced through senses and recollections (his Irish, hers Jewish) still alien or ethnic and not wholly domesticated or "naturalized," which really means "denatured." One gets the sense of poetry, which "makes nothing happen" (Auden, 1939) and "does not matter" (Eliot, 1940), conscripted or impressed into a guerrilla campaign of Harmony, however imaginary, against Irony, however potent.

From *Poetry* 142 (April 1983). Copyright © 1983 by The Modern Poetry Association. Reprinted by permission of the Editor of *Poetry* and William Harmon.

It is not that one has influenced the other, and there is no question of theft or even borrowing or sharing. It is just that both Kumin and Kinnell have inhaled the same atmosphere and exhaled the same sorts of art, which one could fairly typify as *the* characteristic "genre" poetry of the American Northeast since the Second World War. . . .

Kinnell's *Selected Poems* takes its turn at lapsing now and then into "thinking of Eden and the fallen state": "I think the first inkling of the lesson / Was when we watched him" (pp. 19–20); "I think of a few bones" (p. 54); "I think of how I / Sat by a dying woman" (p. 60); "And tonight I think I prowl broken / skulled or vacant" (p. 91); "until I think I must rise up / and dance" and "I awaken I think" (p. 94); "I thought suddenly / I could read the cosmos spelling itself" (p. 105); "I could only think / that one looks relieved" (p. 146). The textures of these passages show, however, some of the difference between Kinnell's verse and Kumin's (or Kilmer's). At its strongest, Kinnell's idiom seems to issue from that extreme sort of "mind so fine that no idea could violate it," for which Eliot praised Henry James. Eliot's point is not so very far, after all, from Williams's "no-idea" aesthetic or from Hopkins's neo-Scotist linguistic individualism. This position is not at all some species of Know-Nothing anti-intellectual political philosophy. It is a practical matter. Neither language nor literature exists for the recording of ideas. Any poet who says, without irony, "I think" might as well go ahead and complete the sentence with "that I shall never see" etc., because nothing that anyone can say he thinks, not even the sublimest thought ever thought, will fit, as such, into a work of art.

Kinnell can come very close to the eloquent wording of noble sentiment, as in a poem addressed to his daughter, Maud:

> Little sleep's-head sprouting hair in the moonlight,
> when I come back
> we will go out together,
> we will walk out together among
> the ten thousand things,
> each scratched in time with such knowledge, *the wages*
> *of dying is love.*

But, I believe, a reader's deepest hunger for poetry is left unsatisfied. We have here such a sentiment and such eloquence—abetted by the Chinese language ("the ten thousand things") and italics and the Bible and "Gerontion"—that we must acknowledge the sentiment and the eloquence, but, as we do, we remain nostalgic for some old authentic totemic bloody muddy bodily poetry below sentiment and beyond eloquence.

Why ought we to feel so? The immediate reason is that Kinnell's *Selected Poems* contains one absolutely magnificent piece of very great poetry indeed: "The Avenue Bearing the Initial of Christ into the New World." Here, from the terrific title and gripping first line ("pcheek pcheek pcheek pcheek pcheek") all the way to the final "oi weih," without slackness, alloy, or editorial interruption, we have what must rank among the dozen most inspired and most stimulating visions in American literature. The only bad thing about this poem is that it makes every other piece by Kinnell seem relatively insipid.

DANIEL L. GUILLORY

# The Past

Kinnell opens *The Past* with moving evocations of his life in Sheffield, Vermont some thirty years ago. But his real subject is the eerie passage of time which, like "the pay phone at the abandoned / filling station . . . rang, off and on, an entire day." Time is the "me-here-it-gone" paradox of our daily lives, containing "all the elsewheres, so far away, where children cry. . . ."

Time is acutely real for lovers, trying to prolong their bliss in a moment of *déjà-prévu,* "the already-memory of what has just happened." Time, finally, implies death, as Kinnell recognizes in poignant elegies for Richard Hugo and James Wright. Readers will join him in asserting, on the final page, "I have always intended to live forever, / but even more, to live now." A major book by a major poet, highly recommended.

Reprinted from *Library Journal,* 15 November 1985. Published by R. R. Bowker Co., Div. of Reed Publishing, USA. Copyright © 1985 by Reed Publishing, USA, Div. of Reed Holdings, Inc.

PHOEBE PETTINGELL

# From "Songs of Science"
## [*The Past*]

History was the controlling trope for nineteenth-century writ-
ers: Novelists, essayists, poets, and playwrights all affirmed
their hopes for mankind's progress, or their fears about the de-
cline and fall of civilization, by pointing to the record. The
discoveries of Darwin and Einstein seem, at first glance, to have
shifted our metaphor to science. Even biblical fundamentalists
who reject evolutionary theory will often subscribe to "Social
Darwinian" demonstrations of survival of the fittest in the mar-
ketplace. Though physics may be too technical for a mass au-
dience, "relativity" has revolutionized moral attitudes. But liter-
ature still frequently shrinks from science. Old-fashioned
narratives continue to treat time as if it operated like a piece of
thread unwinding from a spool, and man as if he were a unique
phenomenon of nature. In *The Past* Galway Kinnell reports a
dinner table discussion on this problem with Richard Hugo
shortly before his death:

> We agreed that eighteenth- and nineteenth-century poets
> almost *had* to personify, it was like mouth-to-mouth
> resuscitation, the only way they could imagine to keep the
> world from turning into dead matter.
> And that as post-Darwinians it was up to us to
> anthropomorphize the world less and animalize,
> vegetablize, and mineralize ourselves more.
> We doubted that pre-Darwinian language would let us.

Although Kinnell has not invented an evolutionary mode of speech, his poems certainly exemplify a way of thinking that has embraced a biological perception of the world. Much of *The Past* was inspired by personal changes in his life: divorce, children growing up, the death of friends. Yet his consideration of these losses forms around his conviction that man is part of the animal kingdom, and must be stripped "back down / to hair, flesh, blood, bone, the base metals," to be seen for what he is.

Kinnell is a descendant of Rilke, the poet who first suggested that the material world may be superior to the heavenly one. In "The Olive Wood Fire," Kinnell borrows his mentor's sense that God no longer watches over the world by describing how he used to rock his son, Fergus, before the fireplace when the boy had awakened from nightmares. The flames remind the father of the horrors of the Vietnam War as seen on television:

> One such time, fallen half-asleep myself,
> I thought I heard a scream
> —a flier crying out in horror
> as he dropped fire on he didn't know what or whom,
> or else a child thus set aflame—
> and sat up alert. The olive wood fire
> had burned low. In my arms lay Fergus,
> fast asleep, left cheek glowing, God.

This vision of a childlike deity who sleeps through human horrors manages to combine Christian iconography with twentieth-century agnosticism.

Speaking both of history and his own youth, Kinnell recalls that "back then, dryads lived in these oaks; / these rocks were altars, which often asked / blood offerings." This personification of nature remains dear to many contemporary poets, who see themselves as shamans. Kinnell has abjured it, however. In "The Seekonk Woods," his image for a kind of afterlife becomes the stink of a muskrat-skin cap that cannot lose the scent of its dead animal. A lucky person can, like James Wright, feel kinship with "salamanders, spiders and mosquitoes," and so imaginatively pick up "back evolutionary stages"—rather like dropped stitches in knitting, evidently. In "The Waking," lovers during

the act imagine that they are demigods lost in an arcadian land-
scape, but must come to "and remember they are bones and at
once laugh / naturally again."

The irony of Darwin's title, *The Descent of Man,* was not lost
on the language-conscious Victorians, who felt that in this new
perspective they had suffered a fall from the hope of Divine
ordinance, especially an eternal life of which the earthly one was
merely a shadow. *The Past* is an attempt to reconcile oneself to
the fact that one cannot reenter times that are gone. "I have
always intended to live forever, / but even more, to live now.
The moment / I have done one or the other, I here swear, / I
will come back from the living and enter / death everlasting:
consciousness defeated." In Kinnell's post-Darwinian world,
truth means facing the knowledge that our life-cycle consists of
no more or less than growth, propagation and decay, and that
we fulfill our function by living it:

> The rails may never meet, O Fellow Euclideans,
> for you, for me. So what if we groan?
> That's our noise. Laughter is our stuttering
> in a language we can't speak yet. Behind,
> the world made of wishes goes dark. Ahead,
> if not tomorrow then never, shines only what is.

PART THREE *Appraisals—Notes and Essays*

# Fragments

*by various hands*

I read the whole *Book of Nightmares* to my class at our final meeting, a grand farewell, and everyone, including me, thought it magnificent. "A universe," said one, after the last words and a long silence. It encompasses within the breadth of it both political rage and satire, and the most lyrical tenderness, and holds them together: coheres.

> —Denise Levertov, comment from jacket of
> *The Book of Nightmares*

The problem for Kinnell, I believe (and if I single him out . . . it is not because I think his blindness is greater but his potential for vision more)—the problem for Kinnell is the problem of the masculine writer—how to break through the veils that his language, his reading of the handed-down myths (and, I am forced to say, his very convenience), have cast over his sight; and what that will cost him. To become truly universal he will have to confront the closed ego of man in its most private and political mode: his confused relationship to his own femininity, and his fear and guilt towards women.

> —Adrienne Rich, in *Field,* no. 7 (Fall 1972)

In a poem coyly entitled "There Are Things I Tell to No One" [Kinnell] writes: "I say 'God'; I believe, / rather, in a music of grace / that we hear, sometimes, playing to us / from the other side of happiness." Kinnell's talent isn't well served by such ideas. Quite a number of great poems have been inspired by faith in God; how many have issued from a belief in a music of grace from the other side of happiness? Precious few.

> —Robert B. Shaw, in the *Nation,* 8 November 1980

Kinnell tackles ambitious subjects with a wide scope, yet he always makes them real and related to real people. His early end rhymes changed to tense, pared-down lines whose force comes from their vivid imagery. At his best he shows the grotesque and human caught in huge issues, like an idiosyncratic gargoyle on an immense cathedral.

—Roberta Berke, in *Bounds Out of Bounds* (1981)

*Is* the need for the new love faithfulness to old [. . .]? *Does* happiness hide inside the last tear?

—Katha Pollitt, in the *Nation*, 5 July 1980

Kinnell knows that much of poetry comes from below the head. He could have learned this from Lawrence but he learned it from life, from himself. His personalism and passion, his unrelenting look at the truth, preserve his deep knowledge in poems about the porcupine and the bear, the latter one of the best animal poems, surrogate for the animal man, of these times.

—Richard Eberhart, in Introductory Note to
*Cry of the Human* by Ralph J. Mills (1975)

Kinnell is least good where his point gets lost in gloomy, portentous scrutiny of the scenes and topics that most fascinate him, things about which he is often asking rhetorical questions that one wants to answer in a ribald way: dank rivers, frog-ponds, nastier bits of insect life.

—Alan Brownjohn, in the *New Statesman,* 12 September 1969

Galway Kinnell is now speaking quietly, over the noise of cars and ambulances, voices, the urgent background of city life. "Some kind of music that strikes us as grace seems to rule the lives of the other creatures more than it does ours, and we like to hear it any way we can," he says. "One way is through music and poetry. But another way is through listening to the singing of the insects."

—Cathleen Medwick, in *Vogue,* November 1985

There are few others writing today in whose work we feel so strongly the full human presence. His language tantalizes us with a foretaste of meaning, an underlying emotional logic that recalls Whitman's "I am the man, I suffer'd, I was there." Like all good poetry, his finest poems attract and mesmerize us before we really understand them.

—Morris Dickstein, in the *New York Times Book Review*,
19 September 1982

Galway Kinnell's poems are about mortality in the way rivers are about water.

—Robert Hass, In *Book World*, 5 September 1982

If Kinnell is "slogging toward the absolute," he begins with a recognition of the dense and stubborn particularity of the world he wishes to transcend. And his quest is ballasted—as in Frost and Dickinson—by the colloquial tone that represents, for all the temptations of the night, a commitment to waking consciousness.

—Terry Comito, in *Modern Poetry Studies* 6 (1975)

CHARLES ALTIERI

# From "The Dominant Poetic Mode
# of the Late Seventies"

Galway Kinnell's *Book of Nightmares* has often been attacked for
its strained rhetoric, but the important question is why a poet of
such talent should get trapped in problems very similar to
Bly's.* The answer lies, I think, in the task Kinnell sets himself:
In order to sustain and to resolve the level of intense, the-
atricalized suffering of the poem's often brilliant nightmare vi-
sions, Kinnell must be able to elaborate a metaphysical scheme
equal to his demonic moments and capacious enough to justify a
fully bardic stance. But Kinnell's ideas are very thin, and so he is
forced to rely on the verbal gestures of intense emotion grafted
onto conventional romantic postures. Here is the dramatic cli-
max in the central fourth section of the eighth poem:

> and the bodies of our hearts
> opened
> under the knowledge
> of tree, on the grass of the knowledge
> of graves, and among the flowers of the flowers.
>
> And the brain kept blossoming
> all through the body, until the bones themselves could think,

From *Self and Sensibility in Contemporary American Poetry,* by Charles Altieri
(New York: Cambridge University Press, 1984). Reprinted by permission.

*Altieri criticizes Bly on several points, especially for setting forth "poetic ex-
citement" as a criterion for poetry's function. The "problems" he refers to here
are an insistence on intense emotion and "the effects on lyric voice when a poem
is asked to carry the burden of restoring to a culture large religious vision,
however secularized or psychological."—ED.

and the genitals sent out wave after wave of holy desire
. . . . . . . . . . . .

and I understood
the unicorn's phallus could have risen, after all,
directly out of thought itself.

This section continually affirms the onset of knowledge, but after such knowledge, what but bathos can follow? What do trees know or bones think, and, above all, what more than a small lyric can be resolved by such a limited moment of final understanding? Knowledge and holy desire belong here to the realm of unicorns because only an abstract mythic frame will not immediately reveal the ultimate triviality of this resolution. As he reaches for a high style, Kinnell's general Rilkean stance collapses into a Blakean version of "Dover Beach," and the very attempt to transcend the personal by ontological reflection leads only to restating the basic problem as a solution; we are back with the dream of intense personal relations and isolated pastoral moments as the only alternative to the lucidity of nightmare vision. If one persists in seeking resolutions, nightmares demand not a momentary intuition but a sustained imaginative framework akin to a religion. Instead Kinnell's poem offers mostly exercises in lyric sensibility masquerading as thought. The skeptic might glory here in exposing such poetry as a pathetic and portentous attempt to take God's place, with an imaginary phallus our only weapon.

DAVID YOUNG

# From "Galway Kinnell"

In a poem called "Spindrift," Galway Kinnell sits on a beach, looking back the way he has come, noting that "My footprints / Slogging for the absolute / Already begin vanishing." The moment is typical in many ways. The poet presents himself as the protagonist of his poem, moving through a natural setting but preoccupied with metaphysical questions and concerned, not to say obsessed, with his own ephemerality. The edge of wry self-deprecation in the ironic distance between his romantic quest for the absolute and his very temporary impact on the world, as well as in the characterization implied by "slogging," is typical too. Kinnell is a visionary who is also perfectly capable of laughing at himself, though the humor does not so much undermine the seriousness as make it modern and palatable: any poet who can introduce an experience of mystical knowledge with the phrase "Just now I had a funny sensation" ("Ruins Under the Stars") is someone we are apt to feel we can trust.

The poet-protagonist who walks beaches, climbs mountains, encounters animals, meditates in ruins, and stares at the night sky, "the old stars rustling and whispering," is looking for comforts in a harsh and violent universe; and they are few and far between. Civilization, for example a "SAC bomber . . . crawling across heaven," seems confused and purposeless much of the time. Wilderness, wildness, violence, the upsurge of primitive energies in the self and in nature: these are more real but they are also frightening, awesome. Art's role is to provide a little music, something to go with the crickets' shrilling, the elegies of birds, the crunch and crackle of porcupines, to cheer us up even as we

From *The Longman Anthology of Contemporary American Poetry 1950–80*, edited by David Young and Stuart Friebert (New York: Longman, 1983). Reprinted by permission of David Young.

are consumed by the fires and energies of life, as we face the death that is a part of us ("the pre-trembling of a house that falls") as soon as we are born. Were it not for Kinnell's ability to create unlikely but convincing music, like the boys in "Freedom, New Hampshire" improvising on their tissue-covered combs, his world and his poems would be gloomy indeed.

The present selection . . . emphasizes Kinnell's musical talents. These lie partly in his ability to manipulate rich patterns of sound; reading the first section of "Ruins Under the Stars" aloud is a good place to start tasting and savoring his distinctive verbal music. But his musical gifts are organizational as well, and one can trace in these poems his development as a poet through experimentation with poems of musical structure, "suites" in which short lyrical sections accumulate around a major theme. The form is a descendant of the Romantic ode, and its great modern practitioner is Yeats. Spiritually, Kinnell may be closer to some of his declared favorites—Villon, Rilke, Frost—but formally he is a successor to Yeats, and the progress he has made with a poem organized like a musical composition is evident in the present selection. "Freedom, New Hampshire," his memorable elegy for his brother from his first volume, *What a Kingdom It Was* (1960), gives us three sections in which we watch the two boys encountering birth, death, and the generative energies of nature in the country setting where they grew up. In the fourth section, these experiences are recapitulated as the poem moves on to the experience of human loss and grief; the bitter, beautiful conclusion is the stronger for our having been prepared by the sections preceding it, each with its own scenery, music, and movement.

In "Ruins Under the Stars," from Kinnell's next collection, the suite structure has reached a more clearly musical and less temporal formulation. No implied narrative exists, and the temporal notations—"All day," "Every night," "Sometimes," "This morning," "Just now"—act to discount linear progression as important to the poem's variations on the theme of living in time and sensing the presence of the timeless. This same investigation of the interaction of physical and spiritual, visible and invisible, is the main enterprise of the even more dazzling set of variations, "Flower Herding on Mount Monadnock," the title poem of the second collection (1964). By having as many as ten sections, by using the archetypal structure of the quest as a climb toward knowledge, with the poet as a kind of daft shepherd of the wildflowers, and by teasing us with narrative features, this poem invites our delight in its inventive play with contradictions and paradoxes. There is certainly no "slogging" here, and the climb is more like an elated rise, an acceptance as well as a conquering of gravity and decay, accomplished by a strong musical sense and musical order, a dance up the mountainside.

The interest in longer poems that accumulate from shorter sections led Kinnell finally to the writing of a book-length poem in ten parts, modeled loosely on Rilke's *Duino Elegies,* each part a musical suite or sequence in seven sections, of the kind that earlier poems had developed so successfully. From that major effort, *The Book of Nightmares* (1971), we have included one sequence, the seventh of ten, "Little Sleep's-Head Sprouting Hair in the Moonlight." Any excerpting from *The Book of Nightmares* does it an injustice, since common lines of imagery and recurrent themes run through the entire poem, developing a cumulative meaning and force. Readers who wish to experience the full effect of "Little Sleep's-Head" are urged to read the whole poem from which it is taken. They will find it a fascinating and risky enterprise. In it the poet, thinking about his children and the fact of their mortality, seems less able to come to terms with death and change than he did in, say, "Freedom, New Hampshire," so that the book's appeal will be greatest to those readers most able to share its obsession with impermanence. At the same time, Kinnell pushes his characteristic humor and self-mockery into gothic and macabre regions where the excess is apt either to overwhelm the reader with admiration or produce a strong negative reaction. Still controversial, and still being digested and assessed ten years after its appearance, *The Book of Nightmares* is probably the most interesting poem of its kind since Hart Crane's *The Bridge* or Williams's *Paterson.*

# DONALD DAVIE

# Slogging for the Absolute

Galway Kinnell is a man who hungers for the spiritual, who has no special capacity for spiritual apprehensions, who has been culturally conditioned moreover to resist the very disciplines that might have opened him up to the spiritual apprehensions he hungers for. By writing poems which thrash in and out of the impasse thus created, Kinnell has made a great reputation—which suggests that there are many readers who are walled up in the same bind, and ask nothing better than to churn and agonize within it. And Kinnell isn't alone; the same or a similar pattern shows up in other poetic careers which, like his, span the last twenty years. The effect has been to disperse and dissipate the artistic and intellectual riches accumulated by the great decades of American poetry earlier in this century. More specifically the effect has been to take American poetry back out of the twentieth century into the nineteenth, from the astringent and sophisticated world of Allen Tate or Yvor Winters back into the world of Emerson and Whitman. For the impasse that we are talking of—a spiritual hunger which refuses to take the steps necessary to appease itself—is not a modern impasse at all, but is really no more than the tediously familiar dilemma of those late Victorians who vociferously "lost their faith."

This is not the commonly accepted notion about what has happened to American poetry in the last twenty years. For the received opinion, we can go to Ralph J. Mills, Jr.,* in the *Iowa Review* in 1970: "Galway Kinnell's first collection, *What a Kingdom It Was* (1960), can be viewed in retrospect now as one of those volumes signalling decisive changes in the mood and char-

From *Parnassus* 3, no. 1 (Fall/Winter 1974). Reprinted by permission.

*There is a letter by Mills in response to this essay, with a reply by Davie, in *Parnassus* 3, no. 2 (Spring/Summer 1975).—ED.

acter of American poetry as it departed from the witty, pseudo-mythic verse, apparently written to critical prescription, of the 1950s to arrive at the more authentic, liberated work of the 1960s." Similarly "liberated" (from what, is as yet unclear) were also "Theodore Roethke, Kenneth Patchen, John Berryman, Robert Lowell, James Wright, Anne Sexton, James Dickey, W. S. Merwin, and . . . Sylvia Plath," as also swarming onto the field before Mills's essay is half over, "Robert Bly, Louis Simpson . . . Frank O'Hara, Donald Hall . . . John Ashbery." (What a cornucopia of talent! One recalls the extraordinary scenario of Richard Howard's *Alone with America,* wherein America, a whore with a full engagement book, gets to have forty-one living poets alone with her, one after another.) It's to be hoped that some of these poets would resent the company they are made to keep to satisfy Ralph Mills's anxious program of safety in numbers. But there is plenty of evidence that a lot of them have invested heavily in Mills's reading of recent history, and are ready to come to one another's assistance. There will be rather fierce resistance, therefore, to any attempt to reopen a question so comfortably closed. Yet Kinnell himself, with an earnest candor that is characteristic, now forces us to reopen the question, by presenting us with the poems that *he* was writing in the 1950s, from in fact as long ago as 1946. We can't do anything other, faced with this instructive and fascinating collection, than ask how far "witty," "pseudo-mythic," and "written to critical prescription" are indeed acceptable labels for American poetry of the 1950s, how far and in what sense "authentic" and "liberated" are the words for the 1960s.

It turns out that *What a Kingdom It Was* is not, as Ralph Mills thought, Kinnell's first collection. It had been preceded by *First Poems 1946–1954,* which came out in a limited edition; and these are the poems reprinted on the first thirty-eight pages of this new book.* I will say at once that one or two of them seem to me as valuable as any of the more pretentious pieces that Kinnell was to write later. Charles G. Bell, the poet who was Kinnell's

*The occasion for this essay was a review of *The Avenue Bearing the Initial of Christ into the New World. First Poems 1946–1954* was not published until 1970.—ED.

mentor (as he touchingly acknowledges), some years ago saluted two of these early poems: "Island of Night," and "A Walk in the Country." Just as good, to my mind, is "The Feast":

> Juniper and cedar in the sand,
> The lake beyond, here deer-flesh smoking
> On the driftwood fire. And we two
> Touching each other by the wash of the blue
> On the warm sand together lying
> As careless as the water on the land.
>
> Now across the water the sunset blooms.
> A few pebbles wearing each other
> Back into sand speak in the silence;
> Or else under the cliff the surf begins,
> Telling of another evening, and another,
> Beside lapping waters and the small, lapped stones.
>
> The sand turns cold—or the body warms.
> If love had not smiled we would never grieve.
> But on every earthly place its turning crown
> Flashes and fades. We will feast on love again
> In the purple light, and rise again and leave
> Our two shapes dying in each other's arms.

Witty? Pseudo-mythic? Written to critical prescription? Of course there was a distinctive kind of bad poem written in the 1950s, and some of us who were writing them then are the first to laugh at them now; the two longest pieces among Kinnell's juvenilia, "Conversation at Tea" and "Meditation among the Tombs," are touchingly incompetent poems which accordingly display the vices characteristic of the period, notably a lot of unassimilated Yeats. But the extraordinary limpidity of "The Feast," the unemphatic tact with which the metaphor, the lovers wearing each other into sand as the pebbles do, is divulged by a stroke here and a stroke there, neither "built up" nor having the poem laboriously built about it—this has nothing to do with the New Criticism, nor with wit, nor with "myth." It is exquisitely beautiful; it is also exquisitely civilized and mannerly. And we shall look a long way to find such good manners in much that Kinnell was to write later.

One exception, however, is the poem that stood first in *What a Kingdom It Was*. For as Charles Bell noticed, this poem, "First Song," goes along with "Island of Night" and "A Walk in the Country" and "The Feast." And accordingly Ralph Mills is considerably flustered by "First Song" when he encounters it at the start of his appreciation of the later Kinnell who traffics in "stringent realities": in "First Song," Mills concedes with some agitation, these realities "are softened, almost sentimentalized, by pleasant details"; moreover, "pleasurable nostalgia fills the poem" and passages in it are unfortunately "muted." But of course it is possible, and not self-evidently wrong, to admire the poem for just those things in it which worry a reader like Mills:

> Then it was dusk in Illinois, the small boy
> After an afternoon of carting dung
> Hung on the rail fence, a sapped thing
> Weary to crying. Dark was growing tall
> And he began to hear the pond frogs all
> Calling on his ear with what seemed their joy.
>
> Soon their sound was pleasant for a boy
> Listening in the smoky dusk and the nightfall
> Of Illinois, and from the fields two small
> Boys came bearing cornstalk violins
> And they rubbed the cornstalk bows with resins
> And the three sat there scraping of their joy.
>
> It was now fine music the frogs and the boys
> Did in the towering Illinois twilight make
> And into dark in spite of a shoulder's ache
> A boy's hunched body loved out of a stalk
> The first song of his happiness, and the song woke
> His heart to the darkness and into the sadness of joy.

We can certainly agree with Ralph Mills that it's a matter of general interest and public concern how a poet who could write with this tenderness and delicacy should be writing ten or twelve years later (in *Body Rags,* 1968):

> The light goes out. In the darkness
> a letter for the blind
> arrives in my stunned hands.
>
> Did I come all this way only for this, only
> to feel out the world-braille of my complicity,
> only to choke down these last poison wafers?
>
> *For Galway alone.*
> *I send you my mortality.*
> *Which leans out from itself, to spit on itself.*
> *Which you would not touch.*
> *All you have known.*

In between had come the Vietnam War? Yes, indeed. And does such strident writing, or the blood-boltered primitivism of "The Bear," show poetry resisting the brutalizing of war, or surrendering to it?

Charles Bell, who recognized the beauty of some early Kinnell—and even, it appears, preserved early manuscripts which the poet himself had lost—nevertheless does not differ from Ralph Mills about the shape of Kinnell's career to date. For him, too, it is a story of "upward and onward." In Bell's note on Kinnell in *Contemporary Poets of the English Language,* we learn that already when Kinnell was putting together *What a Kingdom It Was,* ". . . his matter was the reaffirmation of the Promethean and pioneer daring of America, to which I also, after the neo-Augustinian resignations of the war, was committed." This is enough to make one weep. Did it not occur to Bell, nor to Kinnell even as he composed his brave and effective poems protesting the war, that it was precisely "the Promethean and pioneer daring of America" that was drowning Vietnamese hamlets in a sea of fire? Prometheus the fire-bringer in literal fact! And yet Richard Howard, who notes the pyromaniac imagery of later Kinnell, seems not to be troubled by it nor to notice any moral ambiguity.

Bell insists that Kinnell's vision was Promethean from the start: "What distinguishes that vision from anything else on the contemporary scene is its continuation of the titanism of the last century." The last century—well, precisely! The later Kinnell, like much American poetry of the 1960s, is an anachronism. The very vocabulary in which it is extolled by its admirers—"the basic urge for transcendence," "a primal level of being which is associated with the earth" (both these gems from Ralph Mills)—comes with an unmistakable whiff of some late Victorian critic like Stopford Brooke. It is not to the point that the American titan who comes first to mind should bear the sacred name of Walt Whitman. In the nineteenth century the U.S.A. had no monopoly of titans. Prometheans were the order of the day. And should we think better of French poetry since 1945 if French poets had found a way to sound like Victor Hugo or Claudel, of Italian poetry if it were once again sounding like Carducci and D'Annunzio, of English poetry if it had recovered the strenuous vehemence of Robert Browning, of German poetry if it sounded like Wagner and Nietzsche? Is it not the case on the contrary that two world wars and sundry other enormities have proved to the sensitive and humane man of our times that the confident affirmations of the last century, however understandable and even admirable in that age of innocence, are unthinkable for us? And why should the American be an exception? If he makes himself the exception, does this not prove that he has *still* not taken the true murderous imprint of the times that we are living in?

None of this is irrelevant to the case of Galway Kinnell, nor will Kinnell fail to understand what I am talking about. The proof is in another early poem now reprinted. It is called "Primer for the Last Judgment," and it is ill-written, yet an honest declaration of attitude toward very troublesome matters, an attitude, moreover, which throws its shadow forward over much that Kinnell has written since:

> When Jesus bruised his toe on stone
> Men crowned him—all of them,
> The pure and the impure—punctured him

Finger and toe, and pinned him there,
And coughed less from conscience than phlegm;
Then called for traditional values, unaware
They were asking their own liquidation.
"The end is at hand," said Paul.
But it did not arrive, that looked-for day
Of devastation, except at its own slow gait.
Daily the spent heart came home to find
A space with the dimensions of home
Ambiguously empty like the three-days' tomb.

And now with us: only a few
Years back, at war's close, the sun
Touching the Pacific found
Two cities crumbled. And men
World over asked, "Has the end begun?"
Maybe it has; maybe it shall come
Exploding flesh off the innocent bones,
Mechanized, official, and at once.
Or maybe it has crueler ways—
Dread of the body, the passion to subdue—
Not to be announced until it is done,
Which is each day from this day
Until the last tomb clutches the last bone.

From all of us who were writing in the early 1950s, the incineration of Hiroshima and Nagasaki seemed to demand a moral stock-taking, as it demands it of Kinnell here. We should respect him for rising to the challenge. Yet one cannot help noting that his speculation about the form which the gradual Last Judgment will take—"Dread of the body, the passion to subdue"—is the merest guess. It would have been equally plausible then, and is equally plausible now, to guess that the judgment on humankind would take the form of an excessive trust in the body, an ever more feverish carnality, and a passion not to subdue others but to wash one's hands of them, leaving the realm of public affairs to others more callous. Obviously, if the second alternatives had seemed more likely than the first, the subsequent career of the poet, as a moral agent and a responsible artist, would have been very different. It would, for instance, have been less Promethean.

Clearly, for the proper understanding of the decisive turn that Kinnell took at the end of the 1950s, a great deal turns on the matter of the poet's openness. Ralph Mills is very sure about this, and eloquent about it:

> This kind of openness—a sensitive receptivity in which the poet, to borrow a phrase of Heidegger's about Holderlin, "is exposed to the divine lightnings" that can easily exact their toll on nerves and emotional balance—extends, in many instances, beyond matters of social and political experience to naked metaphysical confrontation: with the universe, the identity of the self, the possibilities of an absent or present God, or the prospect of a vast, overwhelming nothingness. In such poets as Theodore Roethke, Kenneth Patchen, John Berryman, Robert Lowell, James Wright, Anne Sexton, James Dickey, W. S. Merwin, and the late Sylvia Plath, for example, with all differences set aside, the pursuit of personal vision often leads toward a precipitous, dizzying boundary where the self stands alone, unaided but for its own resources, before the seemingly tangible earth at hand with its bewildering multiplicity of life, the remoteness of space, the endless rhythms of nature, the turns of night and day, and within, the elusive images of memory and dream, the irrationality and uncertainty of human behavior, the griefs and ecstasies that living accumulates. Here the poet—and Galway Kinnell is certainly of this company—is thrown back upon his own perceptions; his art must be the authoritative testimony to a man's own experience, or it is meaningless; its basic validity rests upon that premise.

This is heady stuff, in a mode we have grown inured to: the reformulation for our times of the nineteenth-century myth of the artist as sacrificial Promethean scapegoat. It is of course necessarily blasphemous, since it involves denying the Christian contention that we have indeed known one such scapegoat, just one, unique and unrepeatable, whose name was Jesus. And that is a name that Kinnell has always made great play with, as in the poem just quoted or in the well known Whitmanesque poem which gives its name to this volume. It is very hard to see what "Jesus" or "Christ" signifies for Kinnell. So far as I can make out, it means in his mouth roughly what it means in the mouth of a Unitarian. But it really would be nice to know. And until we *do* know, his making so free with it cannot but seem—and not just in the eyes of Christians—an unpardonable vulgarity. It is in any case very nearly related to what we mean if we counter Mills's praise of his "openness," by accusing Kinnell of having resisted "the very disciplines that might have opened him up to the spiritual apprehensions he hungers for." Those disciplines are the disciplines of Christian worship; and Kinnell's resistance to them, his inability even to stand still long enough to understand them, is documented in three poems early in *What a Kingdom It Was:* "First Communion," "To Christ Our Lord," and "Easter."

No poet can be blamed for his inability to make the act of Christian faith. But what one can ask of any such poet is, first, that the impediments to faith be real, substantial, and such as to command respect; second, that having declared his incapacity for the sacramental and incarnational act of the imagination in the forms inherited from his own culture, he should be wary of pretending to make those acts in the terms presented by cultures that are not his at all; and, third, that he should not, having turned his back on the Christian dispensation, continue to trade surreptitiously in scraps torn arbitrarily from the body of doctrine he has renounced. On all three counts, whereas an honest atheist like Hardy is in the clear, Kinnell stands convicted. For in the first place, in both of the poems which most explicitly deny the validity of the Christian Incarnation (in "Easter" its invalidity is already taken for granted), the case is argued through the experience of a child; and in at least one of those cases, "First Communion," the objections are appropriately puerile, a misplaced matter-of-factness, materialistic and indeed mercenary. The claims of Christianity are nowhere in Kinnell brought to the bar of an adult intelligence. On the third count, we have seen how Kinnell continues to import a religiose fervor by tossing the name of Jesus around. But it's on the second count that the case against him is most flagrant and most far-reaching, since it's something that he shares with many other poets of his generation.

For what has been more common in recent decades than to find poets who reject Christianity (often, it seems, without thinking about it), embracing more or less seriously various forms of Hinduism, Buddhism, shamanism? And, while we must not rule out the possibility that some of these professions of exotic faith are genuine, yet is it not in the highest degree unlikely that a man who cannot profess the traditional faith of his own culture should be able to profess, in all seriousness, the faith of a culture in which, try as he may, he cannot be other than an outsider, a spiritual tourist? Here once again we perceive the lonely titan making his anachronistic reappearance out of the nineteenth century where he belongs, the Byronic or Faustian world-wanderer who disdains to consider his untamable mind as in any way conditioned by the times he was born to, the culture or the nation he was raised in. In Kinnell's case, the clearest and most guileless expression of this is probably his essay, "The Poetics of the Physical World," where, having tossed off some predictably cheap gibes about rhyme and meter ("Had Whitman been more clever, conceivably he could have turned out to be as good a poet as Whittier or Longfellow"), he proceeds to declare himself unable to sympathize with the treatment of death by Tennyson in *In Memoriam* or Milton in *Paradise Lost,* at the same time as he can enter fervently into treatments of the same theme by a Bathurst Islander, an Australian aborigine, and a Tamil from two thousand years ago. And this is of course the claim implicitly made by his already famous and profoundly regressive poem, "The Bear." At this point in Kinnell's career (and we encounter the same thing in many of his contemporaries) the titan who makes his reappearance comes to us not from the last century but from the century before that, from the Rousseauistic heyday of "the noble savage."

It is not really surprising that in this essay, Kinnell should present us with the Bathurst Islander's poem and the Tamil poem, as well as poems by Lorca and Yesenin, as if they were available to us on just the same basis as poems composed in

English. Translator though he is himself, Kinnell makes no allowances for what is lost and distorted in even the most sensitive translation. Thus he tells the reader: "One of the greatest of all death poems is Lorca's lament for Ignacio Sanchez Mejias." And the poem is then quoted in English, quite as if we could take the force of it in isolation both from the particular Spanish words in which it was written, and from the entire context of Andalusian life out of which it emerges. Instead, "The courage of this poem is awesome. Pain, rage, torn love, mingle undiluted, unconsoled." We are in a world where poems are written by courage, pain, rage, and love quite immediately, not as screened and filtered and diffracted through the fabric of any one of the tongues of men. And Kinnell's admirers have dutifully applied the same vocabulary to him. "Courage" and "rage" and "pain," "torn," "undiluted," and "unconsoled"—these are the terms in which they offer us for admiration such late Kinnell poems as "The Porcupine" or "The Bear"; any more manageable and less emotive language would bring down the poem to a level which they would call, doubtless, "*merely* verbal." Accordingly, it would be foolish to look in *Body Rags* for any of the self-effacing and feelingful dexterities that we applaud in the best of Kinnell's poems of the 1950s, or for that matter in *Flower Herding on Mount Monadnock*. If we are still uncertain about this, we should ponder what Kinnell says about the revisions he has made in that collection and in *What a Kingdom It Was*: "Most of the changes were made while I was reading the poems to audiences. Standing at the podium, just about to say a line, I would feel come over me a definite reluctance to say it as written. Gradually I learned to trust this reluctance. I would either drop the line altogether . . . or else invent on the spot a revision of it." I think we are meant to admire the bold trustingness of this procedure, how "existential" it is. But may we not reflect instead how approximate the wording must have been in the first place, how "optional" the expressions must have been, if they could be changed on an impulse thus lightheartedly? We need not deny that improvements can come in this way; "Spindrift," for instance, has profited from losing its last three lines. But it's obvious that poetry composed for or at "the podium" must be, as compared with poetry for the solitary reader, loose in weave and coarse in texture. So it is in "The Avenue Bearing the Initial of Christ into the New World." Certainly the poem is powerful, certainly it is inventive, yes it *is* keenly observed; but inevitably for the solitary reader it telegraphs its punches, as when, needing to allude to the Nazi extermination camps, it can do so only by printing in full a blank form announcing death over the signature of a Camp Commandant.

Kinnell may mistake this point, and his admirers certainly will. We are not asking for more beauty and less power, or for feelings that are tenuous and fugitive rather than those that are vehement; we are asking for feelings that shall be tracked with scrupulous and sinuous fidelity, rather than a general area of feeling expansively gestured at.

The best of Kinnell's collections to date is surely *Flower Herding on Mount Monadnock.* It represents a notable recovery from the much coarser writing of *What a Kingdom It Was,* and it is good to have it back in print. Many pages here can be read with very keen pleasure. But in these poems no more than any others has Kinnell escaped the self-contradiction that snarled him almost from the start. He still wants to experience the transcendent without paying the entrance fee, for instance, in the currency of humility. It is all very well to say, as by 1964 he had said many times already, that man's "lech for transcendence" is unappeasable, because directed toward what is an illusion, an illusion that he must learn to do without. But in that case let him indeed do without it, and settle for the perceivable and perishing world of the creatures as being all the good he will find, and as much as he has any right to. In *Flower Herding on Mount Monadnock* Kinnell repeatedly approaches this position, yet always in the end he shies away from it or tries to go beyond it. In a rare moment of (almost) ironical self-knowledge, he speaks of himself, in "Spindrift," as "slogging for the absolute":

> Across gull tracks
> And wind ripples in the sand
> The wind seethes. My footprints
> Slogging for the absolute
> Already begin vanishing.

Even as he declares that the perceivable is all there is, he continually runs his head against its limits as if to bash his way through by main force into the transcendent, the "absolute." It is not hard to recognize the same phenomenon in the late poems of Roethke. And many readers of both poets apparently find the spectacle both touching and heroic; but equally, as we go through the same foredoomed motions over and over again, we may come to think them simply unintelligent and boring.

What is certain is that a poet who thus thrashes about in a manifest self-contradiction cannot but do damage to the language that he bends to his purposes. In *Flower Herding on Mount Monadnock,* "old" is one word made to carry more weight than it will bear, and "amazed" is another. But the most flagrant case is that familiar telltale, "mystic" (or "mystical"). A cabdriver in Calcutta regards the poet through his rearview mirror "with black, mystical eyes"; Robert Frost is spoken of as "a man who was cursed / Neither with the mystical all-lovingness of Walt Whitman / Nor with Melville's anguish to know and to suffer" (Kinnell of course is with Melville and Whitman); and in "Spindrift," we are presented with "the soft, mystical shine the wind / Blows over the dunes as they creep," and also with a swan who "dips her head / And peers at the mystic / In-life of the sea." In none of these cases does "mystic" or "mystical" bear the tautly defined meaning which saints and theologians have honed fine and sharp through centuries, the meaning which a responsible poet like Eliot was at pains to master before he wrote *Four Quartets.* In Kinnell's lines the words have more to do with "misty" or "mysterious" than with St. John of the Cross. And how could it be otherwise, since the word gestures towards a realm of which by his own confession the poet has no experience? This is what Hulme pungently and truthfully called poetry as "spilt religion." And the spilling, the slopping and spattering, is there in what happens to a word and its meaning; whereas a poet, one supposes, should use words more responsibly than other people, here we see him deliberately fuzzing and blurring, like any adman or politician. And perhaps indeed that is why many readers find such a use of words in poetry natural and acceptable. Eliot, it will be remembered, spoke of "spilt religion" as a vice of nineteenth-century poetry, something which his and Pound's exertions had made disreputable. But we can see that he spoke too soon.

Kinnell, we must suppose, is more intelligent than his admirers. When he hears Ralph Mills talking of a poet who "is thrown back upon his own perceptions," practising an art that "must be the authoritative testimony to a man's own experience," of which the "basic validity rests upon that premise," perhaps Kinnell points out to him gently that this is a description of all worthwhile poetry whatever, not of some novel kind of poetry discovered in the United States about 1960. I should like to think so. For I should like to believe also (though I know it is unlikely) that when Galway Kinnell agreed to collect and reprint these poems of his youth, he was asking in effect whether there was any way back for him into the twentieth century from the blowsy nineteenth-century titanism in which he has snared himself. For a poet of such talent and such earnestness, the answer of course is: Yes! And what after all is the alternative? In a poem like "The Bear" the poet, determined to reach the absolute one way if not another, and unable to leap above his humanity into the divine, chooses to sink beneath it into the bestial. It is a sort of transcendence certainly. But what a fearsome responsibility for a poet, to lead his readers into bestiality. . . . A challenge worthy of a titan! So Charles Manson may have thought. Will Galway Kinnell choose to be a titan, or a human being?

DONALD HALL

# From "Text as Test"

. . . Galway Kinnell's poems began to appear in the 1950s. At first I was unimpressed, I suppose for a reason I was not aware of: now when I read the early poems, reprinted in *Selected Poems,* I hear the pale brogue of early Yeats—and it was Yeats whom my own youthful poems mimicked. Here is Kinnell:

> I looked into your heart that dying summer
> And found your silent woman's heart grown wild
> Whereupon you turned to me and smiled,
> Saying you felt afraid but that you were
> Weary of being mute and undefiled.

Early Yeats patented "weary"; then there is the conflation from "Schoolchildren"'s "And thereupon my heart is driven wild. . . ." I think that Galway Kinnell's poetry begins—no matter how many years it took to get started—with "The Avenue Bearing the Initial of Christ into the New World." This poem derives from Whitman without mimicking his manners, a poem of generosity and inclusiveness; a poem of experience in which experience is never subsumed by form—or by intellectual resolution, which for some critics is the rub.

When Harold Bloom condescended to Kinnell's *Mortal Acts* in the *New York Times Book Review,* he implied that Kinnell's poetry ended with the Avenue C poem, where I claim it began. Earlier Christopher Ricks performed a similar condescension in the same place. And when I had lunch with our leading magazine-critic, and praised Kinnell, I was astonished to hear the

From *American Poetry Review* 12 (November/December 1983). Reprinted by permission of Donald Hall.

reply: "A bit too life-affirming for me." (Who needs to make straw men, when people supply their own straw?)

It seems that Kinnell is a point at which critics and readers define themselves.

At this moment, the public reputation of American poets is anomalous. There is gross disparity between the short-list of leading poets as perceived in the Eastern academy—I avoid the ecclesiastical metaphor; I speak of the *New York Review of Books,* the *New Yorker,* mostly the *Times Book Review*—and the best poets as perceived in the rest of America by poetry's readers and by other poets.

First, it is necessary to affirm—in the face of willful ignorance—that poetry *has* readers, that poetry's audience has increased tenfold in recent years. . . . Otherwise-sophisticated literary folk will look you in the eye and claim that poetry has few readers. Nonsense: there are *many* serious American poets who sell in the tens of thousands, including Merrill and Ashbery of the academy short-list; including Bly, Levertov, and Snyder who are not on the short-list; including Adrienne Rich demoted from that eminence when she became a radical feminist; including Galway Kinnell: *The Book of Nightmares* has sold over forty thousand copies and *Body Rags* almost as many.

(Please do not misunderstand: I know that numbers are always irrelevant to quality—or Lois Wyse and Charles Bukowski would be better than Philip Levine and Ruth Stone; Edgar Guest would be better than Robert Frost, Martin Tupper than Tennyson. But neither can you say that numbers prove incompetence; one cannot blame Frost because he won four Pulitzers any more than one can praise him by the same standard. Nor does one praise Wallace Stevens by saying that *Harmonium* was remaindered: the worst poets in the universe are remaindered.)

Let me assert: there is a public for poetry, out there, which perceives a poetic landscape quite different from the topography mapped by Irvin Ehrenpreis and Helen Vendler.

It is useful to consider why critics feel uneasy with Kinnell. The strongest attack comes from a first-rate poet-critic: Donald Davie knows what is happening—and in large part he does not like it. In an essay called "Slogging for the Absolute" (originally published in *Parnassus,* reprinted in *The Poet in the Imaginary Museum*) Davie begins: "Galway Kinnell is a man who hungers for the spiritual, who has no special capacity for spiritual apprehensions, who has been culturally conditioned moreover to resist the very disciplines that might have opened him up to the spiritual apprehensions he hungers for." Then he quotes Charles Bell's praise of Kinnell's poems as a "continuation of the titanism of the last century." Davie agrees with the ascription of Titanism—but not the praise. Later, Davie finds that Kinnell "import[s] a religiose fervor by tossing the name of Jesus around," and goes on: "For what has been more common in recent decades than to find poets who reject Christianity (often, it seems, without thinking about it) embracing more or less seriously various forms of Hinduism, Buddhism, shamanism?"

Here I think Davie accuses Kinnell of something that others are guilty of. Just to be literal about it, I don't believe that the name "Jesus" occurs in the *Selected Poems.* (Of course Davie was not writing about the *Selected Poems,* and quotes an early poem called "Primer for the Last Judgment" which speaks of Jesus.) In this *Selected Poems,* Kinnell reprints "To Christ Our Lord," in which the cross is the emblem of suffering—as it is throughout his work; for "cross" is a frequent verb, and carries suffering with it but neither the name of Jesus nor the theology of Christianity. In one of the latest poems here, Kinnell puts "God" in quotation marks and corrects himself with the phrase "a music of grace," lines which sound like an animism infected with a reminiscence of Christianity. (*That* much I give Davie.)

But I do not find brutality or primitivism inappropriate to twentieth-century experience, or unbalanced by compensatory gentleness. And—especially—I find him less of a tourist among spiritual things than many of his contemporaries—subscribers to the God-of-the-Month-Club, worshippers at brief shrines like Castenada's Don Juan. . . .

In his charge against poets in general, I largely agree with Davie: the myth of the seeker gathers, but what is the quality of the search? and what is sought? Alas, what most seek is irresponsibility, fatedness, the sense of being controlled—even if it is by a little calculator manufactured to reveal biorhythms. Never have so many people hungered so much after God while wholly

lacking the ability to meditate or concentrate, to study or sur-
render—for the quality of the search is vitiated by ignorance,
narcissism, passivity, and terror. This search is characterized by
the desire *not* to discover, *not* to find repose, *not* to reside in
truth. Variety provides a method of unrest—a pretend-poly-
theism like a Roman's. Belief, after all, may imply responsibility
to act for some purpose other than the moment's comfort. . . .
Better to drift on, from Shaman to Sufi. . . . Better to entertain
the self-serving lies of Carlos Castenada than to study theology.

But *not* Kinnell. If Kinnell cannot be a Christian as Davie is,
Kinnell respects the Christian icon of suffering, and takes with
profound seriousness issues that Christian theology struggles
with.

But if Kinnell is not an easy polytheist, what about the notion
of Titanism?

Insofar as Kinnell names the evils, they are technological,
which separates him from the nineteenth-century Titanism of
his master Whitman, for whom technology was a risen god. But
for Whitman the locomotive and the telegraph were not the only
objects of worship. A moment ago as I denounced the faddish
seekers, I might have included among the false gods Mesmerism
or phrenology—if I had been writing a hundred years ago. Here
are two nineteenth-century pseudo-scientific pseudo-religions
with which Whitman amused himself, and from which he de-
rived lines of poetry. . . .

Apparently Americans seek after fads—American poets of the
last century as well as ourselves. (I have remarked elsewhere that
William Randolph Hearst is the true type of the American poet,
who picked up castles and cultures from all over the world and
assembled them in California.) The nationalist Longfellow pur-
sued nationality by turning Indian, not as a Shaman but as a
Victorian mythmaker, a library Indian. Emerson and Thoreau
studied Eastern religion and philosophy—like the eventually
orthodox Eliot; like Pound with the secular Confucius. And the
New Yorkers Poe and Whitman investigated the *technology* of
self-improvement: phrenology, Mesmerism.

I do not claim that this shopping in the flea market of divinity
is correct or useful, but that it is *American*.

And when I make this claim, what do I imply? Two sides to

this claim leave me skeptical. First, it is yet another invocation of determinism, historical and national this time rather than planetary; I remain skeptical of claims of powerlessness as "it is my upbringing" replaces the Calvinist notion of Election. Second, to call something *American* is not to praise it. Or it should not be.

When American poets or critics name a quality of poetry or criticism as *American,* criticism usually ceases. If we prove it *American* to be violent or sentimental or ruthless or ignorant, we seem to prove that it is good (or democratic or egalitarian or sincere—or at least inevitable: but that returns us to the first skepticism) to be violent or sentimental or ruthless or ignorant. Not only are we determined by nationality we are blessed by it! Of course in this bias we resemble all nationalists everywhere, be they resident in England, Tibet, or Australia. How the French thrill to the nature of *Frenchness!* Literary Americans remain cynical about the patriotism of used-car dealers, veteran's organizations, and college presidents—but when we identify a characteristic of our poetry as American we remove it from criticism.

I mean to suggest (what Davie implies) that the restlessness of the American seeker, of the national spirit as revealed in our poetry, is a fault not a virtue of the American spirit and American poetry.

And I find Kinnell less restless and more settled, more secure in a system of values and beliefs than most contemporary American poets; more settled in a landscape, a loved place that holds him to the earth, that keeps him from flying off into impalpability: the temptation of transcendence.

But can I really ascribe to Galway Kinnell "a system of values and beliefs"? He despises technology; he understands that life is suffering, therefore requiring compassion and "tenderness toward existence. . . ." If we call these notions Galway Kinnell's "philosophy," we call his thought inadequate—and we are guilty of irrelevance. For the poet is not a philosopher nor a theologian nor may we connect the value of the poetry with the wisdom of its derivable axioms. In his last letter Yeats said that we could embody truth but that we could not know it; we could refute Hegel, he said, but not the Song of Sixpence. . . .

It remains to question, as Pontius Pilate might have put it, what Yeats had in mind by "truth." When Sidney claimed that the poet "never affirmeth," did he set to the side notions like truth? In fact, "the poet affirmeth" all sorts of things: Neruda, alas, affirmeth Stalin as well as Mari Moru's knitting; Ezra Pound affirmeth Mussolini—and also a lost coherence; surely Dante affirmeth certain Christian doctrines. . . . Maybe Sidney speaks not of the fallible poet's intentions but of the finished object—the excellent poem. Now, poems are impure and composite: they make statements, tell stories, draw morals—and as poetry they dance, resolve, sing, and draw circles. *As* poetry the poem never affirmeth; it must win through *as* poetry, *as* art, in order to exist—after which it may, in addition to its shapely dance (and in conjunction with the accomplishment of that shapely dance) do all sorts of affirming . . . or not do. Thus a painting resolves formal problems whether it represents anything or not. Once it has paid homage to the separate universe of Art, it can turn into a late Rembrandt Self-Portrait or it can remain cubes and cylinders. When poetry becomes philosophical or theological—as when it becomes political or ichthyological—it invites comparison with usages of philosophy, theology, politics, and ichthyology. . . . But when poetry is neither philosophical nor theological (for instance) it is not by this absence inferior in its theology or philosophy.

The material Kinnell manipulates is mainly not ideas but experience and the feelings engendered by experience. These poems embody the intensities of a life and attitudes requisite or appropriate to these intensities. We may derive moral attitudes from juxtapositions—of course a property of form. (As ever, style is not only the man but the meaning, a statement in which all parts are perfectly interchangeable. Interchangeability indicates tautology. Let it be.) Now if the method is juxtaposition the manner is diversity—opposites are juxtaposed—and the means is multiplicity.

But what of Yeats? His example denies that we can know Hegel, which is philosophy and doctrine, but affirms the body of "A Song of Sixpence"; the song embodies form—two legs, two eyes, as Aristotle would have it—and attitude. I believe that contemporary American poetry—Galway Kinnell and Hayden

Carruth are two examples and James Wright is another—mostly lives to embody emotion. Or: experiences of feeling; experiences and the feelings they give rise to; experiences and appropriate responses in attitude. I think that the unconscious raison d'être for this poetry (it is *not* the only kind of poetry possible; certain contemporary movements, like the Language Poets, rigorously exclude feeling) is to validate or to test feelings. In a culture increasingly assaulted by pseudo-feelings, assumed for purposes of commerce or power, much of our poetry exists in order to ring true. We test our feelings by striking them against the surface of this poem; or we learn how to feel by using the poem as a model of feeling.

And the poet, I suggest, learns how to feel by writing the poem. I do not speak of sincerity. I don't know how to speak of it. When I spoke of "pseudo-feelings" above, I spoke as if with confidence—but when the copywriter invents scenes to praise a beer or a hairspray, how do I know that he/she is insincere? If I have trouble telling when *I* am sincere, how can I know about anyone else? Yet when I read someone else's writing, I feel a clear response to the language as adequate, fresh, and requisite— or as derivative, inappropriate, and ingratiating. I suggest that the reader's conviction of the poem's sincerity derives from form and thought, which the poet discovers not through spontaneity—spontaneity often recollects the words of others—but through slow and difficult rumination, chewing over words, testing them until they feel right. . . . Thus, the poet learns how to feel by writing the poem.

And if poetry claims to validate, test, and model emotions, the claim is surely Titanic. . . .

Years ago in an interview I quoted Galway, a sentence which people have picked up and run away with—and I sympathize, for the sentence makes a trumpet call. I had been praising some unambitious poets and Galway looked black and disapproving. Out of a long Kinnell-silence he spoke: "I have no interest in any poem to which the poet does not bring everything he knows."

I took it as a trumpet call to ambition, and as a statement of methods; he was writing the *Book of Nightmares* at the time.

Of course as a standard, if followed strictly, this trumpet call

omits from the canon two-thirds of the English poems I admire:
it omits wonderful lyrics by Hardy and Herrick, Richard Wilbur
and William Stafford together. . . . It omits as well a good many
charming and intelligent small poems from *Mortal Acts, Mortal
Words,* including:

BLACKBERRY EATING

I love to go out in late September
among the fat, overripe, icy, black blackberries
to eat blackberries for breakfast,
the stalks very prickly, a penalty
they earn for knowing the black art
of blackberry-making; and as I stand among them
lifting the stalks to my mouth, the ripest berries
fall almost unbidden to my tongue,
as words sometimes do, certain peculiar words
like *strengths* or *squinched,*
many-lettered, one-syllabled lumps,
which I squeeze, squinch open, and splurge well
in the silent, startled, icy, black language
of blackberry-eating in late September.

Certainly Galway Kinnell has not brought everything he knows
to this poem. The trumpet call may not be taken literally.
  But.
  When Whitman wrote "Song of Myself" he brought to it
everything he knew. "Out of the Cradle" and other Whitman
poems of the middle-distance also act like great magnets draw-
ing experience out of memory, bringing everything to bear. As
with many of the best poets, Galway Kinnell's genius lies in the
poem of the middle-distance—say, lengths from the brevity of
"Among School Children" to the Intimations ode or "Out of
the Cradle" or "Lycidas." Kinnell first essayed this length with
"The Avenue Bearing the Initial of Christ," then "The Bear"
and "The Porcupine." Then he used the form arrived at in these
last poems—seven parts accumulating to about five pages; sym-
metrical, highly musical free verse; a structure of multiple jux-
taposed   contrasts,   embodying   ambivalence   and   enan-

tiodromia—in the ten sections of *The Book of Nightmares.* (I count "The Last River" as intermediary, a success in its gathering; not so lucky in its resolving.) More recently—having used up the Bear/Nightmare form; one must keep moving or pack it in—he has traveled further into asymmetry and speech, abjuring obvious lyric resolutions; and he is surely successful in a poem like "Fergus Falling."

The new style is headlong, characterized by the extended compound-complex sentence; even the graceful "Blackberries" is a single sentence; later the sentences hurtle on for pages. Where the earlier poems paused to savor their vowels—not even James Wright is more musical than Nightmare-Kinnell—the newer lines make rough music, avoiding any hint of the performance that boasts: "Look at how beautifully I speak of ugliness." This brings Kinnell closer to Carruth.

Meantime both poets are ambitious, and take intensity of feeling, together with inclusiveness, as measure of their success. This ambition, this "bringing everything to bear," is Galway Kinnell's Titanism. Some readers find such ambition offensive, immodest. . . . I call it brave and excellent.

Of course it would not be brave and excellent (it would be naive and bumptious) if Kinnell did not pay continuous, successful homage to the separate universe of Art. Technique is test of sincerity, as the man said—defining sincerity as discernible in the object. The music, the purity of metaphor, the progress of the symbolic landscape—Kinnell performs his art with a shrewd and memorable dexterity. Why then do critics miss him? Davie misses him for serious reasons, deriving from features of modern culture which he finds reprehensible, and of which he finds Kinnell representative. And I think that the literary traditions of the American academy have deteriorated so much that most American academicians cannot hear poetry, have no sense of its *art,* lack a prosody or a notion of metaphor: our leading critics of the contemporary read without leg-muscles or tongues, read without bodies.

"Death is the mother of beauty." Poetry always enacts this confrontation, which lives at the center of consciousness. In the oldest poem, Gilgamesh's lamentation over Enkidu's death begins literature. Or: "*The wages of dying is love,*" in Kinnell's line—more fundamental to his work than the frequently-quoted "tenderness toward existence," because "dying" requires this "tenderness." A poet may survive with only one thing to say, if it is serious enough and if he says it memorably. Kinnell's *love* is multiply related to *dying*. He feels a lust for vanishing—as the soul longs for repose. Mostly, of course, it is the skull of things that makes flesh sweetest. "St. Francis and the Sow" ends erecting "the long, perfect loveliness of sow." Is this, perhaps, "a bit too life-affirming for me"? Well, it is not the Booster Club: it is affirmation in death's face because of death's face.

I ought to admit that—for me, too—there is a lot of American poetry which is too damned life-affirming; not seriously *life*-affirming, just "affirmative" like the Boosters and the *Reader's Digest*—good-natured, soft, optimistic, sweet, melancholy, cheerful, affectionate, warm-hearted, friendly, uncritical, and dumb.

It is the Nice Doggie School of Contemporary American Verse. It is a handsome dog, maybe an Irish Setter, and it will lie beside your chair for hours, napping with one eye opened, but if you stir for just half a second, its head will bob up, it will look up at you with its doggie eyes, tilt its head attractively to one side, and whimper seductively. It *loves* you. It bounds across the room when you let it in from outside, putting its muddy paws all over you, licking your face. . . . It scratches fleas; it spends much of its time licking itself. . . . It is loyal, true, affectionate, *sincere*. . . . It is perhaps a little deficient in irony, even in intelligence. . . .

But not Kinnell, who understands that we live by emptying ourselves. This is from "The Porcupine"—Kinnell wholly in command of his stately lyric middle-manner:

> A farmer shot a porcupine three times
> as it dozed on a tree limb. On
> the way down it tore open its belly
> on a broken
> branch, hooked its gut,
> and went on falling. On the ground
> it sprang to its feet, and

                    paying out gut heaved
                    and spartled through a hundred feet of goldenrod
                    before
                    the abrupt emptiness.

It is typical of Kinnell, in any of his incarnations, that this image of horror is glorious—having it both ways at once. In this sense, Kinnell is ironic as he performs his ambivalence; the suggestion of *up* always summons the implication of *down*. . . .

But he is seldom ironic in the manner of poets *who doubt their own instrument*. Of course he knows to distrust language and its beauties, "the tongue's atrocities" in Geoffrey Hill's phrase, but this distrust seldom enters the poetry. I contrast Kinnell (and most American poets of his generation) with Richard Wilbur, John Hollander, and especially with the best current poets of England—Geoffrey Hill for instance, Philip Larkin, C. H. Sisson, Donald Davie himself, Charles Tomlinson, Thom Gunn (and not Ted Hughes). Their writing is usefully corroded by doubt of poetry itself, doubt of eloquence, of wit, of metaphor, of language. These poets suspect distortions created by the instrument. What if literature creates only literary emotions, *referring* to the sufferings of human beings, but really removing us from them by substituting literary effigies? We are aware of the familiar axis of sentimentality and cruelty, whereby someone who weeps at a movie over the misfortunes of imagined others wreaks unutterable savagery on husband or wife. What if literature allows us to play at pseudo-feelings, and harden our hearts?

And that, abruptly enough, empties me out also. I speak more words about a *Selected Poems* than I speak about one long poem* because it covers more years of change—and also because I want to address the anomaly of Kinnell's reputation. Carruth's poem ought to inspire critics, because it is intellectual history as well as shape, experience, and embodied feeling—but if they attend to it, most of them will speak of little except its

---

*This selection is an edited (and slightly revised) version of an essay/review that dealt with Hayden Carruth's book-length poem *The Sleeping Beauty* in addition to Kinnell's *Selected Poems*.—ED.

myth. My praise of Carruth, like my praise of Kinnell, is praise for the formal integration not of system and idea but of feeling.

This poetry by its shape and import provides continual tests of feeling, emotional litmus paper: texts as tests. Against these lines—under the assault of falsehood, increasingly amplified by technology—we measure and validate the emotional life.

ALAN WILLIAMSON

# From "Language Against Itself: The Middle Generation of Contemporary Poets"

Sylvia Plath's poetry often expresses a desire to leave the personal sense of self behind, to attain to some mode of being that is conscious yet impersonal, transparent, the "eye" of "Ariel," the newborn universe at the end of "A Birthday Present." Yet her poetry remains a personal poetry, because it represents that wish itself as rising from a matrix of individual and social history, and also, perhaps, because it despairs of fulfilling that wish in life. Other poets of Plath's generation have tried to realize and inhabit a larger than personal—in some cases even a larger than human—mode of selfhood, which for them becomes the paradigm of health. Galway Kinnell has given the theme an extreme, and now rather notorious, formulation, speaking of a progress inward "until you're just a person. If you could keep going deeper and deeper, you'd finally not be a person either; you'd be an animal; and if you kept going deeper and deeper, you'd be a blade of grass or ultimately perhaps a stone. And if a stone could read, [poetry] would speak for it."[1] If this inverted hierarchy savors a little of the Freudian conservatism of the instincts that resists life and evolution, Gary Snyder's essay "Poetry and the Primitive: Notes on Poetry as an Ecological Survival Technique" offers us a conservatism that is deeply, though ahistorically, humanistic: "Poetry must sing or speak from authentic experience. Of all the streams of civilized tradition with roots in the paleolithic, poetry is one of the few that can realistically claim an unchanged function and a relevance which will outlast most of the activities that surround us today. Poets, as few others, must live close to the world that primitive men are in: the world, in its nakedness, which is fundamental for all of us—birth, love, death; the sheer fact of being alive."

In poetry written under such premises, the personal self is underplayed not out of shame, or an Impersonal Theory, but because it is seen—as in Rimbaud—as internalized history. Snyder writes, "Class-structured civilized society is a kind of mass ego. To transcend the ego is to go beyond society as well. 'Beyond' there lies, inwardly, the unconscious. Outwardly, the equivalent of the unconscious is the wilderness: both of these terms meet, one step even farther on, as *one*."[2] The truly important educative experiences become, then, experiences of unlearning: empathy with animals, primitive and peasant cultures, the wilderness; a reacclimatization to solitude in nature; the evocation of a Jungian collective unconscious through meditation or surrealism. And so a new (and at the same time an old, a Wordsworthian) repertory of characteristic subjects is established.

With this attitude toward the ego comes a special and in some ways hostile attitude toward language itself. Most of these poets share the view that language is one of the most powerful agents of our socialization, leading us to internalize our parents', our world's, definitions, and to ignore the portions of our authentic experience—the experience of the body and of the unconscious—that do not express themselves directly in verbal terms. (The poets I chiefly have in mind are James Wright, Robert Bly, W. S. Merwin, Snyder, and Kinnell. But the impulse toward the primitive, and away from language, affected many if not most of the poets who were in their thirties during the 1960s—notably Denise Levertov, A. R. Ammons, Robert Creeley, and Adrienne Rich, who in fact coined the famous phrase "the oppressor's language.")

The essential project, then, is to force language to transcend itself. These poets desire not a *mot juste,* but a word we can hear meant by the entire man who speaks it, his heart, lungs, and musculature as well as brain and voice box. Galway Kinnell speaks of "breaking to a sacred, bloodier speech"; James Wright of "the pure clear word" and "the poetry of a grown man." Wright defines this "grown man" in terms that are characteristically bodily, proletarian, and of the dream life, as well as antiverbal:

> The long body of his dream is the beginning of a dark
> Hair under an illiterate
> Girl's ear.

When Snyder, in the essay quoted above, follows on Charles Olson in laying great emphasis on the breath, he gives it an almost mystical significance, as locating man in the physical world and in his own full self. It is "the outer world coming into one's body," and "with pulse . . . the source of our inward sense of rhythm"; while "the voice, in everyone, is a mirror of his own deepest self" (pp. 123–25).

The reasons for the emergence of this shared poetic at this particular time are obviously complex. Some, no doubt, belong to literary history. All of these poets began writing in the early 1950s, at a time when most accepted poetry was orderly, cerebral, and, through the influence and the very sophistication of the New Criticism, a little codified; and some (Wright and Merwin, and, to a degree, Kinnell) had early successes in this mode. (Snyder's more Poundian skills, on the other hand, went unappreciated—in Eastern circles, at least—because of his identification with the "Beats," until sometime in the 1960s.) In one sense, then, these poets distrust rational organization and literary convention because they had to fight their wars of poetic identity against an overvaluation of these things. But one cannot ignore the larger history, the fact that this was the first generation to confront concentration camps and the atomic bomb, the fully revealed destructiveness of civilized man, while still growing up, before private values had had a chance to solidify. Like many other people in the 1960s, these poets came to hold, at least briefly, the scathing view of our collective moral history expressed by Kinnell in *The Book of Nightmares:*

> In the Twentieth Century of my trespass on earth,
> having exterminated one billion heathens,

heretics, Jews, Moslems, witches, mystical seekers,
black men, Asians, and Christian brothers,
every one of them for his own good,

a whole continent of red men for living in unnatural
    community
and at the same time having relations with the land,
one billion species of animals for being sub-human,
and ready to take on the bloodthirsty creatures from the other
    planets,
I, Christian man, groan out this testament of my last will.

For this generation, the search for values before and behind
civilization became an "ecological survival technique" in deadly
earnest; and (also for the first time in recent history) there were
tools other than Fancy available to the task, in modern an-
thropology and depth psychology. When Snyder defies at least
fifty years of taste by calling Rousseau's Noble Savage "one of
the most remarkable intuitions in Western thought" (p. 120), his
choice of words is worth pondering; what was once considered a
myth, whether appealing or noxious, is now seen as an inspired
scientific hypothesis, opening new areas of exploration and
discovery.

If "to transcend the ego is to go beyond society as well," we
might well begin our stylistic consideration with the "I" of the
poet. The poets we have been concerned with up to this point—
Lowell, Berryman, even Plath—intend a descriptive "I," a
voice we recognize complexly as we do a friend's, a social ego at
its richest and most individual. Their "I" seldom begins a poem;
it arrives politely late, surrounded by phrases that cast back its
idiosyncrasy, intelligence, tone, like so many mirrors. The "I"
beginning, on the other hand, is ubiquitous in Wright ("I am
bone lonely"; "I am delighted"; "I woke"), and not uncommon
in any of his contemporaries. But more remarkable is the shared
penchant for putting the "I" in the simplest of possible sentence
structures, pronoun plus active or linking verb, with no modi-
fiers before or between. The "I" becomes numb, neutral, uni-
versal: a transparency through which we look directly to the
state of being or feeling. (Snyder, on the other hand, prefers to

omit the pronoun entirely—following on Pound and the ideogram.)

The preference for simple sentence structures is not limited to first-person utterances. With these poets, no matter how wild or surrealistic the content becomes, the syntax tends to remain clear and enumerative. When Robert Bly describes the kind of free-associative poetry he desires, his metaphors are of motion from point to point, acrobatic enough, but still essentially linear: "a leaping about the psyche," "that swift movement all over the psyche . . . from a pine table to mad inward desires."[3] This constitutes a strong break with the hitherto dominant mode of irrationalist poetry in English (that of Hart Crane, Dylan Thomas, et al.), which, following from Rimbaud and Mallarmé, tends to suspend or confuse the normal syntactic flow, and create spaces for mystery and free association between the words themselves. Perhaps it is the location of the mystery *in* language, or in an operation performed on language, that repels a poet like Bly; better, for him, that the true complexity of feeling perish unuttered than that it become ambiguously intertwined with the studied complexity of the intellect.

But there is a strictly literary, as well as a psychological or epistemological, aspect to the search for simplicity. These poets are Wordsworthian questioners, bent on isolating the poetry in poems from all that serves essentially mundane ends: to prepare or seduce the reader, to shield the writer from anticipated criticisms, aesthetic or moral, to move the poem mechanically from place to place. Beginnings and endings in these poems are as abrupt and direct as the grammar is simple. There is an implicit aversion to all rhetorical devices which set an image in an "improving"—or even an interpretive—perspective; the image is intended to flash, like a spontaneous mental picture, and is usually coterminous with the line. Indeed, the whole aesthetic of "rendering" is suspect for these poets; its necessarily overburdened descriptions seem cold and predictable, its theory a rejection of the spontaneity and subjective validity of feelings. Often, these poets deliberately reinstate the outlawed nineteenth-century vocabulary of feeling and awe: Wright is devoted to the words "lovely" and "strange," Kinnell to forbidden abstractions like "infinite," "reality," "nothingness." (There is a similar forthrightness about human loves and loyalties, a refusal to let the fear of sentimentality—which after all implies forced emotion—interfere with deep commitments.) Perhaps it is all summed up in the mannerism—frequent even with Merwin and Kinnell, poets whose natural breath-unit is as long as Whitman's—of placing a single word alone on a line. There could be no clearer statement that the artifice in poems is finally peripheral; the poetry must, and can, spring from "the pure clear word," the meant word. . . .

. . . If James Wright is the most lyrical of the poets treated here, Galway Kinnell is the most energetic. He attained early fame with his very ambitious poem "The Avenue Bearing the Initial of Christ into the New World," which is still arguably as good as anything he has written. It can remind one of Crane and early Lowell in its sonority, but more of *The Waste Land* in its ability to include a seething cauldron of urban sensations, of randomness and ugliness, yet hold its own poetic shape. What it lacks, however, is a controlling or interpretive vision, beyond mere awe at the weight of humanity, the "instants of transcendence" and the "oceans of loathing and fear." At the rare points where it tries to conceal this lack through rhetoric, the poem becomes abruptly stagey.

Both the strengths and the weaknesses here are prophetic for Kinnell's later work. He continues to have the most over-vaulting and Marlovian style of his contemporaries, but it is a double-edged advantage, since his share of the generational directness, and his personal fondness for metaphysical clichés, make any hamming more obvious, and less likely to be mitigated by surrounding beauties, than it would be in a poet like Crane. On the other hand, his later poems succeed in uncovering the real feeling behind the Avenue C poem and making it, itself, the subject. It is the sense of a violent, impersonal, unseemly energy behind life, stunning the ego and bringing both "transcendence"—because it makes a continuum of the personal self and the cosmos—and "loathing and fear," because it is inseparable from the threat of change and death, "the pre-trembling of a house that falls." In poem after poem, Kinnell resuffers one identical ordeal, accepting death in order to be able to accept life, and concomitantly—like his Thoreau in "The Last River"—accepting cruel appetites in order to accept his full animal being and to avoid a crueler sadomasochistic simulacrum of spirituality. At times, the acceptance seems as negative as that, at least; but at other times it has its own special serenity, as at the end of "La Bagarède," where "the seventh / of the Sisters, she who hid herself / for shame / at having loved one who dies, is shining."

Kinnell's form has not altered substantially since his second book, just as his central experience has not. It is a sequence of generally very short, always numbered free verse units; the isolations somewhat take the place of rhetoric in conferring a brooding intensity on details; and the poet is free to move quickly from himself to nature to vignettes of other lives, while keeping our primary attention on the pattern that moves us into terror and out again into some form of resolution. Kinnell's poetry has a very narrow range of purely personal experiences. He can really handle only those that touch directly on his cosmic vision— passionate love, being with the dying and the newly born, the vulnerability of political imprisonment in the South—but of these he writes extraordinarily well (offhand, at least, I can think of no poetry about the first year of life better than that in *The Book of Nightmares*). But one looks in vain, in Kinnell's poetry, for the personal roots of his own vision and his repeated self-trial; though I am struck by the recurring theme of self-hatred, the special self-hatred of the large man presumed to be brutal by others, to be imprecise and blundering by himself—as it appears, for instance, in his discussion of his size at birth ("It was eight days before the doctor / Would scare my mother with me"). But I have dwelt too much on limitations, not enough on what makes the poetry convincing, remarkable—those frequent moments of stunned sensation in which human beings turn into force and object, and nature into embodied metaphysics, before our eyes; in which a tear is

> one of those bottom-heavy, glittering, saccadic bits
> of salt water that splash down
> the haunted ravines of a human face

and the dawn happens so: "The song of the whippoorwill stops / And the dimension of depth seizes everything."...

It is hard to evaluate these poets, as a group, in comparison to their predecessors. More distance may be needed before we can intelligently measure the cost of renouncing so many of the enhancements, the structures, the tacts of earlier poetry, against the qualities of consciousness—the poets might say, of being—rendered newly, or at least more sharply, articulate through their daring. It does seem to me, however, that all of these poets have gone through an unusually marked crisis of confidence in midcareer, in which their poetic self-definition—being so highly ethical to begin with—tempted them to exchange a problematic aesthetic merit for an imperishable moral one, and to allow themselves self-repetition with the same excuse a first-grade teacher has: the lesson is not yet adequately learned. (Perhaps the political climate of the late 1960s played a role, with its promise of an immensely enlarged, but less literary, audience sympathetic to the poets' collective vision.) In any case, the books published around 1970, when the poets were in their early forties (Wright's *Collected Poems,* Bly's *The Light Around the Body,* Snyder's *Regarding Wave,* Kinnell's *The Book of Nightmares,* Merwin's *The Carrier of Ladders*), become more ambitious ideologically, but at the same time more given to abstract self-explanation and to formula. Few are free of the kind of moral pomposity, the self-importance about the act of writing, regardless of the aesthetic value of the result, evident in Wright's

> If you do not care one way or another about
> The preceding lines,
> Please do not go on listening
> On any account of mine.
> Please leave the poem.
> Thank you.

or in Kinnell's bombastic peroration:

> The foregoing scribed down
> in March, of the year Seventy,

> on my sixteen-thousandth night of war and madness,
> in the Hotel of Lost Light, under the freeway.

The most cogent and successful of the ideological or prophetic books produced in this period seems to me to be Snyder's *Turtle Island*—it, too, weakened by preachiness, but given weight by the quality of such central poems as "The Bath" and "The Hudsonian Curlew." Later in the 1970s the didactic impulse seems to have receded, though at some cost to the level of ambition—witness the return to fine but small-scale nature epiphanies in Merwin's *The Compass Flower* and in some, though not all, of Bly's recent work. James Wright alone managed, before his premature death in 1980, to reinvent the very premises of his style, in order to encompass a more capacious and public subject matter in a more dramatic and, in some sense, objectified way.

Individual declines and recoveries aside, there is something of the tightrope act about this generation's work, even at its best. On the far side lies the real choice of silence, or of some purely physical or gestural art form. On the near side lies a kind of routine rhetorical religiosity—visible, already, in the slacker work from the early 1970s—in which the preverbal state is asserted, rather than conjured up, and the antiverbal doctrine serves mainly to relax critical standards. . . . Perhaps a poetry at once so exploratory and so denuded could be written only on the very edge, or hinge, of such a crisis of cultural self-confidence as we have been going through. It requires a very special combination of love and hatred to succeed in making language do exactly what, by one's own definitions, it cannot.

## NOTES

1. Cited in A. Poulin, *Contemporary American Poetry*, 2d ed. (Boston: Houghton Mifflin, 1975), 435.

2. Gary Snyder, *Earth House Hold* (New York: New Directions, 1969), 118, 122.

3. Robert Bly, "Looking for Dragon Smoke," in *Naked Poetry*, edited by Stephen Berg and Robert Mezey (Indianapolis: Bobbs Merrill, 1969), 161–64.

# Galway Kinnell and the Old Farmer

Galway Kinnell often refers to a transformative power that gives
radiance to the gross life of flesh; and transfigures the flesh be-
cause the radiance comes from beyond the flesh. He imagines
and represents two movements: the movement down into earthly
body, dirt, appetite, gross desire, death; and a movement to-
ward sunlight, time, fulfillment, lily blossoms, purity, narcissus
flowers, beauty, opening. Through the bee he represents the
second movement:

> The bee is beautiful.
> She is the fleur-de-lis in the flesh.
> She has a tuft of the sun on her back.
> She brings sexual love to the narcissus flower.
> She sings of fulfillment only
> and stings and dies.
> And everything she ever touches
> is opening! opening!

In the same poem he praises the fly:

> The fly
> I've just brushed
> from my face keeps buzzing
> about me, flesh-
> eater
> starved for the soul.
> One day I may learn to suffer
> his mizzling, sporadic stroll over eyelid and cheek,
> even be glad of his burnt singing . . .

---

Printed by permission of Robert Bly.

And yet we say our last goodbye
to the fly last,
the flesh-fly last,
the absolute last,
the naked dirty reality of him last.

Here Kinnell resists too easy transcendence; he resists spirituality that urges us to lift too quickly away from the flesh, and warns against fulfillment before the heavy work of incarnation has been done. He fears that the upward movement may result in bloodless purity and narcissistic self-obsession. Thoreau, referred to mockingly in "The Last River," has taught Kinnell the dangers in such upward movement:

> a man of noble face
> sits on the iron bunk, wiping
> a pile of knifeblades clean
> in the rags of his body.
> My old hero. Should I be surprised? . . .

> "Seeking love . . . love
> without human blood in it,
> that leaps above
> men and women, flesh and erections,
> which I thought I had found
> in a Massachusetts gravel bank one spring . . .
> seeking love . . .
> failing to know I loved most
> my purity . . ."

Kinnell distrusts German idealists and poets too angelic and overly transcendent persons who may misuse the transformative power. But he understands that although it may be misused, the transformative power exists. When a lucky moment comes, light seems to shine from inside matter.

> When the fallen apple rolls
> into the grass, the apple worm
> stops, then goes

all the way through and looks out
at the creation unopposed, the world
made entirely of lovers.

In fallen apples or fallen nature there remains something eternal and shining. To "go through" is to inhabit the world "made entirely of lovers": "And now everything changes. Look: / Ahead of us the meantimes is overflowing." Kinnell will not use angels as a metaphor for the streaming; instead he chooses milk bottles, or bees, or a moment by an ordinary wood fire.

> On the path,
> by this wet site
> of old fires—
> black ashes, black stones, where tramps
> must have squatted down,
> gnawing on stream water,
> unhouseling themselves on cursed bread,
> failing to get warm at a twigfire—
>
> I stop,
> gather wet wood,
> cut dry shavings, and for her,
> whose face
> I held in my hands
> a few hours, whom I gave back
> only to keep holding the space where she was,
>
> I light
> a small fire in the rain.
>
> ("Under the Maud Moon")

A critic might apply biographical detail to explain this passage, but such explanation is beside the point. The honoring of the transfigurative power is present, and Kinnell suggests that it is feminine in tone.

What is the proper route then to take toward this "world made entirely by lovers"? As I understand it Kinnell says the fly or the porcupine may be more helpful than the bee. His suspicion of the transcendent, or the falsely or too easily transcendent, invigorates each step he takes, and he would rather go the way of the porcupine, no matter how many blows to the snout he receives, than to reach heaven through purity. He is not put off by porcupine behavior in human beings:

> In character
> he resembles us in seven ways:
> he puts his mark on outhouses,
> he alchemizes by moonlight,
> he shits on the run,
> he uses his tail for climbing,
> he chuckles softly to himself when scared,
> he's overcrowded if there's more than one of him per five
>     acres,
> his eyes have their own inner redness.

Ascension is not for the porcupine, nor the starfish. Kinnell insists on water, mud, and descent.

### DAYBREAK

> On the tidal mud, just before sunset,
> dozens of starfishes
> were creeping. It was
> as though the mud were a sky
> and enormous, imperfect stars
> moved across it as slowly
> as the actual stars cross heaven.
> All at once they stopped,
> and as if they had simply
> increased their receptivity
> to gravity they sank down
> into the mud; they faded down
> into it and lay still; and by the time
> pink of sunset broke across them
> they were as invisible
> as the true stars at daybreak.

In this masterpiece, Kinnell describes the process of sinking with utter clarity. One simply sinks down into matter; there is no apparent effort. When one sinks in the psyche, one does not lose touch with the world above earth. On the contrary, the starfish resembles—in a way the physical eyes cannot see—"the true stars at daybreak." The aim then is to sink in such a way as to retain contact with the stars.

Keeping in mind these thoughts about rising and sinking, I'd like to turn our attention to Kinnell's new book, *The Past*. As the title suggests, the poetry in the book does not attach itself to the eternal, but to time. The imagination dwells on men getting older and weaker, on memories of a childhood friend calling to him at dawn, on events that took place on a certain stretch of road often passed, on a woman loved one night and missed since, on mornings spent with poets now dead. His imagination finds it hard to pull away from what is, from the chunky, the death-bound, the pig and the fly, though the "I" complains lightly all the while of insufficiency.

> . . . I want to lie out
> on my back under the thousand stars and think
> my way up among them, through them,
> and a little distance past them, and attain
> a moment of nearly absolute ignorance,
> if I can, if human mentality lets us.
>
> ("The Seekonk Woods")

It is the "I" that is aware of the moments when the past overlaps the future, and aware of the streaming that sometimes comes through.

> . . . Then I will go back
> to that silent evening, when the past just managed
> to overlap the future, if just by a trace, and the light
> that lives inside the eclipse doubles and shines
> through the darkness the sparkling that heavens the earth.
>
> ("That Silent Evening")

I am more and more aware of two separate beings living inside Kinnell's poems. In these passages, the "I" hovers observant, witnessing, aware of incompleteness and completeness, of moments when a shining "heavens the earth," of moments of bodiless love, an intense union of two souls, transfiguration. Another being, ancient and powerful, remains in matter, loves matter, holds to matter, and persists in that love like the huge log he describes that rolls up the Oregon beach and down into the water over and over again, is once more tossed up, plunges down and submerges. The log knows only matter. This earthlike, loglike personality is obsessive. Though not imaginative by its nature, it controls the imagination. Whatever the earthlike being dwells on, the imagination will dwell on. "Does the imagination dwell the most / On woman won or woman lost?" Yeats asked, feeling helpless. Kinnell's imagination dwells on blackberries, sows, wet wood, frog ponds, and in language on words so squinchy they are like blackberries or frog ponds. I see this earthlike personality as the persistent lover of matter, embodied at last in the old farmer Kinnell evokes in his poem called "Farm Picture," whose title comes from Whitman:

> Black earth
> turned up, clods
> shining on their
> western sides, hay
> sprouting on top
> of bales of spoiled
> hay, an old
> farmer bent far
> over like *Australopithecus*
> *robustus,* carrying two dented
> pails of water out
> to the hen yard.

How bent over the old farmer is! How ancient he is! Elsewhere in Kinnell's poems, the "I" is young and light. With the most wonderful faithfulness, Kinnell sustains the tension between these two. For Galway Kinnell is neither one. He is the one who remains alive and remains alert to the tension between these two. He keeps them in conversation.

The earthlike personality, the old farmer, lives by being attached. The old farmer is attached to mother, to milk, to fireplace, to children in the father's arms, to pigs in a sack, bears hibernating, bears being hunted, bears licking their young. Kinnell has strengthened his old farmer by paying attention to his language, by recalling the scenes he has enjoyed seeing. Whatever he loves, the imagination will dwell on, no matter what the "I" wants.

I now look on Galway Kinnell's poems as the product not of an integrated personality, but as a conversation between two personalities. I referred to them earlier as "rising" and "sinking," and just now as "I" and the "old farmer." We have all experienced a similar split, and we don't know what to do, for lack of instruction, about the dance that needs to go on between the two personalities. As a man or woman gets older, the relationship between the two is bound to change. This ancient and bent over farmer that goes into the henyard with his dented pails—what will he do now as the longing of the "I" gets stronger? What will the young fresh "I" do now?

PART FOUR  *Focus on Poems*

CARY NELSON

# From "Ecclesiastical Whitman: On 'The Avenue Bearing the Initial of Christ into the New World'"

Kinnell's verbal machinery (I use the word in Kenneth Burke's sense) acts repeatedly to apply that formal, nominative seal to whatever particular events provide the poem's ostensible occasion. Relative quality in Kinnell's poetry is partly a question of how far this continually renewed project succeeds. As we read a succession of his poems, we have to ask how much of our common experience is channeled through each new instance of a familiar ritual.

As Kinnell has acknowledged, he succeeds more fully in long poems. His short visionary poems are unconvincing because his key words are not very powerful without a more elaborate context. His short poems can work, however, when they are chiefly ironic. In a short poem, irony can provide a sufficient emotional ground and can even make a limited subject seem representative. But Kinnell's irony works only as a form of relief, or a signature for closure. Given larger ambitions, his irony tends toward sentimentality, so it will not in itself support a long poem.[1] Kinnell's verbal motives require not deftly managed synecdoche but a sense of broad inclusiveness established through accumulated detail. So long as the details are American, the method is patently Whitmanesque, and by now culturally approved and politically safe. Yet our history has soured us for such projects. If the sequential naming of American things, places, and people survives at all without ironic compromise, it is only, as Susan Sontag has shown, in the austerity of the black and white pho-

From *Our Last First Poets,* by Cary Nelson (Urbana: University of Illinois Press, Illini Books, 1984). Copyright © 1984 by the Board of Trustees of The University of Illinois. Reprinted by permission.

tograph.[2] We can now *see* with Whitman's eyes; the vast poem of America founders all about us. Visually, we can cross the continent in a minute. If the trip takes longer, the poem of community succumbs to the obvious visual evidence of violence and greed.

Kinnell's first major long poem, "The Avenue Bearing the Initial of Christ into the New World," naively ignores these cultural realities, and, I think, largely fails as a result. As anyone who has read much poetry by young people in New York will readily confirm, the subjects Kinnell selects cry out for poetic canonization. The "crone who sells the *News* and the *Mirror*, / The oldest living thing on Avenue C," may not have read Dostoevsky, but she seems to know instinctively that "she is Pulchería mother of murderers and madmen." In London, fishmongers sometimes exaggerate their Cockney accents when they hear American voices; more brutally, the residents of Avenue C conveniently suffer in Kinnell's presence.

There are at least partial solutions to these problems. Ginsberg sometimes succeeds by limiting himself to a particularly flat form of description and by acknowledging that the panoramic listing, in so far as it demonstrates community, is a lie the American poet revives because he needs it. Such poems must either deal overtly with the poet's motives, or they must court disaster (as Robert Duncan does) through deliberate formal subversion. Kinnell in these earlier poems is not yet able to confront his own cynicism and anguish. He is simply used by the tradition. Moreover, in "The Avenue Bearing the Initial of Christ into the New World" he supplies an unfortunate barrage of mythological, biblical, and literary allusions that turn his pathos into Camp sentiment and his avenue into a Hollywood set. The poem fails (and its ready acceptance by reviewers is a sign of that failure) even though its descriptions, which I confirm as a former resident of the avenue, are entirely accurate.

Kinnell's stance in the poem, to the extent that his impulse to write about the poor of Avenue C is benevolent rather than merely colonialist, is that poetry is a public forum where people can be given a voice they could not acquire themselves, a voice they may not consciously miss, but which the poet decides they need. Williams remained in Rutherford all his life in part for the same reason, and the program can be traced in American poetry back to Whitman. Williams, however, had rather less apocalyptic aims in mind; he does, in one way, transpose the whole of his native landscape to the body of *Paterson,* but he does not share Kinnell's troubled need to believe that poetry confers immediate beatitude on its subjects. "The Avenue Bearing the Initial of Christ into the New World" declares itself as a transforming fire where the common poor become heroic, eternal versions of themselves. Yet the poet's will to bestow grace is not quite so altruistic. Sanctity distances those who acquire it. The poem's real drama, its covert pain, is Kinnell's own struggle to unburden himself of the photographs his mind has taken of the avenue. He calls it a place "where the drowned suffer a C-change," but the real stage is not the sordid, extraordinary street but the poem itself. The reference to *The Tempest* hints that not only his subjects but also the artificer himself must be reborn. It is Kinnell who is drowning and would breathe again:

> It is night, and raining. You look down
> Towards Houston in the rain, the living streets,
> Where instants of transcendence
> Drift in oceans of loathing and fear, like lanternfishes,
> Or phosphorus flashings in the sea, or the feverish light
> Skin is said to give off when the swimmer drowns at night.

Kinnell's poem bears within it the seeds of a purgative journey through overwhelming sensation. The poet would immerse himself in the avenue's flood of images so as to acquire a new and broader selfhood. But the journey here is replaced by the special power of mythical vision automatically granted poetry itself. As Terry Comito has pointed out, "All the swarming multiplicity of the scene only emphasizes the ceaselessness of a dissolution in which human life seems to share the fate of what it feeds upon," but Kinnell will not confront the way his descriptions of decay challenge his vision.[3] From the outset, the poem is a secure site of transfiguration. In Comito's words again, "America becomes for Kinnell a special myth for the elusiveness of these 'leaked promises,' for the bitter nostalgia of all our Nicks and Kanes and Gatsbys for the 'secret country' where we can rest and be at one with the world."[4]

Instinctively, Kinnell knows that this America exists only in his poetry, and that the tangible products of history he describes there threaten even this imaginary redemptive landscape. Hence the undertone of brittle desperation in his poetry, for he does not yet know what to do with this knowledge. For Roethke [in his "North American Sequence"] the problem was not so acute; his vision, of course, was more fully worked out, yet he still had to handle his American materials carefully. Roethke could cite, almost with gingerly reticence, the waste acres at the edge of cities, a few sounds of bulldozers and hammers, and the traces of human garbage in a frozen river, without any of this quite forestalling his vision, however much it made his vision a more tentative artifice. Kinnell, writing almost at the same time, describes whole neighborhoods in dissolution, and the vision of communality becomes nearly absurd. By the time he writes *The Book of Nightmares* the process will be complete. . . .

NOTES

1. Charles Molesworth argues that Kinnell's main impulse is to move beyond the irony characteristic of modern poetry toward a poetry of empathy: "Empathy results from a systemic consciousness, an awareness of the field on which and through which the forces of experience act and make themselves visible." Molesworth cites sentimentality, a loose oracular structure, and "a didacticism close to the evangelical" as the pitfalls in Kinnell's chosen mode. *The Fierce Embrace: A Study of Contemporary Poetry* (Columbia, Mo.: University of Missouri Press, 1979), 98–111.

2. See Sontag, *On Photography* (New York: Farrar, 1977).

3. Terry Comito, "Slogging Toward the Absolute," *Modern Poetry Studies* 6, no. 2 (1975): 191.

4. Comito, "Slogging Toward the Absolute," 190.

PAUL MARIANI

# Kinnell's Legacy

On "The Avenue Bearing the Initial of Christ
into the New World"

It is one of those quicksilver pieces, Galway Kinnell's poem with
the impossibly long title, "The Avenue Bearing the Initial of
Christ into the New World," a poem whose parts seem to be
continually sliding through your fingers as you try to hold the
whole of it in the cup of your hands. And it is a young man's
poem: brash, sardonic, hardbitten, overreaching, vulnerable,
earnest, vital. Kinnell was barely thirty when he wrote it—"En
l'an de mon trentiesme aage"—and the length of the rhythms
like the length of the poem in effect make several important
announcements, not unlike Whitman at the beginning of his
poetic career in "Song of Myself."

For one thing, the poem announces its own seriousness, its
eschewal of the earlier formalist techniques which Kinnell had
already employed and even mastered to a degree, these concerns
now giving way to a new sense of freedom to pursue new rhet-
orical models, to see what he could do, for example, with the
Whitmanian catalogue, the language of the image, and—unlike
Whitman but very much like Villon—with the suppression of a
poetic self in favor of allowing the mirror world on the other
side of the poet's window to reveal something of the interiority
of the human condition. This is a poem which attempts, like
Stevens's alter ego Crispin downing his turnip whole in "The
Comedian as the Letter C," to swallow nothing less than the
world itself. The few critics who have paid Kinnell's first long
poem anything like serious attention at all have for the most part
marked its so-called flaws, castigating Kinnell's early poem (ap-

Printed by permission of Paul Mariani.

parently with an arrogance unearned by what they themselves had "seen" in the poem) for doing what the poem itself does not intend at all to do.

To begin with, Kinnell's poem does not intend to incorporate Whitman's vision of a new world stretching from the Atlantic to the Pacific except to demonstrate that we cannot have the mystical union Whitman, like Lincoln, hoped for even as the nation moved toward its own fracturing and annihilation. Such an optimism was a pre–Civil War condition, more a hope, an antimask, a vision of progress, a vision which Kinnell understands Whitman himself lived to reconsider after Shiloh and Antietam and Lincoln's assassination. Nor can Kinnell accept—either intellectually or along his pulse—Whitman's lifelong desire for a vision of sane and sacred death, as attractive as such a vision might be. The voice of the Jew, Isaac—Hebrew for "he who laughs"—Isaac the son of Abraham, who in our time has been consigned to the flames of the Holocaust by the millions, and more specifically the short story writer Isaac Rosenfeld who, reading Whitman back in Chicago, had merely laughed at Whitman's vision of easeful death, commenting on it trenchantly, "Oi! what shit!" Isaac laughs sardonically at any romanticizing of death whatsoever. Death is death: mean, nasty, and inevitable, and Kinnell—who had lost his own brother when he began writing this first long poem—feels the weight of this truth as much as any man.

As Francois Villon, for example, had. Villon, three lines of whose poem, "The Legacy," are evoked near the end of Kinnell's poem by way of counterpoint to Whitman. And why a medieval French poet from the streets of Paris, and a criminal at that? Perhaps because Villon's vision of death and old age and his vivid and realistic sense of medieval Paris chime so well with Kinnell's own brooding sense of death, which is why Kinnell has twice—over an interval of a quarter century—translated Villon's poems into an increasingly spare and vigorous American idiom commensurate with our own time. Consider Villon's sense of impending death brought home in images of corpses burning on Paris's cobbled streets in the wake of the Black Death, which devastated so much of Europe in Villon's century, and then—more directly—Villon's own premature aging (he disappears from history at the age of thirty-two) after being confined, tortured, and sexually debased in the dungeons of Meung and Paris in the 1450s and 1460s. Consider the image of those rotting corpses piled up by the hundreds to be burned and then superimpose upon this image those grainy black and white film clips of corpses at Auschwitz and Buchenwald and the other death camps being bulldozed into mass graves. For it is with the text of the Holocaust very much in mind that I think Kinnell reads the history of mankind along Avenue C, the once-teeming, vigorous Jewish quarter in the New World, which is—after all—one of the cities of the modern Diaspora. Life along Avenue C here in the New World, in other words, has after all merely become a continuation of the life lived in the old cities of Europe and the Near East, in cities like Paris, Damascus, Jerusalem, a people not unlike many of us in the New World, joined in this: that we are "scattered over the lonely seaways, / Over the lonely deserts . . . / [hiding] In dark lanes and alleys."

Asked about the origins of this endlessly fascinating poem, Kinnell has said that "The Avenue Bearing the Initial of Christ into the New World" actually began for him in Jerusalem in the mid-1950s, when he followed the ancient way Jesus followed as he was led off to die, staggering under the weight of the cross on which he would be nailed outside the gates of the holy city (letter to the author, 1 May 1985). That ancient way consists of the fourteen Stations of the Cross, beginning at the place where the tribunal chair of Pilate is thought to have been located and where Pilate, after much waffling, finally condemned Jesus to death, and ending at the place where Jesus was hastily buried before the beginning of the Passover at sundown.

And where are the great religious cities of the New World to vie with those of the old? New York? One would hardly have thought so at first. "When I did settle on Avenue C, living on 5th Street between C and D," Kinnell writes in the same letter, "I noticed that the street had 14 blocks, and that recalled my Jerusalem thoughts. The stations of the cross exist in those 14 sections [of "The Avenue . . ."], but barely, and could be called the [poem's] vanished skeleton." Jerusalem/New York. So, then, the origin of the poem may lie just here, like an early layer in the palimpsest of a life's work, an attempt to deal with the big issues: the problems of love, death, imaginative empathy and the possibility of transfiguration. Seen in such a light, the poem reveals its thematic affinities with such poems as "The Bear," *The Book of Nightmares,* and the poems remembering his dead mother and brother in *Mortal Acts, Mortal Words.*

Kinnell's Christian background—as with James Joyce only imperfectly rejected—seems to stand behind this poem like an early irritant, for the poem holds together best not if it is read as a latter-day "Song of Myself" but rather as a meditation on the inevitability of death, with this twist: that there is a resurrection of sorts possible and poetry is its source. For it is the word itself, the word which carries something of our very flesh and blood with it, the sound of the wind carried through our lungs and thorax and lips, which is the mediating force in this resurrection of the dead.

In *The Book of Nightmares* Kinnell laments Christian man's complicity in the death of his fellow Jews, for surely it was a Christian society—however that Christianity may have been subverted—whose witnesses, either directly or by standing by and doing nothing, essentially abandoned the Jews. This sense of collective shame, I think, stands behind one of the most troubling images in "The Avenue . . ." as well, in the image of Eliot's Fisher King transformed into a Jew (Christ himself) nailing fish to a plank to scrape the scales from them as he turns them—in a parody inversion of the Resurrection—into "flesh for the first time in their lives." For this community living along Avenue C, the remnants of one of the largest Jewish communities in the New World, mixed now with Blacks and Puerto Ricans and others in a swarming, vital, and exotic racial minestrone, is not unlike the Jewish communities Kinnell would have mingled with—Jew, Arab, Christian—in the old divided city of Jerusalem. Kinnell knows too that the Jews have survived the worst threat to their survival in the history of their race. And that tenacity, the miracle of having passed through the fire and been made clean, is a source of both consolation and of inspiration for the poet as creator, for the poet who would raise up this world—a world foreign to the so-called mainstream of America—to the level of the imagination.

Moreover, as Kinnell understands, the locus of his poem—

Avenue C—is central to anyone aware of American place-names and the history of American poetry. Situated in a tenement room a few blocks from the East River and the place where the Brooklyn ferries once docked, Kinnell cannot help but recall Whitman's "Crossing Brooklyn Ferry" and Hart Crane's *The Bridge,* to reconsider the largely failed promise of both these poems: the words of a poetic father and a poetic son haunting the youngest visionary in the triad—Kinnell himself.

In fact, among the catalogue of prelinguistic New World sounds which Kinnell uses to announce his poem is a tugboat on the East River, chuffing by at dawn as it "blasts the bass-note of its passage, lifted / From the infra-bass of the sea." Those who recall "The Tunnel" section of Crane's epic, published thirty years before Kinnell's poem, will remember the tugboat lunging past at midnight at the close of Crane's poem, "wheezing wreathes of steam" and giving its "one galvanic blare" as it moves upriver to disappear into the night. In 1957, though much has changed, the tugs, those workhorses of the river, are with us still. And so are the bums, those misplaced modern-day Daniel Boones, the romantic pioneers and adventurers who populate the "River" section of Crane's epic. In that poem, which Kinnell has very much in mind here, Crane records seeing one such derelict in the guise of Rip van Winkle as Crane moves along Avenue A on his way to work in Manhattan, having crossed over Brooklyn Bridge from his rooms in Brooklyn. In turn the derelicts remind Crane of the rail-hopping hoboes he'd seen as a boy back in Ohio:

> Behind
> My father's cannery works I used to see
> Rail-squatters ranged in nomad raillery,
> The ancient men—wifeless or runaway
> Hobo-trekkers that forever search
> An empire wilderness of freight and rails.
> Each seemed a child, like me, on a loose perch,
> Holding to childhood like some termless play. . . .

By contrast, there are Kinnell's bums along Houston Street, the panhandlers and winos who gob into their handkerchiefs and wipe your windshields for you as you wait cursing under your breath for the light to turn green. The only thing which has changed in the period between Crane's vision at thirty and Kinnell's at the same age—and the change is crucial—is the vitality and despair, the antiromantic posture, in the language Kinnell employs to capture the actual bums inhabiting the same streets Crane once walked and where Kinnell walks now:

> You stood once on Houston, among panhandlers and winos
> Who weave the eastern ranges, learning to be free,
> To not care, to be knocked flat and to get up clear-headed
> Spitting the curses out. "Now be nice,"
> The proprietor threatens; "Be nice," he cajoles.
> "Fuck you," the bum shouts as he is hoisted again,
> "God fuck your mother." . . .

During the academic year 1956–57, Kinnell taught at the University of Grenoble where, as an instructor in American literature, he was asked to give a course on *Leaves of Grass* to French students. It was, coincidentally, as Kinnell has reminded us, the same year in which Allen Ginsberg published *Howl,* the poem which Kinnell says announced "Whitman's return to American poetry after an absence of a century." Any American writer who has worked abroad and been forced by circumstances to speak principally in another tongue can I think understand something of the impact Whitman's fresh and concrete language must have had on Kinnell as he analyzed Whitman's poems for a French audience, using primarily the French tongue to teach his countryman.

Kinnell himself has told us what Whitman's example has meant to him. It is nothing so large as transcendentalism or any of a variety of philosophical mysticisms that attracted Kinnell to Whitman; it was music, a particular man's voice alive and present on the page itself long after the man himself was gone. And yet that voice is also, Kinnell reminds us, universal. In one sense, Kinnell's description of Whitman recalls Keats's Negative Capability, the poet's self radically empathizing with the other, a movement out from the self, attaching itself "to the things and creatures of the world." But there is the other side, no less important, which allies Kinnell to poets like James Wright and Philip Levine, one of the central triads in contemporary American poetry, the voice which "speaks at the same time of a life far within. In this double character, of intimacy and commonplace, [Whitman's poetry] resembles prayer" (see Kinnell's 1971 essay, "Whitman's Indicative Words").

Kinnell could be—and probably is—describing the particular effect his own poems so often have on readers as well. In fact, the curve of Kinnell's "Avenue" poem moves from an imitation of pure, virginal sound, the sounds along his street, and ends in a failing attempt at the unitive moment, a moment which attempts to incorporate the various antagonistic elements of Kinnell's world into an instant of transcendence. It is night and it is raining. It is the night of our history, the night of the soul, a night whose correlative is the blackness of the polluted East River rushing blindly and relentlessly into the North Atlantic. The poet looks down the Avenue where he sees a lone wildcat cab trying to make time crosstown on 7th. And then he notices the traffic lights:

> You knew even the traffic lights were made by God,
> The red splashes growing dimmer the farther away
> You looked, and away up at 14th, a few green stars;
> And without sequence, and nearly all at once,
> The red lights blinked into green,
> And just before there was one complete Avenue of green,
> The little green stars in the distance blinked.

What this is is a parody of American transcendentalism, the nightmare vision of an earlier and somewhat naive belief in the ultimate rightness of things, what has become for Kinnell, in spite of himself, an instant of transcendence adrift in—recalling Kierkegaard—"oceans of loathing and fear." If there is a light in that darkness, Kinnell tells us, it is merely the "feverish light / Skin is said to give off when the swimmer drowns at night."

"The Avenue Bearing the Initial of Christ into the New World" reads, then, like a prelude to Kinnell's own *Book of Nightmares,* filled as it is with Bosch-like images of grotesque death, images like the doomed goats in the markets of Damascus and seeing the twelve goatheads for sale, all with the rictus of death upon their faces; or the mass-produced impersonal letter from the Nazi camp commandant addressed to the relatives of the deceased—"Your husband, _____, died in the Camp Hospital on _____. May I express my sincere sympathy on your bereavement . . ."; or the fish hacked and scaled, heads lopped and guts dumped into a pail; or, finally, the would-be suicide caught in the searchlight glare of the fire engines, prepared to jump from the top-floor window, and—in an image recalling the reliving of human crucifixion in our time, "nailed in place by the shine."

The more one reads this poem, the more one feels its sense of strangulation, of being forced underwater, as in a dream from which one would awaken if one could. That sense is everywhere, from the image of the old man wading toward his last hour, to the sun shining down on the New York ghetto like some jellyfish, to the pigeons who fountain out from a rooftop. We live in a world cut off from the light, Kinnell suggests, and know the light only obliquely and in isolated moments, like fish, exactly like these dead fish. In this Kinnell reminds us of Shelley at La Spezia, recalling the fish moving in darkness toward the beckoning light, only to be smashed on their heads by night fishermen who have lured them to their deaths.

So, toward the end of the poem Kinnell hears the solace of bells,

> The bells of Saint Brigid's
> On Tompkins Square
> Toll for someone who has died . . .

These lines are immediately followed by three lines from Villon's "Legacy"—

> J'öis la cloche de Sorbonne,
> Qui toujours à neuf heures sonne
> Le Salut que l'Ange prédit . . .

which Kinnell himself has translated as

> I heard the bell of the Sorbonne
> Which always tolls at nine o'clock
> The salutation the Angel foretold . . .

What Villon says he did in "The Legacy" at precisely this juncture is what Kinnell also attempts failingly to do: "So I stopped and wrote no further / In order to pray as the heart bid." Kinnell's ellipses invite us to consider Villon's response and his own. It is one of the darkest moments in the poem, and the suicide caught for a moment in the glare of the searchlights surely recalls the figure of the despairing suicide at the beginning of Hart Crane's *The Bridge,* the poet as bedlamite, as jest, tilting from the Brooklyn Bridge momentarily before plunging into the darkness of the river below.

Kinnell too waits in his poem, lying awake in his bed, "expecting the vision," and hearing the "dead spirituals" of Blacks singing outside his window as the songs are converted out of the poet's intense loneliness and necessity back into prayers. But there is nothing, no response, except for the sound of garbage cans in the early morning hours being emptied surrealistically into the anus of a garbage disposal truck. Perhaps, the image suggests, we are all eventually swept into the darkness, a compost meant merely to seed the next dying generation.

In the harbor at the head of the River that is East there is a woman. She has stood there for a century beckoning the teeming millions from around the world. "Give me your poor," she says in a language recalling the Gospels. But for Kinnell the promise of the New World is more problematic, the Avenue at its entrance

> A roadway of refuse from the teeming shores and ghettos
> And the Caribbean Paradise, into the new ghetto and new
> paradise,
> This God-forsaken Avenue bearing the initial of Christ
> Through the haste and carelessness of the ages,
> The sea standing in heaps, which keeps on collapsing,
> Where the drowned suffer a C-change,
> And remain the common poor.

"God-forsaken": And we recall that this passage is from the fourteenth section of the poem, parallel with the entombment of the dead Christ, the suffering servant who had cried out to his father, echoing the Psalms: *Eloi, eloi, lama sabacthani,* that is, "My God, my God, why have you forsaken me?"

"Behind the Power Station on 14th, the held breath / Of light, as God is a held breath, withheld." Thus, Kinnell opens this the fourteenth station, waiting for a God who does not answer, while the river of history flows on into the coming darkness, where the teeming masses dissolve and die like the fish Kinnell has been at pains to paint for us in their various attitudes of death, "pale / Bloated socks of riverwater and rotted seed, / That swirl on the tide . . . and on the ebb / Stream seaward, seeding the sea."

But there is another side to all of this: the light which flares all the brighter for the darkness. What is the nature of the delight we feel in Rembrandt's painting depicting a side of beef, or those French still-lifes of dead fish and poultry? Kinnell suggests two answers: the answer which Rilke gives in the Ninth Duino Elegy, an answer Kinnell describes as "the resurrection of the world within us which Rilke strains his whole being to describe":

> Sind wir vielleicht *hier,* um zu sagen: Haus,
> Brüke, Brunnen, Tor, Krug, Obstbaum, Fenster,—
> höchstens: Säule, Turm. . . . aber zu *sagen,* verstehs,
> oh zu sagen *so,* wie selber die Dinge niemals
> innig meinten zu sein.

> (Perhaps we are *here* in order to say: house,
> bridge, fountain, gate, pitcher, fruit-tree, window—
> at most: column, tower. . . . But to *say* them, you must
> understand,
> oh to say them more intensely than the Things themselves
> ever dreamed of existing [Stephen Mitchell's translation]).

The other is the answer Kinnell believes Whitman offers us, the ability of words to indicate and restore the things they describe, something possible because poetry is not only a Virgilian or Wordsworthian elegy for what has been, but—even more importantly—a physical act, an act of love and intimacy by which words "rescue things and creatures from time and death." And so even the most "unspeakable" acts are resurrected and renewed by the poet, for the energy inherent in all physical things offers itself freely to the poet who accurately names those things. This is why Kinnell can give us his catalogues of sounds and the detritus of the world—dead fish, burnt matresses, the stores along Avenue C, the derelicts—and why we return to them to celebrate what would otherwise have long emptied into oblivion's river. Consider the splendid and distinctive catalogue of fish which Kinnell gives us at the eleventh station. If these symbolize at some level ourselves in various attitudes of death, still, there is energy and precision in what Kinnell has given us, the naming of a thing so that we see it freshly, as if for the first time:

> Porgies with receding jaws hinged apart
> In a grimace of dejection, as if like cows
> They had died under the sledgehammer, perches
> In grass-green armor, spotted squeteagues
> In the melting ice meek-faced and croaking no more,
> Mud-eating mullets buried in crushed ice,
> Tilefishes with scales like bits of chickenfat.

Just prior to this scene Kinnell had evoked the fire in Gold's junkhouse which had destroyed the offscourings of a thousand lives in its flames. But we know now what the meaning of that fire was. Gold's junkhouse: the alchemist's fire, in which the baser materials are transformed into gold, after first having passed through the refining fire. We know what made up that fire: love, human passion, the "bedbugged matresses, springs / The stubbornness has been loved out of . . . / Carriages a single woman's work has brought to wreck. . . ." And so with the self-reflective aspects of Kinnell's poem, as he tries out with his own indicative words to remake the detritus of the world in which he lives. Perhaps part of what he understands is that the Jewish people have survived their terrible ordeal by fire, though they have, like the old Jew in the second station, lost their sons.

But their example, their very survival, gives the poet hope, hope in the power of language to resurrect the dead, to give life to the precious, rejected things of this world, another life in words. And not merely a memorial or elegiac life, a Virgilian or Words-worthian remembrance, as important as those may be, but a sense of a world alive and shimmering in the act of the poem's being reenacted over and over, the polyvalved human voice fleshing things and reviving them for an instant again. That resurrection of the thing in the reincarnating words, it seems, is Kinnell's great discovery in Whitman and one which he attempted to emulate himself in this first long poem of his career.

Like life itself, the poem is rife with tensions and cross-purposes, the flames playing against the overwhelming flood of loss and darkness which is the human condition. But what joy in the words Kinnell must experience even as he questions the efficacy of those words, spilled out from lungs which

> put out the light of the world as they
> Heave and collapse [while] the brain turns and rattles
> In its own black axlegrease. . . .

And yet, and yet, in spite of this "nighttime / Of the blood" the words themselves "are laughing" like Isaac—the man who is laughing—on the pyre of our fallen human history. At thirty Kinnell has learned a secret about words which most of us, critics included, suffer a lifetime of discourse without ever grasping.

JOSEPH BRUCHAC

# I Have Come to Myself Empty
*Galway Kinnell's Bear and Porcupine*

"I think I could turn and live with animals. . . ." So said Walt
Whitman in "Song of Myself." It is a sentiment echoed in two
of Galway Kinnell's best-known poems, "The Porcupine" and
"The Bear." In fact, in those poems Kinnell does not just live
with the animals, he becomes one with them, goes through
death with them, "coming to himself empty" and then experi-
ences a new life within their skins.

In a way, Kinnell's experience in these poems is like the initia-
tion rite which shamans the world over have spoken of (as ex-
pressed in Mircea Eliade's landmark *Shamanism*). He travels in a
sort of dream-state to a place where animals and humans are
deeply connected, dies, and is reincarnated. In "The Bear," after
hunting and killing the animal, he climbs into its belly and
sleeps. When he wakes up, it is as the dying bear. In "The
Porcupine," he dreams his way into that bristly and strangely
sexual shape. Then, somehow, like the mortally wounded por-
cupine whose long intestines are caught on a limb, he jogs across
fields of goldenrod, guts emptying out behind him until he
reaches the final emptiness. That emptiness is another sort of
awakening, I think, both like that emptiness one may feel after
the "little death" of sexual intercourse and, strangely enough,
that awakening into an enlightened awareness sought by stu-
dents of Zen.

In his essay "Poetry, Personality and Death," Kinnell's words
relate directly to the attitude toward animals we see in the two
poems. After criticizing what he calls the "closed I," found in
both the confessional writers and the poets whose use of the first

Printed by permission of Joseph Bruchac.

person pronoun separates them from anything outside them-
selves, he quotes Whitman as follows:

> Latent in a great user of words, must be all passions, crimes,
> trades, animals, stars, God, sex, the past, might, space, met-
> als, and the like—because these are the words and he who is
> not these, plays with a foreign tongue, turning helplessly to
> dictionaries and authorities.

He also cites Gary Snyder's words from *Earth House Hold:*

> The archaic and primitive ritual dramas, which acknowl-
> edged all sides of human nature, including the destructive,
> demonic, and ambivalent, were liberating and harmonizing.

The words "archaic," "primitive," and "harmonizing" have a
very special meaning for Kinnell. They relate, of course, to the
more "natural" life of the animals he identifies with and be-
comes in those two powerful evocations of transformation,
death, and rebirth. What Kinnell wants is to transcend "that ego
which separates us from the life of the planet, which keeps us
apart from one another, which makes us feel self-conscious,
inadequate, lonely, suspicious, possessive, jealous, awkward,
fearful, and hostile; which thwarts our deepest desire, which is
to be one with all creation."

Perhaps not all human beings have that noble a desire, but it is
at the heart of what is going on in "The Porcupine" and "The
Bear." To quote Kinnell one more time from that essay,

> The death of the self I seek, in poetry and out of poetry, is not
> a drying up or withering. It is a death, yes, but a death out of
> which one might hope to be reborn more giving, more alive,
> more open, more related to the natural life.

Kinnell then closes the essay with the well-known Washington
Matthews translation of one of the oral poems of the Navajo
Indian people, the night chant which has influenced and moved
many, including Pulitzer Prize–winning Kiowa Indian novelist
N. Scott Momaday, who took the title of his novel *House Made*

*of Dawn* from that same ritual poem. It is, though Kinnell does not mention it, a poem of healing and a part of one of the extended rituals of the Navajo people used to return a person back to balance with nature and the community.

> Restore my feet for me.
> Restore my legs for me.
> Restore my body for me.
> Restore my mind for me.

So reads the translation, concluding "May it be beautiful all around me. / In beauty it is finished." The word "beauty" in the poem is only one translation of the Navajo word which also means "balance." Though I am not sure that Kinnell was aware of that double meaning of the word, I am sure he would have liked it.

Let's look at each of those two well-known poems. What (and this is, I think, crucial) is the identity and the point of view of the narrator? In "The Bear" Kinnell takes on the persona of a hunter, one who kills the bear by a hunting technique well known to Native American people. One sharpens a bone at both ends and then ties it so that it is bent like a bow. It is frozen in a ball of fat and the string cut so that when the fat thaws the bone will snap straight, piercing the stomach of the animal which picks it up and eats it. There are many Inuit, Athabascan, and Cree stories of using that method for wolves or bears. Thus, we might assume the speaker of the poem to be an Eskimo, especially when we see the landscape of the poem—frozen water, white wasteland without any shelter except that of the bear's body itself.

Yet I think Kinnell does not mean that narrator to be that far from himself. It is not a real hunter who speaks but Kinnell's image of himself as a hunter, one who seeks not just to kill the bear, but to kill himself, strip away his old life and be born again in that longed-for natural world. It is Kinnell who hunts the bear, setting out without the supplies that an Eskimo hunter would carry, desperate in his need to feed from and subsume and be subsumed by his prey. It is a powerful and revealing stance. He eats the bear's blood-drenched feces to survive on that seven-day-long chase and, after drinking the bear's blood, an old ritual suggestive not just of ingesting nourishment to stay alive but also the taking on of the spiritual power of the victim, cuts open the bear's dead body and goes to sleep within it—again a method of survival which was used often by Native American hunters.

At that point, his purely human narrator disappears. In his place is a sort of were-bear, a being neither man nor truly natural animal. Though Kinnell longs for that connection, I think the evidence of the poem is that it is a partial one, a faulty one, even a tragic one. He dreams himself into the bear's life and experiences with it the pain of its death—a death he caused by his whittled wolf rib. Its death matches his sleep at the end of the fourth stanza of the poem and when he wakes up ("I awaken I think") it is as a bear again, but a bear which moves in a sort of dream state, "one / hairy-soled trudge stuck out before me, / the next groaned out, / the next, / the next. . . ." And he is a bear who moves without purpose while still dimly remembering Kinnell's former life as hunter and writer (the two blending together as solidly as the identity of man and bear have blended), "that sticky infusion, that rank flavor of blood, that poetry, by which I lived."

Thus, though the details are accurate, the event, one which has happened and could happen again, the psychic dimension of this poem, the empathic direction it takes, make this bear of Kinnell's as far removed from a real animal as is the totem animal of a true Eskimo hunter, and also as spiritually close. It is an attempt on Kinnell's part, I think, to move as far as he honestly can in the direction of that fusion with the natural world which his self-consciousness and his Western-trained mind have divorced him from. He goes further than most, and far enough to make a poem which is strange, powerful, and convincingly painful.

Like "The Bear," "The Porcupine" is in seven parts. It also moves back and forth between animal and human, though the human in this poem is more clearly Kinnell himself, not a Native American persona. The porcupine is linked, like the bear, with humanity, but not as an animal to be hunted so much as an animal drawn to that which Kinnell clearly sees as a symbol of our human passions, the sweat from the body. At certain times of the year in particular, when their diet of leaves and bark has left their bodies starved for salt, porcupines will eat anything which has been moistened by human perspiration, whether it is the bow of an aluminum boat or, as Kinnell puts it, "goings across floors . . . hesitations / at thresholds . . . handprints of dread. . . ." In one sense the porcupine cleanses the earth of our presence, in another he is drawn to us. It is a wonderfully paradoxical image and its complexity is no less complex than those human passions which both draw us to and distance us from our animal lives.

One major difference between the two poems is that, while Kinnell's narrator perceives the bear first as hunted animal and then as self, the movement in "The Porcupine" is largely through comparison. Not only is the porcupine compared with the human, but there are other comparisons throughout the poem, both explicit and implied. Angels, saints shot full of arrows, and empty seed-heads are some of those figures.

The comparing begins when we are told how the porcupine resembles us in character in seven ways (seven is a significant number for Kinnell, full of magical associations), comparisons which vary from the accurate to the sardonic, sometimes combining both, and which are in no way flattering to the human species. We are told that "he uses his tail for climbing," that "he shits on the run," that "he chuckles softly to himself when scared." All of our imperfect, sexually driven morality can be read into those varyingly funny and frightening comparisons.

When Kinnell "becomes" the porcupine itself in the last three stanzas of the poem (the same stanzas where the transformation into an ursine being takes place in "The Bear") the shift is neither as dramatic as that in "The Bear" nor is it stressed in any way. Kinnell can remain within his own body, in a sense, the bristles of his own self-consciousness, his sometimes wounding sexuality alternately stabbing himself within or turning out to prick the woman beside him, for we already know that the human *is* the porcupine. And though the transformation makes the terms of his existence more clear, it cannot save him. The perception of the autumn-dried plants at the end of the poem (no food for a porcupine or a human) is only redeemed by that tenuous possibility of a vision of beauty (and completeness), "the forced-fire / of roses."

In addition to such literary and Christian images as Saint Sebastian and an "ultra-Rilkean angel," the poem also contains a reference to another, older tradition, that of ancient Persia. We find it in the first stanza of part 5:

> The Avesta
> puts porcupine killers
> into hell for nine generations, sentencing them
> to gnaw out
> each other's hearts for the
> salts of desire.

Kinnell's interest in the religions and people of the Near East is manifested in his one, intensely written novel *Black Light,* which tells the story of an Iranian rug-mender who during the days of the Shah's regime murders and then flees. It is a novel filled with irony and an awareness of human imperfection, as well as a lyricism as carefully wrought as in any poem. The evidence of that novel alone should indicate that there is significance in his mention of the Zend-Avesta, the mythology of the ancient Iranians which was put down in written form sometime around 600 B.C., during the time of Zoroaster. (Kinnell, I feel, seldom makes a purely offhand reference.) The Avesta is a highly hierarchical religion which has the worship of fire and the sun at its center (and this may be a reason for the stricture against the killing of the porcupine, whose quills have been seen by other peoples, including the North American Iroquois, as radiating from its body like the rays of the sun). It led toward a pre-Christian vision (as embodied in Zoroaster's teachings) of the struggle between the forces of Good and Evil and the moral imperative to strive after perfection in word, thought, and deed. That striving is evident not only in Kinnell's animal poems, but in all of his work. I do not mean to imply that Kinnell is a Zoroastrian, only that the tenets of the Avesta—like those of the night chant—seem, as Kinnell interprets them, to work well into the worldview of his poetry.

Kinnell's animals are on one level very true to life, the natural history about them quite accurate. One has only to read the article on the porcupine in the June 1985 issue of *Natural History* magazine to see how good an observer of the animal's behavior and characteristics Kinnell really is. Yet it is not just their reality which makes them memorable; they also exist as powerful symbols, archaic and archetypal. When Kinnell encounters porcupine and bear in his poems, he does not do so on the level of "man" the conqueror or as a representative of that human species which has been given "dominion." Perhaps his poems may begin that way, with the man as hunter or elevated observer, but, like the Zen teacher who urges the student to pour out the cup so that it may be filled, Kinnell tries to get rid of that painful barrier between himself and the natural world. Each of the poems moves toward that moment of emptiness, of transcendence into the body of the beast. It is a motion which takes courage, for it risks not just failure, but ridicule. Though the transformation may not be a completely successful one—for Kinnell in neither poem finds himself in an Edenic state after that shift of skins—it is a journey which gives his voice a power and authority like that of the man who disappeared from his village long ago and came back, many seasons later, clothes tattered, with stories of having lived among the animals. And because he told his story so well, because of a strange new light in his eyes, the people gathered around and listened to visions which widened their world.

CONRAD HILBERRY

# The Structure of Galway Kinnell's
## *The Book of Nightmares*

Writing about Galway Kinnell's long poem, I feel as I imagine I might feel if I were lecturing about *Paradise Lost* with John Milton in the back of the hall. Why doesn't everybody just turn around and ask *him?* In fact, Kinnell has said some helpful things about the structure of *The Book of Nightmares* (e.g., in the *Ohio Review* interview, Fall 1972)—and may say more. But I suppose, like other poets, he will leave a great deal unsaid. This, of course, is not coyness or obstinacy. When another person comments on a poem, we see that commentary as illuminating or not illuminating, right on certain points and wrong on others, etc. But no one sees it as the last word, equivalent to the poem itself. We always assume there is more to be said as the complexities of the poem take different configurations for other readers. But when a poet speaks about his own work, the statements sound with an uncomfortable finality. Who can dispute the man himself? And whenever a reading is taken as final, the poem is diminished.

I believe the best place to begin with a work as large as *The Book of Nightmares* is its structure. When the architecture of the book begins to come clear, when we have a confident sense of the movement of individual parts and the development of the whole poem as the parts build on each other, then there will be time to look more closely at recurring details or motifs, at variations of tone, at the texture of allusions, or at literary parallels. Certainly there will be things to be said about mythological elements. A glance at Joseph Campbell's *Hero with a Thousand Faces* draws to the surface countless pieces of myth in the poem:

From *Field* 12 (Spring 1975). Reprinted by permission of Conrad Hilberry.

the road of trials through rocks and mountains, the helpful crone, the death of self, the descent into the underworld, the hero united with his missing female half, etc. But to begin with, what are the parts and how do they fit together?

# I

I propose to look first at the structure of poem I, "Under the Maud Moon," in the belief that the structure of that poem is analogous, in a backwards way, to the structure of the whole book. I will go on, then, to the overall movement of the book and then back to look at several other individual poems in the context of the whole.

The first section of "Maud Moon" is a desolate one. It establishes the scene—Kinnell following a mountain path, lighting a fire, remembering a woman. (The speaker calls himself Kinnell.) Almost every detail reiterates a sense of brokenness, separation. He imagines tramps before him "unhouseling themselves on cursed bread." The tramps are doing the reverse of what the Eucharist intends; they are breaking themselves off from the sacred. So, too, with other details in this section. The woman is absent and Kinnell's hands hold only the empty space. The limbs, longing for the universe, snap, their embrace torn. The oath that made the universe one, holding together earth and water, flesh and spirit, is broken—resworn and broken over and over. Maud is not mentioned in this first section, nor is the song. The wholeness or oneness of the world is noticed only in its absence.

In the second section, the scene is the same—Kinnell is alone by the small fire in the rain. But he moves both back and forward in time, thinking back, by way of his singing, to the songs he used to croak for his daughter in her nightmares and forward to the bear out ahead of him, the one he will see later, nodding from side to side, eating flowers, his fur glistening in the rain. All three of the elements here, his daughter Maud, the bear, and the song, tend to bring some unity to the desolate brokenness of the first section. The child is closer than she will ever be again to the underlife, the "underglimmer of the beginning"; the bear moves with his own motion, perfectly at home among the blossom-smells on the rained earth; and the song, a love-note, "like the coyote's bark, curving off, into a howl," may bring us as close as we can come, with our torn speech, to a unison with the natural world.

The restorative elements are present again, and less hesitantly, in section 3. It moves back, in present tense now, to Maud waking in her crib. Throughout the section she is associated with plants, flowers: her hair sprouts out, her gums bud for her first spring, her green swaddlings tear and the blue flower opens. She is torn from the primal oneness, to be sure, but she is still natural, linked with flowers as the bear was in section 2. At the end of this section, she reaches into her father's mouth, to take hold of his song, to learn from him a second-best way toward wholeness.

Section 4, the center one of the seven sections, is crucial to the movement of "Maud Moon." (This tends to be true of each of the poems; to understand its structure, notice the movement into and away from its fourth section.) Here Kinnell takes us back to wholeness, the child in the womb, flipping and over-leaping, "somersaulting alone in the oneness under the hill." Here, for a while, the place is her own; she presses a knee or elbow along a slippery wall, "sculpting the world with each thrash." And the song she hears is not words spoken from mouth to ear but the stream of omphalos blood humming all about her. Effortlessly, she is the song. Without losing the gaiety, the comedy, of the child somersaulting "under the old, lonely bellybutton," Kinnell can slip in a phrase like "in re-membrance," which must bring to mind Christian communion; inconspicuously he links the womb-leaping with the sacramen-tal bread. Here flesh and spirit are put together—as they were not for the unhoused tramps in section 1.

A passage from Kinnell's essay "Poetry, Personality, and Death" makes plain how much emphasis he intends to place on "the oneness under the hill":

What do we want more than that oneness which bestows—which *is*—life? We want only to be more alive, not less. And the standard of what it is to be alive is very high. It was set in our infancy. Not yet divided into mind and body, our mind still a function of our senses, we laughed, we felt joyous connection with the things around us. In adult life don't we often feel half-dead, as if we were just brains walking around in corpses? The only sense we still respect is eyesight, probably because it is so closely attached to the brain. Go into any American house at random, you will find something—a plastic flower, false tiles, some imitation panelling—*something* which can be appreciated as material only if apprehended by eyesight alone. Don't we go sight-seeing in cars, thinking we can experience a landscape by looking at it through glass? A baby takes pleasure in seeing a thing, yes, but seeing is a first act. For fulfillment the baby must reach out, grasp it, put it in his mouth, suck it, savor it, taste it, manipulate it, smell it, physically be one with it. From here comes our notion of heaven itself. Every experience of happiness in later life is a stirring of that ineradicable memory of once belonging wholly to the life of the planet.

Another sentence, from "The Poetics of the Physical World," explicitly follows our sense of oneness with the world back to the womb itself: "Isn't the very concept of paradise also only a metaphor? Our idea of that place of bliss must be a dream extrapolated from our rapturous moments on earth, moments perhaps of our infancy, perhaps beyond that, of our foetal existence."

The first three sections of poem I have moved in toward the foetal somersaulting of section 4, the sense of "belonging wholly to the life of the planet." The last three sections move out again into the torn world. Chronologically, Maud's residence in the womb is the earliest event in "Maud Moon"; the first four sections moved progressively back in time to that original paradise. The next three sections move forward again to her birth, to her crying in the crib, and finally to a glimpse of her later life.

Section 5 is the birth. "Being itself" gives her into the shuddering grip of departure; separation is built into the nature of things. She skids out, in section 6, still clotted with celestial cheesiness, still glowing with the astral violet of the underlife. But they cut her umbilical tie to the darkness and her limbs shake as the memories rush out of them. She screams her first song and her arms clutch at the emptiness—as Kinnell's hands, in section 1, kept holding the empty space where the woman's face had been.

Section 7 becomes more distant, more reflective. Maud is now remembered in the past tense, as she was in section 2, after the more immediate present-tense birthing in the middle sections. Here, Kinnell, still by the mountain fire presumably, thinks back to Maud in her crib and his own singing to her. The song itself is the main subject of this last section. It is no angel song but a blacker rasping; nonetheless it has cosmic allegiances. He learned the song under the Maud moon, when Sagittarius sucked the biestings, the first milk, of the cosmos. And he learned it from marshes where he could hear the "long rustle of being and perishing," where earth oozed up, "touching the world / with the underglimmer of the beginning." The song carries intimations of a larger life beneath and above this one.

As the tramps in section 1 unhouseled themselves on cursed bread, so here in the last section Kinnell foresees a time when Maud will be orphaned, emptied of wind-singing, with pieces of cursed bread on her tongue. The poem has moved from the brokenness and desolation of the first section into the miraculous "oneness under the hill" and back to separation and cold and curse again at the end. But in the last section there is the song, the poem, the *Book of Nightmares,* doing what it can to make connections. As Maud, crying in her crib, knew sadness "flowing from the other world," so she will remember the specter of her father, with ghostly forefathers behind him, singing to her in the nighttime. This section states, indirectly, the hope of the book: to be there, a raspy, spectral voice reminding us that wholeness is at least conceivable, as Maud and the rest of us see the oath broken between flesh and spirit, between our lives and the life of the planet.

## II

I have emphasized the symmetry of the first poem. The whole *Book of Nightmares,* though extremely various in its moods and inclusive in its details, is built on a similarly symmetrical pattern—in fact, the mirror image of the structure we have seen in "Maud Moon." That poem moves from fragmentation to wholeness and back to fragmentation; the whole book moves from Maud's birth with its affecting glimpse of the oneness we must have experienced in the womb or in infancy, to the relentless meditation on death in poem V and the hellish picture of human depravity in poem VI, and then back to the birth of Kinnell's son Sancho Fergus and the qualified celebration in the last poem. This symmetry is reinforced by details recurring in poems I and X: the path, stream, and fire on the mountain, the bear, the two births, the constellation the Archer, references to communion, etc. More than that, some images or details that occur at the beginning or end of the book occur also in the desperate center parts but with connotations reversed. For example, as we have seen, the pregnant belly appears in an exuberant passage in the first poem. In the eighth poem, the swollen belly has similar connotations. But in poems V and VI the belly is big with death. In VI, 5, the belly of a dead soldier "opens like a poison nightflower" reminding us, by contrast, of Maud's flowering in I, 3. Poem V, 5, develops more fully the deadly birth image. Here the drunk dies, his flesh turns violet, and "the whine / of omphalos blood starts up again, the puffed / belly-button explodes, the carnal / nightmare soars back to the beginning."

A couple of other details similarly link the dead center of the book with the beginning or end. In II, 5, the Northern Lights flashed and disappeared until Kinnell thought he could "read the cosmos spelling itself, / the huge broken letters / shuddering across the black sky and vanishing." The comparable detail in V, 4, has none of this sense of ambiguity and wonder, no sense that the cosmos might magically flicker its meaning above the horizon. Here the message is man-made, definite, and final: "I saw the ferris wheel writing its huge, desolate zeroes in neon on the evening skies." One other instance: in VI, 2, the air force gunner, Burnsie, says,

> remember that pilot
> who'd bailed out over the North,
> how I shredded him down to catgut on his strings?

one of his slant eyes, a piece
of his smile, sail past me
every night right after the sleeping pill . . .

That catgut comes back in X, 5 as the strings out of which the violinist draws his music.

Even these two small details, the writing on the night sky and the catgut, give some sense of the structural movement of the book. It begins aware of death and torn lives, to be sure, but nonetheless buoyed up in the first two or three poems by glimmers of cosmic writing, remnants of celestial cheesiness, or intimations of the underlife. By V and VI, the book moves under "the absolute spell of departure," the neon zeroes of death. Men detest the sweat of their own bodies and shred other men to catgut because they love the sound of the guns and the feel of them in their hands. In the last poems love is again possible— under the pear tree which grows out of the boneyard, the Aceldama bought with Judas's silver. Deeply acquainted with death, the wood and catgut will open again to love's singing.

## III

The introduction of the mountain scene in I and the return to it in X suggests that this place may be taken as the literal location of the poem, with all the rest being the hiker's mental journeying. This much is evident: as the book opens, Kinnell, the speaker, is making a fire on a path by a stream in the rain, remembering a woman whose face he has held in his hands, thinking of the bear he has not yet encountered out ahead of him, and, as he sings into the fire, thinking of his daughter. By the final poem he has climbed further up the mountain. The fire is now behind him, still flaring in the rain, and the stream is now skinny waterfalls that wander out of heaven and strike the cliffside. The bear that was out ahead is now present, his fur glistening in the rain, like Sancho Fergus's hair. Standing in the old shoes flowed over by rainbows of hen oil, Kinnell calls out toward the cliff and listens for an echo, hears the clatter of elk hooves, and looks down on the river below. This scene does contain many details that develop into prominent motifs as the book grows: the path, the stream, the bear, the stones, the woman who is his torn half and whom he has just left in Waterloo, Iowa, the fire, the daughter and son, even the old shoes and the hen—or at least the grease from the hen. It seems to me plausible to think of this as the literal setting of the poem, made intense partly by his having just let necessity draw him away from the woman in Waterloo. "The Hen Flower," "The Shoes of Wandering," and the rest then become meditations triggered by elements in that literal scene. They are the imaginative or spiritual journey the speaker takes as he is climbing a few hundred yards or a mile or two up the mountain from the site of the fire to the clearing where the bear nods and turns.

One hesitates to push this reading too hard, for a couple of reasons. For one thing, even though the stream, the shoes, the hen, the children, the divided lovers, etc., recur throughout the book, there are few references between I and X to the mountain scene itself. (In fact, four: V, 4; VII, 4; VIII, 7; and IX, 1.) Can we travel through all the rich and emotional material in between and still hold in mind the mountain location? If Kinnell had intended us to do that, would he not have brought us back to that scene more often? Second, the description of Maud's birth in the first poem and Fergus's birth in the last gives a strong sense of time elapsed. (Probably our knowing that Kinnell wrote the book over a four-year period contributes, illegitimately, to that feeling.) But those reasons do not seem to me conclusive. There the hiker is, further up the mountain in the tenth poem, and if we find it helpful to see the book as an internal journey, a series of meditations bracketed by the literal fire and bear on the mountain, I believe we are justified in doing so.

## IV

Now a few observations about Poems II, IV, VII, and X and their place in the progress of the book. Again, I am dealing with the general contours of these poems, their structure, saying little about the lovely modulations of tone and texture that draw us along, surprising us and engaging our feelings page after page.

If "Maud Moon" recalls the glimmers of the celestial, the

intimations of immortality that we knew from before birth and still could touch in earliest childhood, "The Hen Flower" considers death and the mysteries, if any, that lie beyond it. It is as though Kinnell, in order to write Maud a true book for the days when she finds herself orphaned, must discover as much as can be known about death. He begins that exploration here in the second poem.

In the first and last sections of II Kinnell is sprawled face down on the mattress of hen feathers, aware of how little there is between himself and the long shaft of darkness shaped as himself, and wishing he could let go, throw himself on the mercy of darkness like the hen who woozes off when its throat is stroked, throws its head back on the chopping block, and longs to die. The "letting go" that Kinnell wishes to instruct himself in is probably, in part, a literal willingness to die when the time calls for it. It may be, as well, the death of the self that he speaks of in "Poetry, Personality, and Death" as when in the deepest love-making "the separate egos vanish; the wand of cosmic sexuality rules." A paragraph from that essay may clarify this death-longing:

> The death of the self I seek, in poetry and out of poetry, is not a drying up or withering. It is a death, yes, but a death out of which one might hope to be reborn more giving, more alive, more open, more related to the natural life. I have never felt the appeal of that death of self certain kinds of Buddhism describe—that death which purges us of desire, which removes us from our loves. For myself, I would like a death that would give me more loves, not fewer. And greater desire, not less. Isn't it possible that to desire a thing, to truly desire it, is a form of having it? I suppose nothing is stronger than fate—if fate is that amount of vital energy allotted each of us—but if anything were stronger, it would not be acquiescence, the coming to want only what one already has, it would be desire, desire which rises from the roots of one's life and transfigures it.

"The Hen Flower" has its symmetries, as does "Maud Moon," but the internal organization is different. Here, in sections 2 through 6, two views of death alternate, one prevailing for a section or a paragraph and then the other having its say. The first sees death as simple extinction, the cheeks of the axed hen caving in, the gizzard convulsing, the next egg skidding forth, ridding her of the life to come. This is the tone of the passage in 5 in which the mockingbird sings the cry of the rifle, the tree holds the bones of the sniper, and the chameleon is not changed, not raised incorruptible, but remains the color of blood. It is the tone of the paragraph in 6 in which the rooster groans out for Kinnell, as for the stonily doctrinaire Peter, *it is the empty morning*. But playing off against this view of death as literal and final are those wonderful, half-comic hen-resurrection passages—the one in which the beheaded hen waits for the blaze in the genes that according to gospel shall carry it back into pink skies, where geese cross at twilight honking in tongues. And the one in which the Northern Lights, seen through the spealbone of a ram, appear to spell mysteries against the black sky. And the one in which Kinnell flings high the carcass of the hen and watches the dead wings creak open as she soars across the arms of the Bear.

Section 4, at the center of "The Hen Flower," takes us into the opened cadaver of the hen, back to the mystery of hen-death past the diminishing eggs toward the icy pulp of what is. There zero freezes itself around the finger. If there is any ambiguity here, it lies in our knowledge that zero is not only the end of the diminishing series of positive numbers but also the beginning of the series of negative numbers. But this may be too hopeful a reading for that cold cipher. Oneness was at the center of I; the center of II is zero.

In II Kinnell has instructed himself to let go, to throw himself on the mercy of darkness, "to say all," as he says in the *Ohio Review* interview (Fall 1972, p. 30). In III, the dangerous journey begins. After a kind of vigil at the Xvarna Hotel (a Zoroastrian word, Kinnell says, meaning "hidden light"), he sets out, lost to his old self and aware of his inadequacy on this strange road where even the most elementary questions are a puzzle.

The fourth poem, "Dear Stranger Extant in Memory by the Blue Juniata," is one of the most complex and difficult. The first three sections describe three different places where one might

look for help or insight or guidance on the uncertain journey—
and all three fail to provide it. No longer hoping for some
mythic gatekeeper, or deskman, to swing open the steel doors
and announce a new day, Kinnell still listens for the church's
tinny sacring-bell, rung during the Eucharist at the elevation of
the bread and wine. He hopes for some instruction from this old
ceremony. But the *chime* is just *chyme,* a mass of semidigested
food. Instead of the bread and wine of our loves being trans-
formed into the sacred body and blood, they are chewed and
swallowed. The physical remains physical, subject to maggots.
In section 2, Virginia is in touch with something supernatural,
some force that can lead her hand to draw circles and figure
eights and mandalas—all symbols of wholeness, infinity, or per-
fection. But she sees this magic not as benevolent but as terrify-
ing and demonic. In 3, the natural landscape of rural America,
the primal garden, has also lost its efficacy. The root-hunters are
pulling up ginseng, violating the virginal woods so that they
may sell artificial aphrodisiacs. (The first chapter of Malcolm
Cowley's *Exile's Return,* titled "Blue Juniata," evokes just this
sense of irrecoverable innocence, a lost world: "Somewhere the
turn of a dirt road or the unexpected crest of a hill reveals your
own childhood, the fields where you once played barefoot, the
kindly trees, the landscape by which all others are measured and
condemned.")

Section 4 provides a recipe for the only potion that we can
hope may remake us. It is an unsavory concoction of salvaged
bits of magic and religion, the fragments of belief or intuition
"that mortality could not grind down into the meal of blood and
laughter." It is here, drawn through terrors by this imperfect
magic, that we may find one more love, a face to be held in the
hands, or one more poem whose title must be "Tenderness
toward Existence." What stands against nothingness, the
vacuum, here in section 4 is far more modest than the oneness
asserted at the center of I. But it is something, a love or a poem
to tie one to existence.

The world is not transformed by the potion. In the last three
sections the Juniata (which flows through the Appalachians in
south central Pennsylvania) is no longer blue or virginal, the
sanctus bell dies against the sheetglass city, there is no second

coming of resurrected hen, people do not share their darkness to make one light. As the primal garden of 3 becomes the dark shore of 5, so the letter of 2 is balanced by the even more desperate letter of 6. For Virginia, the supernatural holds nothing but terror. And the final section is Kinnell's acceptance of distances and wounds.

With the fifth poem, "In the Hotel of Lost Light," the traveler becomes an intimate of death. In the sixth, "The Dead Shall Be Raised Incorruptible," he goes far beyond that, touching the very bottom of human depravity, especially American depravity. The deaths are no longer individual or personal; they have become institutional. (Both poems have the quality of legal documents—V a sort of death certificate, signed and dated in V, 7, and VI a last will and testament.) The title of VI is heavily ironic. In this poem, there is no sign that flesh will be changed, raised incorruptible. Corruption reigns. Only the prayer in the last section, "*do not remove this last, poison cup from our lips,*" may be intended without irony. Perhaps we must drink horror to the bottom of the cup if we are to have any hope of recovering from it.

Poem VII, "Little Sleep's-Head Sprouting Hair in the Moonlight," opens with this sentence: "You scream, waking from a nightmare." Here the book wakes from the nightmare of VI. Maud, whom we have not seen since "Maud Moon" (except perhaps in IV, 5, if that is Maud crying in her bed by the Juniata) reappears, Kinnell's arms heal themselves holding her, and the tone changes to a relaxed, affectionate one. Death is still very much part of the poem, as it will be to the end, but now the emphasis shifts to the effect that the awareness of death has on our loves.

The center of VII seems to me to fall in section 5, rather than 4, and in general VII is less symmetrical than its predecessors. Perhaps the somewhat looser organization contributes to the change of pace and tone.

The subject of VII is permanence—or, rather, the inevitability of change. In the opening scene, Maud clings to her father as though he would never die, and in the second section Kinnell wishes he might hold Maud forever out of the world of decay. But both of them sense the pretrembling of a house that falls. In the restaurant, Maud shouted once, stopped all the devouring in midair—but only for a moment.

In section 4, Kinnell imagines the time, in 2009, when Maud will be the age he is now and will walk, as he is, in the rain, among the black stones that repeat one word *ci-gît* ("here lies . . ."). In another glimpse of Maud's future, in 5, Kinnell sees her with a lover in a café at one end of the Pont Mirabeau, again reenacting Kinnell's experience, thinking that the bridge arcs from love into enduring love. For Maud, as she lives these events for herself, Kinnell has one piece of advice—that she should reach more deeply into the sorrows to come, touch the bones under the face, hear under the laughter the wind across the black stones, not to lessen the intensity of the moment but to increase it. She should know that *"here is the world:* this mouth, this laughter, these temple bones." The cadence of vanishing is the only measure she can dance to.

As section 4 and 5 moved forward in time, section 6 moves back to connect, in a lovely metaphor, Maud's mortality with that of Kinnell's father:

> I can see in your eyes
>
> the hand that waved once
> in my father's eyes, a tiny kite
> wobbling far up in the twilight of his last look:
>
> and the angel
> of all mortal things lets go the string.

Then he puts her back into her crib and promises that when he comes back (from climbing that stony mountain?) they will walk out together with the knowledge that *"the wages / of dying is love."* This idea, love's dependence on death, is critical in understanding the rest of the book. The force of it comes through clearly in this paragraph from "The Poetics of the Physical World":

> It is through something radiant in our lives that we have been able to dream of paradise, that we have been able to invent the realm of eternity. But there is another kind of glory in our

lives which derives precisely from our inability to enter that paradise or to experience eternity. That we last only for a time, that everyone and everything around us lasts only for a time, that we know this, radiates a thrilling, tragic light on all our loves, all our relationships, even on those moments when the world, through its poetry, becomes almost capable of spurning time and death.

This meditation on mutability prepares us for "The Call Across the Valley of Not-Knowing," the book's strongest and most eloquent statement of the coming-together that is possible in love. Poem VIII is organized much as I is, moving from incomplete or partly broken love (the split half-persons Aristophanes speaks of in Plato's *Symposium*) toward a remembered moment of wholeness in section 4, and back to separation across the valley of not-knowing. But here the wholeness is not recalled from the womb but experienced in adult life—the coming together for a moment of body and thought, of man and unviolated nature, of love and the knowledge of death, of lover and lover.

"The Path Among the Stones" (IX), for me the least energetic of the poems, recapitulates the movement of the whole book down into the dismal mineshaft where a man squats by his hell-flames and then, tentatively, back up.

The magnificent tenth poem, "Lastness," has a structure of its own, but more important than this internal shape, perhaps, is its function in drawing together, into an ambiguous resolution, the themes and images that have twisted and grown through the whole book. The organization of X may be summarized very briefly: the first section reestablishes the mountain scene. The second and third sections present the positive and negative halves of the dichotomy that has played all through the book: wholeness is possible, yet everything breaks, falls apart, dies. The fourth section brings together those two opposites in the figure 10. The rest of the poem shows what follows from that conjunction of one and nothing, what kind of music, or poetry, may be sung out of it and what kind of life it implies.

Consider the cluster of images in each section. Even the first section, made of three direct sentences, holds the double vision that pervades the book. At this height, the stream is a series of skinny waterfalls, footpaths wandering out of heaven and shattering on the cliffside—reminiscent of the oath (I, 1) sworn in the clouds and broken on earth, sworn and broken over and over. There is—and is not—a communion between the cosmos and our torn selves. Similarly, this section brings back all the water and fire that have gone before. The desolation of wet ashes, cursed bread in the rain, is eased by a twig fire, kindled out of a particular human love but, now that the self does not clutch for its own so greedily, part of a less personal vitality that keeps flaring up in a dying world.

Section 2, a touchstone if there ever was one, catches up in the bear and Sancho Fergus all the poem's images of what it is to belong wholly to the life of the planet. Here is the primal garden (IV), the blossoming of brain and body under the knowledge of tree (VIII) encompassed in the glistening of this new birth. The man watching the bear from the fringe of the trees is still a death-creature, still capable of the perversions and violations catalogued in poem VI, but at this moment he can become bear watching bear. That innocence echoes in the pride and freshness of Sancho Fergus's birth. Though Fergus's smile acknowledges disasters to follow, the force of this section is wonder at the glistening oneness of bear fur, boy fur, and the grasslands and fern of the newborn planet.

As Kinnell walks toward the cliff, in section 3, calling out to the stone, the stone calls back—and then does not, turns to stone, sending nothing back. He stands between the answer and nothing, as he stood in "The Hen Flower" between the resurrected hen soaring across the arms of the Bear and the cold cadaver of hen, the icy pulp of what is. This is where the shoes have stood all along; this is where the journey into the future must be made—between the answer and nothing. At the end of the section, the negative half of the truth bears in more heavily. He learns again what he has been learning throughout the book, that *To Live* has a poor cousin, who pronounces the family name *To Leave*. In a clatter of elk hooves, the empyrean has emptied itself of whatever eternal truths it may have held. The truth now is that the earth is all there is and the earth does not last. The journey stops here. Living brings you to death, there is no other road.

The central section of the tenth poem pulls together all the ones and zeroes that have gone before: the oneness under the hill, the oneness of two loving halves put together, the oneness, perhaps, of man and bear and boy and planet in X, 2; and the freezing zero of hen corpse, the desolate neon zeroes of the ferris wheel, the zeroes the skipped wafer-stone leaves on the water. There can be no resolution. One and zero walk off the pages together, one creature side by side with the emptiness. The two need each other. Our brightness, gathered up out of time, takes some of its radiance from the fact that it will end, leaving nothing behind. And the death that resides in old cars, river-mist, and constellations is a beginning, too, as in the woodcut on the cover of *Book of Nightmares* new words are drawn out of the mouth of the man about to be devoured by the raven.

Out of love and the awareness of death, one and zero, comes the only music worthy of us. The ladies and gentlemen in the chandeliered room may look as though they would never die, but the violinist who puts the irreversible sorrow of his face into the palm of the wood knows better. As the rasping song of "Maud Moon" is at once a love-note and a howl, so the violinist's music knows the waves of holy desire of VIII and the flesh of the pilot, in VI, shredded to catgut. It is made out of the sexual wail of back-alleys and the sliced intestine of cat.

The book is not just song, or poem, but a life as well (as Kinnell says in response to a question about X, 6 in the *Ohio Review* interview). We are left with an image of how one may live: the sky-diver, floating free, opening his arms into the attitude of flight, as he obeys the necessity and falls. He has come back to the instructions of "The Hen Flower," to let go, to throw himself on the mercy of darkness. The ambiguity persists to the end. The worms on his back are still spinning forth the silk of his loves and already gnawing away at them. And for a son whose father's body will be laid out, both reactions are fitting: Don't cry! Or else, cry.

# V

In reply to Robert Frost's dictum that writing free verse is like playing tennis with the net down, Kinnell writes, "It is an apt analogy, except that the poem is less like a game than like a journey. . . ." ("Poetics of the Physical World") Kinnell's poems have frequently been journeys literally, as well as figuratively. Even in his first book, *What a Kingdom It Was,* "Westport," "Where the Track Vanishes," and "The Descent" are all traveling poems. So is "The Bear." So are many others. But *The Book of Nightmares* is the big journey, the one that encompasses the whole passage of our lives. The scope of its motion makes one think of *Paradise Lost* or the *Odyssey.* It is the hiker's journey up the mountain (on the Olympic Peninsula, Kinnell says), but inside that journey the poem travels back to the beginning, to the unborn child complete in its dark world or even further back to man before he had evolved away from the bear, when he was wholly at one with the planet. It moves through separation and knowledge of death into the collective depravity and wanton destruction of the Vietnam War. But it leads out of that slough, too, by way of Maud and Fergus, and love for a woman, and a hoarse song.

The traveler reaches no destination. In an interview in the *Iowa Review* (Spring 1970) Kinnell says,

> One of the blessings of being my age is that you need not talk about the *purpose* of your life. When one is young, one perhaps longs for a goal or purpose. But life itself is insulted by having to be justified by a goal; life *is,* and that is all there is to it. And to open oneself to the rhythm of being born and dying, while it is awful, since it means facing your terror of death, it is also glorious, for then you are one with the creation, the cosmos. (P. 129)

When one and zero walk off the end of the poem's pages together, they are not headed toward a conclusion. The lone creature can only keep on journeying, side by side with the emptiness. But now, at the poem's end, the journey reverberates with cosmic terror and grandeur.

JOHN UNTERECKER

# Of Father, of Son

*On "Fergus Falling," "After Making Love
We Hear Footsteps," and "Angling, a Day"*

My project is to talk a little about the three affectionate and, on
the whole, cheerful "Fergus" poems that open Galway Kinnell's
*Mortal Acts, Mortal Words:* a very little about the second and third
and a good deal about the first. I want to talk of them in terms
both of technique and of tone as well as explicit and implicit
statement. I also want to stress that affection Kinnell shows
toward his son, an affection I've already pointed to.

But because these three poems do open the book and because
they anticipate, at least glancingly, all of its major themes, it
seems worthwhile to sketch in the large structure of *Mortal Acts,
Mortal Words,* the big musical context in which the Fergus poems
sound opening notes.

Even the casual reader is likely to notice certain structural pat-
terns: a book divided into four parts, the first, second, and last of
which contain nine poems each and a third longish part that
consists of only five poems (nine poems and fourteen pages in
part I, nine poems and eleven pages in part II, five poems and
fifteen pages in part III, and nine poems and twenty-two pages
in the last part). It feels designed. It's an approximate symmetry.
These "parts" are all labeled as such: Part I, etc., not just I, II,
III, IV. The book is then clearly a book, not four gatherings of
otherwise unrelated poems, a book with sections (parts) and
subsections (poems) and sometimes subsections of subsec-
tions—the latter reminiscent of the way all of the poems in
Kinnell's most symmetrical work, *The Book of Nightmares,* had

Printed by permission of John Unterecker.

been organized (ten poems, each subdivided into seven sections), the impetus for such designed work, as Kinnell once explained in an interview, probably coming from Yeats: "I think my interest in the poem made of sections, of elements that don't come together until the end, probably derives from Yeats . . . I've always loved how all the materials . . . come back woven together and transformed."

*Mortal Acts, Mortal Words* is a tightly structured book; but, as I hinted at the beginning, it also feels musically organized—if not in so rigid a fashion as T. S. Eliot's *Four Quartets,* then casually, a book dominated by musical tonalities that seem to fit the subjects of each part, each section slipping effortlessly into a literary version of what in a score would be marked with an appropriate composers' shorthand for tonality, tempo, or mood.

It is especially easy to think of the first part in musical terms— a section comprising poems that deal with home, family, and friends, poems of the most intimate private involvement that, after an opening acknowledgment of omnipresent death, take on for half the section a jaunty quality, though one that gradually darkens into elegy. It's easy to think of part I as an initial brief *allegretto* that leads to a sustained *allegro vivace,* the latter gradually shifting into *andante,* perhaps one marked *andante elegiaco.*

Once your mind falls into this kind of thinking, it's hard to stop, for the second part—all nine poems—almost demands to be marked *scherzo.* These are the "coolest" poems of the book— poems of observation and wit, where the subjects are by and large drawn from the outdoor world (daybreak, lava, blackberries, an about-to-be-kissed toad) and are more often than not distanced by irony. But even here, as the ninth poem of part II ends, the *scherzo* darkens and four middle-aged tennis players find themselves trapped in a snowbound game, evening darkening into night "as winter comes on, all the winters to come."

There's a verbal linkage—probably accidental—between the last word of part II and the second word of part III: "all the winters to come" / "He comes to me like a mouth." But accidental or not, the impact of the repeated "come" links elegiac material: the ironies of part II have shriveled toward a winter deathlike in tonality and the brother who comes from the grave to begin part III "like a mouth / speaking from under several inches of water," has been made inarticulate: "I can no longer understand what he is saying." Words fail as the middle-aged tennis players of part II, though they hold their ground, are reduced to "grunting," and the waters above the dead brother's mouth drown sound.

But part III is really designed, I believe, to balance part I. The family members of part I are those living now: at the center of them, Kinnell and his wife, Fergus and his sister. On the other hand, the family members of the third part are those of the dead—dead brother, dead father, dead mother—kept alive only in the memories of the living, Kinnell and his own sisters.

There is consequently a strange déjà vu in this part of the book, an inverse recapitulation of what we already know. For just as young Fergus of part I—first child, then not-quite-adolescent youth—is observed by Kinnell in the opening three poems of the book, here young Galway is the principal observer of his own father, mother, brother (though not without vacillation between the boy Kinnell had been and the "fifty-odd-year-old" man whose memory of that boy recovers incidents of childhood and whose memories of the deaths of his parents and brother shape the section). If there is a musical tonality to this part of the book it is explicitly *adagio lamentoso:* a gesture not toward understanding the past but comprehending—embracing—it, and not in the hope of gaining freedom from the losses of the past but freedom through them. The dead must be memorialized both in memory and in words—kept alive—so that the living can truly breathe.

Part IV, finally, seems to me all *allegretto maestoso:* poetry recapitulating earlier materials but now enlarging them to generalization. Here Kinnell tackles all the "big themes." Biblical echoes in "The Rainbow" and "The Apple" explore the brevity of life, its glory in ruin, the transience of and need for love's "bitter knowledge." A poem about a hobo killing a chicken lets Kinnell think of the discoveries of youth ("I was fifteen I think") that link death and pain to laughter and creaking song, just as another poem of childhood, "The Still Time," celebrates the power of memory to create songs of loss that ultimately "heal."

Not just these four, but all nine of these poems stretch back toward the opening poems and toward the title of the book, their common theme the relationship between mortal acts—our gestures in the face of certain death—and mortal words—defiant songs in praise of mortality itself, songs that through recollection reembody lost times and lives and find a way to preserve our most difficult and most breathing experience, human love, love that is "very much like courage," that, indeed, is perhaps even "*only* courage" (Kinnell's italics), love that we localize, when we are lucky, in a word so mundane and shining, finally, as the name we use for the place we live: for Kinnell, a house in Vermont in the first poems of the book, an apartment, probably, in New York City in the last—but in either locale, "home." Though *Mortal Acts, Mortal Words* could from one point of view be classed as a "travel book," the movement is nevertheless from an opening poem of home and its marvelous risks toward the last three words of the last line of the last poem: "the home ground."

This kind of capsule analysis, of course, distorts a book that is made in four carefully distinct parts from closely interwoven materials, for it underplays the unique statement of each poem. Let me make up for it now by focusing in on Fergus himself and the three poems that constitute the first third of part I of *Mortal Acts, Mortal Words*.

Before this book and these poems, we've heard of Fergus only three times: in the dedication to *The Book of Nightmares,* in section 2 of the last poem of that sequence (where, at the moment of birth, his "great shoulders" cause him to stick, "his head out there all alone," as he "almost / smiled . . . almost forgave it all in advance") and in the final section of that last poem where as a babe in arms he is given the option of crying or not crying—and then, in an enormous leap across time, is asked to search "the blued flesh when it is / laid out," presumably the flesh of Kinnell himself, for "the one flea which is laughing." (As Kinnell frequently mentions in interviews and at readings, these last words were intended to provide a relatively happy ending to *The Book of Nightmares*—on the general theory that fleas on the dead body of a man who has led a happy life might reasonably be concluded to be happier than other fleas!)

In any event, by the time we get to *Mortal Acts, Mortal Words,* Fergus is old enough to climb, branch over branch, to the very top of a white pine, fall from it, cry out as he falls, report a discovery to his concerned parents, and then, in this opening poem about the living and the dead, seem for an instant to be swept out of life: "His face went grey, his eyes fluttered closed a frightening moment. . . ."

As I've suggested, "Fergus Falling" introduces most of the major themes of the entire book: the need for taking risks (young Fergus's climb is for the sake of the climb, for no good reason but to prove it can be done—though Kinnell offers as an alternate "to get out / of the shadow / . . . of this father"), the omnipresence of death (all of the catalogued friends and strangers who had lived and all but one of whom had died working or walking or fishing a pond in the evergreen forests—cedar, spruce, new pine, old hemlock—that made and still make Vermont's mountains green), the importance of chance that gives us bad luck (the wards of the state who walked into the woods one Halloween, couldn't be found, froze to death, and whose huddled skeletons waited a year to be discovered; for that matter, the bad luck of Fergus's fall itself) or good luck (Kinnell's shrill electric saw out of order so that Fergus's falling cry can penetrate the casual rasp of a hand saw), and, finally, the fact of human love commingled with love of place (and neither love explicitly spelled out though by indirections most vividly established).

But the poem, appropriately first in the book because it establishes themes, isn't worth reading for that reason alone: no poem is—at least not worth reading more than once.

We reread "Fergus Falling" for two reasons, I think: because it offers us a subtle kind of knowledge, a knowledge difficult to come by in any other medium than poetry and one that satisfies us most, I suspect, in being peculiar to one poem. More of that later. We also read it, however, in order to experience a surge of joy that has nothing to do with explicit or implicit statement, a joy that hinges on pure technique and that is as abstract in execution as the sound progressions of a Bach fugue or the geometric echoes in a cubist painting by Juan Gris.

And here we need a word about technique. I've already quoted Kinnell on his debt to Yeats's compartmentalized yet intricately interwoven poems. But I think he also learned from Yeats or someone very like him—Dylan Thomas, perhaps, or Hopkins, or maybe even Whitman—an equally important lesson in poetic organization. Since Yeats, when asked what accounted for his success as a poet, spelled it out, let's pretend Kinnell learned it from Yeats. Yeats's answer to the impertinent question was extraordinary in that he mentioned nothing about subject matter or even his own or his readers' emotions. Instead, his success as a poet, he told his surprised questioner, hinged on his "powerful syntax"—nothing more than that: his syntax, his powerful arrangement of words into sentences. And Yeats meant exactly what he said. Kinnell, if pressed hard enough, might well make a very similar answer.

For Kinnell is a master craftsman and nothing demonstrates it more clearly than "Fergus Falling," a tour-de-force in parallel structure, with its first three stanzas a single rush of words, a 253-word, twenty-four-line sentence that "ends" in the suspension of a three-dot ellipsis ("and the soft pine cracked . . ."). Within that vast rush of words, repetitions and appositions (for this is literally a poem of ups and downs) shove us relentlessly forward. Some of these combinations glare: Fergus "climbed to the top" of a pine in line 1 and, reminding us where we are in the sentence, "climbed to the top" (still the same climb) again in line 7. What he saw, however, was not up but down: Bruce Pond, "down in its valley," a place where (though Milton Norway once "came up" behind Galway and later put cedar shingles on the house) Clarence Akley "cut down" cedars, a place where Fergus, seeing for the first time "down there" the "oldness" of the pond "in its old place in the valley" (a place where an "old fisherman" still sits in a rowboat), suddenly gained a heaviness in his bones.

The pond itself echoes spectacularly through this three-stanza sentence, established as "Bruce Pond" in the twelve-line first stanza, and then dominating the wildly-stretched-out five lines of the second stanza (no line shorter than twenty-one words and the most-stretched-out-of-all, forty-three words long), each of the five lines either starting with "pond where" or "where": "pond where Clarence Akley . . ." / "where Milton Norway . . ." / "where Gus Newland . . ." / "pond where two

wards of the state . . ." / "pond where an old fisher-
man . . ."—and then carrying over into the seven-line third
stanza (in almost identical words) echoes of Fergus's discovery
of Bruce Pond that he (stanza 1) "saw for the first time": (stanza
3) "and when Fergus / saw the pond for the first time / in the
clear evening."

If the parallel appearances of the pond dominate the beginning
of the long-line second-stanza verses, the mortality of the person
or persons mentioned in each line dominates its close: "he's
gone" / "he's gone" / "he's gone" / "they're gone," the only
variation being the old fisherman of the last line of the stanza:
"when he goes he's replaced and is never gone."

The syntax of the fourth stanza—a long eighty-word, nine-line
sentence containing a short six-line quoted one and a single con-
cluding eleven-word sentence, again ending in the suspension of
an ellipsis ("His face went grey, his eyes fluttered closed a fright-
ening moment . . .") allows Fergus's falling cry to penetrate the
noise of the handsaw and bring his parents to his fallen body.
But the whole drive of the syntax is to focus on chance: the luck
of the noisy electric saw being out of order—all of its imagery
violent body language ("carbide teeth" that would have been
burning into a hemlock plank "black arcs . . . / like dark circles
under eyes / when the brain thinks too close to the skin").
Thanks to the defective saw, Fergus's cry can echo in parallel
structure (line 1, "I would not have heard his cry"; line 7, "but I
was sawing by hand and I heard that cry"). And also thanks to
the defective saw, Fergus's parents reach his fallen body and are
able to hear his ninth-line revelation: "Galway, Inés, I saw a
pond!"

For it is the pond, of course (even more than Fergus or,
perhaps more accurately, interwoven with Fergus) that the
poem is all about. The pond appears in all five stanzas: a con-
stant—like the old fisherman who may die but who is replaced
and so is "never gone." The pond, through its "oldness" at the
instant of Fergus's first glimpse brings on his "fledgling" fall
("he became heavier suddenly / in his bones / the way fledglings
do just before they fly"), is nevertheless a discoverer's vision.
Maybe it is a small vision; and though we smile for a second

thinking how little Fergus's risk has brought him, there is really nothing funny in the fact that, grazing death, he sounds triumphant: "I saw a pond!" For as the last stanza (syntactically a sentence fragment linked to Fergus's word "pond") makes altogether clear, Fergus's discovery is, if not in magnitude then certainly in fact, unique. He has seen from the pine top something no human being alive has ever before spotted from that particular patch of earth. No wonder he's presented as birdlike in his fall or that Icarus flashes into and out of a reader's—this reader's—mind, or a sudden memory of Keats feeling "like some watcher of the skies / When a new planet swims into his ken; / Or like stout Cortez when with eagle eyes / He stared at the Pacific." I'm not arguing, needless to say, that Kinnell is playing a game of literary allusion. The parallels are in my head and weren't, I'm sure, in his. But I am asserting—and for all I'm worth—that *discovery* is an absolute, that discovery may be worth a brush with death, that it invents joy, and that the recognition of a child's discovery, for the sensitive observer, creates a complex emotion of entangled joy and pathos. (When Shakespeare forces Prospero to say " 'Tis new to thee," he knows how quickly the "brave new world" that widens Miranda's discovering eyes fades into the ordinary one. But he knows also that though the experience of discovery fades, a young person's discovery of anything previously unimagined—a pond for Fergus, had Shakespeare have been transported forward in time to know Fergus, a beautiful young man for Miranda—itself remains miraculous.)

So it is the pond we have been trying to see, see in something the same way Fergus saw it as it flashed out of sunset and led to his fall. And it is to that pond that the poem's parallels return us in the last stanza:

> Yes—a pond
> that lets off its mist
> on clear afternoons of August, in that valley
> to which many have come, for their reasons,
> from which many have gone, a few for their reasons, most
>     not,
> where even now an old fisherman only the pinetops can see
> sits in the dry gray wood of his rowboat, waiting for pickerel.

Here in this sentence fragment, Kinnell's powerful syntax is most dramatically evident; for we suddenly realize that we don't know how many sentences there are in the poem: that perhaps what look like independent sentences are interwoven into a complex of one enormous sentence: that the ellipses that surround the fourth stanza make it parenthetical and that the linkage from Fergus's quoted "I saw a pond!" to the last stanza's "Yes—a pond" forms the final link in the chain that begins in the opening stanza of the poem and triumphantly ends in the pond that, now Fergus has fallen, "only the pinetops can see."

And this gives us pleasure, a pure pleasure in having so gracefully been allowed to thread our way through an elaborate structure without once having had to hesitate over sense. Despite all its intricacy, the poem moves effortlessly forward. There is no moment when the statement of this eloquent work isn't luminously clear. The powerful syntax—the powerful form of the sentence or sentences that constitute the poem—creates a joy that is abstract in quality, clean in action, and musical in effect.

I could stop at this. Yet that persistent word *musical* demands a nod toward the sounds rather than the phrases that help orchestrate "Fergus Falling."

I've already made clear enough that the syntactical speed of the poem comes in large part from repeated words and phrases, usually in one form or another of parallel structure. To recapitulate only the most obvious repetitions (words only, this time) there are the seven appearances of *pond,* the three of *down,* the six of *gone,* the six of *where,* the three of *old* (plus *oldness* as a kind of fourth) and all the simple repeats: *climbed, climbed; cedar, cedar; fisherman, fisherman; top, top; out, out; forefathers, forefathers, father; vain, vain; came, came,* etc., etc., etc.—perhaps a dozen more of the same sort. These create a very special kind of music almost identical in its effect on the ear as rhymes or partial rhymes but much more subtle because (unless isolated as I've isolated it here) so inconspicuous. A related kind of music (what the French call *rime riche*) comes when the same spelling carries two different meanings—as in this poem's "and *saw* for the first time," "and when Fergus / *saw* the pond," "if my electric *saw* had been working," "but I was *saw*ing by hand," "I *saw* a pond!" (all italics mine). Here the "rhyme" is a buried pun on seeing and sawing (a seesaw action if ever there was one!) not altogether unlike the echo all the I's of the poem make, in an inverse *rime riche* fashion, in two *eyes* and the buried *I* sound of *Inés*. (The *I* sound is, of course, also caught up in a whole set of virtually inaudible full and partial rhymes, most of them inaudible because syntactically "hidden." For the record, however, here are the ones I noticed: *cl*imbed, *p*ines, *cl*imbed, *t*ime, *I'*d, *I, I, t*ime, *fly, p*ine, *I, cry, eye*s, *I, I, cry, In*és, *I, eye*s, *fr*ightening, *p*inetops, *dry*.) But then rhymes and (especially) partial rhymes ripple through this most integrated poem like gossamer melodies, little threads of linked sound ("*o*ld . . . r*owbo*at," for example), embellishments on the big melodic patterns of straight repetition.

Especially in free verse, it seems to me, sound structures of this sort—some simply fortuitous, most perhaps initially accidental—are by a poet as conscious of his art as Kinnell ultimately recognized and incorporated into a complex harmonic pattern. They are fragile, risky devices but, when successfully handled, flexible yet accurate as the lithe figures that transform *Eine Kleine Nachtmusik* from scraps of sound into most tangible glory.

Like powerful syntax, subtle sounds create a pleasure almost—but never entirely—independent of the statement of the poem. They offer us an analyzable joy; and we can almost—not quite—create from them an aesthetic neat as the calculations that define the speed of light.

But the speed of light is not light. And the marvelous aspects of "Fergus Falling" that I have been discussing, though separable enough from it to stand up under examination, are not the poem.

For the poem is an amalgam of technique and of facts (some accurate, some distorted), at least three points of view (none of them interchangeable), and a conglomerate of Fergus's reported emotions, Kinnell's own feelings—some of them described and some inherent in the process of creating a poem—and your response and mine to the whole shebang.

There are, if you will, at least three poems (I'd make a case for an infinity of them) that relate to but can never accurately translate into each other.

There's one poem that has to do with events and "truth": Fergus's climb, his discovery of a pond, his fall, and his report of that discovery to his parents. (Call this Fergus's poem and try, if you can, to imagine him reading what Kinnell has written.)

The second poem is obviously Galway Kinnell's, a poem constructed from and necessarily transforming the events and the "truth" he experienced, a poem constructed from the knowledge and practice of his own craft, a poem involving decisions about the sequencing of events, about language, about material peripheral to the main action (all the pond men of the second stanza, for example). Those are elements of the poem we can dissect and, if delighted, celebrate. But, crucially for Kinnell, it is also a poem made from pity and terror and love and affection, and these elements of the poem, though incorporated into the text, of necessity speak to Kinnell always privately and in ways none of us can ever experience.

Finally, there is the poem that creates in each reader that unique knowledge I spoke of earlier and about which—for good reason—I was carefully evasive, because the knowledge I want to deal with is incontestably a little different for each of us. It is different not because the poem "changes" for each reader—after all, its words don't change from copy to copy—but because we have no choice but ourselves to be changed by the poem. It is consequently not so much an organizer of Kinnell's knowledge as of our own. Its function—on a surface level—is, of course, communication. But its action is catalytic, and in this it differs from most prose and from some poetry. (I should also quickly say that I believe no work of art, this poem or any other, can be catalytic for all people.) For those people who respond to it, it takes material from private experience and rearranges that material (memories of events; feelings of past and present fear, affection, or love; recollections of persons and places and even poems—mostly, for each of us, different because of our different lives). The minor rearrangement of our literal selves that the poem brings about incorporates the poem in us. It becomes—if other readers love it as much as I do—an ingredient maybe not central to but at least tangentially a part of life itself. For me, there it sits (along with its two companion poems) shoulder to shoulder with the random crowd of poems that have in their ambiguous ways organized within me otherwise untranslatable knowledge: a list far too long to make here but, for a very random sampling, poems by William Stafford and William Shakespeare, by Emily Dickinson, by Gregory Orr, by William Blake and Edward Lear and Hart Crane, by W. B. Yeats and Leonie Adams, by Edmund Waller and Cathy Song and Ernest Dowson and Fred Baysa, poems by Susan Wood and Thomas Traherne, by James Wright and Theodore Roethke and W. S. Merwin and Wallace Stevens. What odd companions! And all the other unnamed ones. Yet everyone who reads poetry has, I'm sure, a storehouse of knowledge-bonding poems that shape a kind of wisdom for him.

After so grand a catalogue, it seems strange to turn to so slight and tender a poem as "After Making Love We Hear Footsteps." Yet, when I think of it, there is no strangeness at all. It's the risks that count, I suppose, the chances an author takes when he opens up private moments not confessionally—for recent confessional poetry seems in nine cases out of ten to lead to chest-pounding self-glorification or self-pity—but, instead, as in this tender poem, casually: "For I can snore like a bullhorn," etc. This story of a boy who can sleep through every deafening racket his father can produce except the whispering noises of lovemaking is indeed tender, but its tenderness is balanced by ironies: whenever the slightest heavy breathing or "stifled come-cry" reaches his sleeping ears, Fergus sets off on a run from his bedroom to his parents' to ask the crucial question: "Are you loving and snuggling? May I join?"

The poem charms us, but its charm is an achieved one. Those same careful devices that move the reader through "Fergus Falling" also operate here. Even in syntax the poems resemble one another: here, a long first sentence (sixteen lines) ends in the two tiny questions from Fergus quoted above. And a relatively short sentence ends the stanza (Fergus flopping down between husband and wife to "snuggle himself to sleep").

Kinnell deliberately holds off the direct quotation from Fergus for as long as he possibly can in both poems. And in the third Fergus poem, "Angling, a Day," it will be held off until the last three lines of an eighty-three-line single-stanza single sentence! "After Making Love," on the other hand, follows the pattern of "Fergus Falling" with the last stanza—a six-line sentence—stressing the mortality of father and mother, their arms and eyes and smiles enclosing the sleeping child, "this one whom habit of memory propels to the ground of his making, / sleeper only the mortal sounds can sing awake."

If the poems resemble each other syntactically in opening with a very long sentence that ends in a quotation from Fergus, a sentence propelled on by repeated *wheres* and other repetitions in "Fergus Falling" and a set of *ors* in "After Making Love," they are also similar in their use of hidden rhymes, off-rhymes, and repetitions to create songlike harmonies. (These are even more numerous in "After Making Love," a positive choir of echoing sound, than in "Fergus Falling." Just listen to a sampling that could virtually be doubled if every echo were accounted for: *for, snore,* bull*horn, or, or, or, for, mor*tal; lo*ud, house, now, down, ground, sounds; sleep, sleep, sleep*er; *I, Irishman, by, cry, lie, quiet, I, smile; awake, make, making, make, making, awake; love, lov*ing, *of, of, love; touch*ing, *touch, touch; baseball, baseball; only, only; snugg*ling, *hugs, snugg*les; *this, this, this; one, wonder, one; arms, arms:* all this and more in a twenty-four-line poem!)

While techniques resemble one another (and startlingly), the tonalities of the poems are radically different. "Fergus Falling" is dominated by mortality: the small triumphs of those who die or will die, even Fergus, whose childhood brush with death anticipates the death that will come, only the race (the old fisherman sitting in the dry gray wood of his rowboat, who will be replaced, as Galway will be replaced by Fergus and Fergus by some other)—only the race enduring, its individuals headed toward death and variously facing it, sometimes pathetically (the frozen wards of the state), most often through the satisfactions of working well (Galway at his saw, the loggers braving cold or chopping in "slow spondees") or simply fishing well or, splendidly, through seeing a pond from the top of a pine. "After Making Love," on the other hand, celebrates the root force of mortality's beginning: not death but the lovemaking that can lead to birth and did, indeed, lead to Fergus's birth. The tone therefore is comic (in both senses of the word—funny and life-affirming: if no divine comedy, then a little mortal one) and the statement altogether celebratory: Fergus, "this blessing love gives again into our arms," drawn by the lovemaking of his parents into the circling enclosure of their affections.

"Angling, a Day" is another kettle of fish—or at least another kettle, since the plot of the poem is that of Fergus and Galway making a before-dawn to well-after-dark tour of the whole upper half of Vermont, unsuccessfully fishing all of the best fishing spots.

Again, structure and technique correspond to the first two Fergus poems. As I've already noted, this poem is one enormous sentence, though I have not noted that it is held in parallel structure by eight repetitions of the word *though*.

This time, Fergus gets the last word, pointing the moral in a couple of final little sentences enclosed in the larger one. Galway, "afraid that Fergus . . . / must be thoroughly / defeated, and his noble passion for fishing / perhaps broken," asks Fergus how he feels:

> "I'm disappointed," he says, "but not discouraged.
> I'm not saying I'm a fisherman, but fishermen know
> there are days when you don't catch anything."

Perhaps the clearest way to see this poem in relation to the other two is to recognize that, while "Fergus Falling" focuses on death, dying, and the various ways an acknowledgment of death can make life valuable, and "After Making Love" focuses on what Yeats calls "honey of generation," the joys of lovemaking that lead to birth and the almost-instinctive yet gloriously conscious love of parents and child, "Angling, a Day" sets us clearly in life itself and Fergus at what staid anthropologists might label a "contemporary rite of passage." For if his initiation ceremony isn't quite as spectacular as an Australian aborigine's "walkabout" or even the initiation of the child who would become King Arthur in T. H. White's *The Sword in the Stone* or, say, that of Huck Finn as he makes his enlightening trip down the Mississippi, yet Fergus gets through it. And this time the wisdom of the poem comes not from Kinnell or from the reader. For Fergus, not catching fish, nevertheless passes his initiation with flying colors and at the end of this poem speaks his own piece. If his creel is empty, his mind is full. His move from child to adolescent, from innocence to experience, is as satisfying as that of any young hero.

Dealing with neither the end of life nor its beginning, "Angling, a Day" sets father and son on a masculine tour. It takes them to fishing spots favored by some friends (Bill Allen, Hayden Carruth, and his friend John Engels) and other spots favored by strangers (a man named Ralph and an unnamed man who recommends spark plugs for freeing snagged lines). But principally it lets Fergus—guided but not guarded by his father—spend, in the words of the title, "a Day" learning something of what it is to be a man, a day in many ways cut out of time, one that starts out as ordinary but that, in Fergus's final understatement, becomes the transforming extraordinary day that moves him fully into life. It is indeed a "rite of passage" that Fergus experiences in the poem, a rite that also invests Fergus with an unstated knowledge of the processes by which fathers and sons guardedly share love.

I don't want to blow up out of proportion Kinnell's accomplishment in these three poems. And I certainly don't want to suggest that Fergus says his say and then vanishes forever from Kinnell's work on page eight of *Mortal Acts, Mortal Words*. Though not named, he seems conjoined with his sister (as well as Galway and his own sister) in "Two Set Out on Their Journey," and he's one of Galway's children in the beautiful elegy for Galway's mother, "The Last Hiding Places of Snow." He is part and parcel of the family Kinnell has increasingly acknowledged as central to man's otherwise lonely journey through life.

"Family and friends," I should have said. But documenting that would involve me not just in another essay but in an entire book on this writer, a writer caught up in an awareness of human mortality and of all our poets the one perhaps most eloquent in defining life's rich, complex, and—though a strange adjective, accurate—gallant possibilities.

WILLIAM MATTHEWS

# On the Tennis Court at Night

"What is it about tennis that appeals to you?" Galway Kinnell was asked by an interviewer in 1975, and here's how he answered.

> If you really concentrate in tennis, mind, body, spirit, all become one thing—in this it's like poetry—a tremendously happy activity. But it's also the opposite of poetry, because it's an entirely escapist activity. I like it for both reasons. When the world is too much with you, you just put on your white vanishing-clothes and enter that court laid out in pure, Euclidean lines—and live for a few hours with increased life, like a wild animal.

Kinnell goes on to name other poets obsessed by tennis: Pound, Hart Crane, Berryman, Roethke (who coached the game as well as played it), and Jarrell.

In a letter written in 1950, Jarrell wrote similarly of how the game can simultaneously lift you out of yourself and remind you of your inescapable home in yourself.

> I played a lot of tennis this summer; I won a singles tournament at Cape Cod in a very long match, the most satisfying I ever played. When one does what one *should,* beyond one's expectations, it's a queer feeling—one gets as much used to one's faults as to the world's, and yet they are an obsessive grief in a way the world's never are.

I can't prove it, but I think the pun of "fault" in Jarrell's letter was probably unconscious. Intentionally made, it would have been lost on his correspondent, whose English was very good

Printed by permission of William Matthews.

but nonetheless a second language, and who was neither an avid tennis player nor the compulsive punster Jarrell was. In any case the passage implies a double purpose, for Jarrell, in playing tennis.

On the one hand, the game is humbling: it teaches you over and over your faults and that you should, more or less, come to terms with those faults. But on the other hand, when and in fact because you do more or less come to terms with those faults, there are times when you play so well and so fluidly that you seem to transcend them, to be, more or less, faultless.

Kinnell's vocabulary is different, but he also invokes in tennis a dual power. On the one hand you are made whole and wholly mortal by the game: mind, body, and spirit converge. But on the other hand you escape into an increased life and are like a wild animal. Notice that the escape is from a "world . . . too much with you," so that you play "out of this world." Current tennis slang has it that you play "in the zone," or, as Martina Navratilova told Bud Collins in a Wimbledon interview, "I really zoned in the third set."

The truth is that you would not want to be long out of this world, for that is quite literally to be dead. But to see only "this humanized, familiar world as if it were all there is," as Kinnell has it in another interview, is a kind of willed blindness. I think Kinnell speaks of tennis the way he does in the passage I quote above because the dual power he finds in tennis rhymes with a dual power in poetry, particularly in Kinnell's own poetry. Kinnell's poems relish and love to describe the physical world, and exult in the kind of loving attention to physical life that makes mind, body, and spirit all become one thing; his poems have great powers of concentration. But at the same time his poems love to peer *through* the physical world toward the vast cosmos in which our world is as but a cinder.

"On the Tennis Court at Night," from *Mortal Acts, Mortal Words* (1980), is a characteristic meditation on these dual impulses in Kinnell's work. Here are the first eleven of the poem's fifty-one lines.

> We step out on the green rectangle
> in moonlight; the lines glow,
> which for many have been the only lines

of justice. We remember
the thousand trajectories the air has erased
of that close-contested last set—
blur of volleys, soft arcs of drop shots,
huge ingrown loops of lobs with topspin
which went running away, crosscourts recrossing
down to each sweet (and in exact proportion, bitter)
❍ in Talbert and Olds' *The Game of Doubles in Tennis*.

The lines glow because of the moonlight, but also, meta-phorically, because they *can* represent, when so little else can, an idea of justice. They're allied to ❍ marks in what most experts—I am not one and so am relying on their testimony—think the best book on doubles strategy; these marks represent the ideal shot placement in various given situations likely to arise in or-derly play. The ❍ marks, the lines, and indeed the idea of or-derly play—as opposed to an improvised play in which accumu-lated wisdoms about the size of the court, the positioning of the players, and the most advantageous shots to play in given situa-tions are ignored—represent a communal and historical achieve-ment of the "humanized, familiar world," and also represent a grid of expected and usually profitable procedure against which brilliant improvisations can be measured. Without the grid cer-tain inspired shots might seem merely random.

The actual play of the last set is lost to memory, and perhaps it is just as well. It would resemble one of those time-lapse photographs of night traffic along a highway, or the surface of much-skated ice. And the more the trajectories obscured our view of the pure, Euclidean lines of the court the less the trajec-tories would have any reason for being.

Here's an excerpt from a 1971 interview:

*NYQ:* In our *New York Quarterly* craft interviews we have tried to be as objective as possible and not to get too involved with feelings and emotions about things, but stay with craft and style.
*Kinnell:* Matters I don't know anything about.

And here's an excerpt from a 1976 interview:

*Interviewer:* I know you've said that you distrust discussions of poetry that are technical—

*Kinnell:* I *think* I distrust them. Perhaps I like them without knowing it.

It's easy to see what's going on in the *New York Quarterly* interview. I can hardly imagine a poet who would find the question—which isn't a question, but a self-congratulation—more obnoxious. Surely Kinnell doesn't mean that he knows nothing about craft and style, but that to talk about what he knows without reference to feelings and emotions about things seems to him nonsense. And I think we can see what's going on in the 1976 interview. He means that he's wary of the terms in which such discussions are often conducted, but that if they did not perforce chop into pieces what the poet struggles to make whole, he'd damn well be interested in the topic.

The circumstances where a poet can write what he best knows about such matters is in writing a poem, and "On the Tennis Court at Night" does so, metaphorically. Metaphor does not discuss "one thing in terms of another," as we may have been wrongly told at some point in our schooling, but discusses several things all in terms of each other. Usually, of course, a poem has an ostensible central topic—in this case, tennis.

Also, a poem can become itself a kind of large metaphor for the capacity of intelligent feeling to resolve what seems paradoxical when it is argued in prose. How can a highly formal and conventional game like doubles release one to feeling like a wild animal? And how can one by extreme concentration on immediate physical life seem to belong both to it and to the larger and essentially inhuman life of the cosmos?

In the "Author's Note" to *The Avenue Bearing the Initial of Christ into the New World: Poems 1946–64* (though the book was published in 1974, the note is dated 1970), Kinnell wrote:

I have chosen these poems out of some hundreds I wrote—and mercilessly revised—in my late teens and early twenties.

It might have turned out better for me if, during that period of my life, I had written less and given myself more to silence and waiting. At least those arduous searches for the right iambic beat and the rhyme word seem now like time which could have been better spent. I will never know, and in any event, it is not possible for me to regret a travail which released in me so much energy and excitement, to which I gave myself so entirely, and which saved me. The leftovers, these few pieces of verse, whatever their worth for someone else, I hold in kindly affection.

As I was preparing this collection, Charles G. Bell produced from his files all the first, unrevised versions of my poems—versions which I myself had long since thrown away. I discovered those first versions were almost always superior to the revised ones—which says little for my powers of recognition and revision. The poems in this book, therefore, are mostly in their earlier form, some of them cut considerably, others patched up here and there with lines from the revisions.

It's a good thing, we speculated earlier, that the trajectories of all those volleys, drop shots, lobs, and cross-courts are erased, and doubly so, for there are two trajectories for every shot in tennis, at least the way I play tennis. There's the imaginary trajectory leading from the racket to the ✪ mark exactly where Talbert and Olds would have me hit the shot, and then there's the trajectory of the shot I actually hit.

Kinnell is describing something similar in his "Author's Note," with "the right iambic beat and the rhyme word" standing for the same purpose as the ✪ mark in Talbert and Olds.

But of course the poem is not made by discovering the right iambic beat or rhyme word, but rather from the tension between some such imaginary ideal and what the poet actually finds for himself to say. The function of forms and conventions may be to enable that tension. In tennis it is that tension against which, even more than against opponents, I play. And in writing it is a similar tension—I think of it as being like an electrical resistance—that a poet hopes will blunt what is merely habitual and facile in what he discovers to say.

> The breeze has carried them off but we still hear
> the mutters, the doublefaulter's groans,

cries of "Deuce!" or "Love two!",
squeak of tennis shoes, grunt of overreaching,
all dozen extant tennis quips—"Just out!"
or, "About right for you?" or, "Want to change partners?"
and *baaah* of sheep translated very occasionally
into *thonk* of well-hit ball, among the pure
right angles and unhesitating lines
of this arena where every man grows old
pursuing that repertoire of perfect shots

"The breeze has carried them off," this passage begins, and "them" refers to the trajectories of all the shots of the last set, but another breeze like it will carry off the mutters, groans, squeaks, grunts, and quips that Kinnell enumerates, and eventual breezes will carry off the players themselves. It might be closer to the spirit of the poem to think of the players as not carried off, when that day comes, but translated, the way sheep gut gets translated to racket strings.

Here's Kinnell speaking in an interview:

Yes, as death has two aspects—the extinction, which we fear, and the flowing away into the universe, which we desire—there is a conflict within us that I want to deal with.

The lines quoted above are characteristic in their loving litany of physical detail and especially characteristic in the way that litany builds along with its own rhetorical momentum a kind of shadow momentum, an accumulating fatigue and sense of the gravity of physical life, so that the prospect of release, of flowing away into the universe, mollifies the more terrifying aspect of death as extinction. For while the "arena" is on its most literal level the tennis court, it is additionally the wearing and memory-laden life of the body:

darkness already in his strokes,
even in death cramps waving an arm back and forth
to the disgust of the night nurse
(to whom the wife whispers, "Well,
at least I always knew where he was!");
and smiling; and a few hours later found dead—

> the smile still in place but the ice bag
> left on the brow now inexplicably
> Scotchtaped to the right elbow—causing
> all those bright trophies to slip permanently,
> though not in fact much farther, out of reach,
> all except the thick-bottomed young man
> about to doublefault in soft metal on the windowsill:
> "Runner-Up Men's Class B Consolation Doubles
> St. Johnsbury Kiwanis Tennis Tournament 1969" . . .

This is a central trope in Kinnell's work, though it has seldom taken such good-natured form. Death is seen not only as the fate but perhaps even the engine of every life, or if not the engine somehow the purpose. The present is a sort of of window, normally opaque, but momentarily clear. And through it can be seen not only the eventuality of the present but the arc connecting the present with its outcome.

Here are some other examples from *Mortal Acts, Mortal Words*. Adam and Eve, biting the apple, are seen as

> . . . poisoning themselves
> into the joy
> that has to watch itself go away.

And here are the final three lines of "Memory of Wilmington":

> I was fifteen, I think. Wilmington then
> was far along on its way to becoming a city
> and already well advanced on its way back to dust.

And in "The Rainbow" life in the womb is described as "that last time we knew / more of happiness than of time."

But this trope has been crucial to Kinnell from the beginning. Here are the first four lines of "Island of Night," the third poem in *The Avenue Bearing the Initial of Christ into the New World*.

> I saw in a dream a beautiful island
> Surrounded by an abrasive river,
> And soon it was all rubbed into river and
> Gone forever, even the sweet millet and the clover.

But Kinnell's tennis poem is now at its only stanza break, and now physical description begins to give off an aura, a prefiguration of being translated.

> Clouds come over the moon;
> all the lines go out. November last year
> in Lyndonville: it is getting dark,
> snow starts falling, Zander Rubin wobble-twists
> his worst serve out of the black woods behind him,
> Stan Albro lobs into a gust of snow,
> Don Bredes smashes at where the ball theoretically
> could be coming down, . . .

This passage may well begin with a November match last year in Lyndonville when the four men played on into the time after a few first flakes of snow came down. But last year from when? From the time the poem's speaker spoke, one unique time in history, this poem? Or from whatever year a reader finds this poem? Each snowflake has *ubi sunt* neatly lettered on it; these are the snows of yesteryear in advance.

In the moon's absence, only these snows provide natural light against the dark and the black woods. The way the phrase "the lines go out" sounds like "the lights go out" is important. Now it is the knowledge of death that provides us what form provided us earlier, and now we can see, intuitively, that form and convention are outward and visible signs of the knowledge of death.

> . . . the snow blows down
> and swirls about our legs, darkness flows
> across a disappearing patch of green-painted asphalt
> in the north country, where four men,
> half-volleying, poaching, missing, grunting,
> begging mercy of their bones, hold their ground,
> as winter comes on, all the winters to come.

In his preface to *Walking Down the Stairs,* the book of interviews from which I have quoted so frequently in this brief essay, Kinnell explains what revisions he did and didn't permit himself in traveling from transcriptions of taped interviews toward the printed page.

I entirely rewrote many perfunctory or muddled answers. A few times when I rewrote answers I found they no longer fit back into their original places. These I put into the interview with Don Bredes and David Brooks, an interview which is partly based on actual conversations, partly a repository of fragments from other interviews, and partly a literary composition.

Surely this is the same Don Bredes who "smashes at where the ball theoretically / could be coming down," and it's pleasant to think of the moment when Kinnell and his interviewers found in the process of putting this particular interview together the ✪ mark where a few words could be gracefully inserted about tennis, the game to which they had given so much energy and excitement, and which had repaid them with an absorbing emblem for the paradoxes of form and freedom, and a durable emblem for how men "hold their ground / as winter comes on, all the winters to come."

MARSHA PETERSON WHITE

# Trusting the Hours

## *On "Wait"*

Among the major sequences, the memorable lyrics, and other often-anthologized pieces of Galway Kinnell, "Wait" is an inconspicuous poem—until you are suffering the desolation that stems from bereavement, abandonment, betrayal, or loss. When you are in need of counsel that is wise, calm, and painfully honest, then you will count the poem among Kinnell's masterpieces. You sense that his advice is right, partly because it is difficult to accept.

Although this short poem is a typical Kinnell poem, it also echoes at least two other poems, T. S. Eliot's "East Coker," the second of the *Four Quartets,* and Theodore Roethke's "It was beginning winter," the fifth and last section of "The Lost Son." All three poems center on what Eliot calls "the sharp compassion of the healer's art."

The bridge between the three poems occurs most fully in "East Coker":

> I said to my soul, be still, and wait without hope
> For hope would be hope for the wrong thing; wait without
>     love
> For love would be love of the wrong thing; there is yet faith
> But the faith and the love and the hope are all in the waiting.

Roethke describes a similar "in-between time" in "It was beginning winter." The tortured persona, represented by "the beautiful surviving bones" of the winter-dead weeds, realizes that he

---

Printed by permission of Marsha Peterson White.

251

is not alone, that an illumination will come; but he only partially apprehends what it will be:

> A lively understandable spirit
> Once entertained you.
> It will come again.
> Be still.
> Wait.

Kinnell's poem begins with the same calm, almost serene tone:

> Wait, for now.
> Distrust everything if you have to.
> But trust the hours. Haven't they
> carried you everywhere, up to now?
> Personal events will become interesting again.
> Hair will become interesting.
> Pain will become interesting.
> Buds that open out of season will become interesting.

Underlying this poem is an essential theme of Kinnell's, which can be traced back to Whitman: that love and loss are inextricably bound together. Kinnell repeats this notion in many of his poems:

> If love had not smiled we would never grieve.
> ("The Feast")

> It is written in our hearts, the emptiness is all.
> This is how we have learned, the embrace is all.
> ("Goodbye")

> No one easily
> survives love; neither the love
> one has, nor the love
> one has not; each breaks down
> in the red smoke blown up
> of the day when all love will have gone on.
> ("The Apple")

And in the haunting, last lines of "Little Sleep's-Head Sprouting Hair in the Moonlight":

> when I come back
> we will go out together,
> we will walk out together among
> the ten thousand things,
> each scratched in time with such knowledge, *the wages*
> *of dying is love.*

The recompense for this burden of awareness is the realization that loving is a perpetual process "which continually must make its way forward, from night / into day, from transcending union always forward into difficult day" ("Flying Home"). In "Lost Loves," the persona not only accepts but even rejoices "that everything changes, that / we go from life / into life // and enter ourselves / quaking / like the tadpole, his time come, tumbling toward the slime." Eliot, like Kinnell, knows that the healing process, if it is genuine, cannot be forced or formulated, "for the pattern is new in every moment / And every moment is a new and shocking / Valuation of all we have been." Hence, that most difficult admonishment in Eliot's, Roethke's, and Kinnell's poems: wait.

Equally difficult, for those of us who have come to Kinnell's poem tired, desolate, and desperately wanting our emptiness to be filled, is the implied but unmistakable message that the resolution lies only in ourselves, in our willingness to acknowledge "that enormous emptiness / carved out of such tiny beings as we are." In *Black Light*, Kinnell's novel, an old opium smoker tells Jamshid that whatever has caused his spiritual death is what will bring him back to life again. Jamshid, who perpetually mourns his wife's death, finally allows himself to suffer his loneliness and to risk his greatest fear—that his own resources will fail him. The beautiful, familiar stars, under which he and his wife used to lie, become "wild stars" that grow larger and rush downward as if to destroy him. After a night of fearful dreams, he awakens refreshed, comforted again by the rhythm of the stars and the steady breathing of the woman lying near him. As the opium smoker predicted he must, Jamshid has danced on his own grave and thus renewed himself. Love, Kinnell says, is very much like courage, / perhaps it *is* courage, and even / perhaps / *only* courage" ("Flying Home").

The healing seems as if it were entirely an inward process, but in fact it is not. Kinnell, like Whitman, believes that the renewal of the world within us depends on our willingness to enter into things outside of ourselves—hair, "buds that open out of season," and second-hand gloves. In an essay on Whitman, Kinnell writes,

> An energy flows between Whitman and the thing. He loves the thing; he enters it, becomes its voice, and expresses it. But to enter a thing is to open oneself to it and let the thing enter oneself, until the presence glows within oneself. Therefore, when Whitman speaks for a leaf of grass, the grass also speaks for him. The light from heaven which shines in Whitman's poetry is often a consequence of these loving unions.

The more common, humble, and mute the thing, the greater the miracle of rescuing it from oblivion. In "East Coker," Eliot expresses a similar thought. He doubts the sincerity of high ideals and abstractions, the "Long hoped for calm, the autumnal serenity / And the wisdom of age." He writes,

> Do not let me hear
> Of the wisdom of old men, but rather of their folly,
> Their fear of fear and frenzy, their fear of possession,
> Of belonging to another, or to others, or to God.
> The only wisdom we can hope to acquire
> Is the wisdom of humility: humility is endless.

Kinnell uses the metaphor of music to describe the painful progress toward full awareness. The song must be your own song, played on "the flute of your whole existence." It may be a lament, a song "rehearsed by the sorrows," but it is the only way through to the joy. In "First Song," Kinnell describes a farm boy, "weary to crying," whose cornstalk violin produces a ragged music which wakes his heart "to the darkness and into the sadness of joy." In a beautiful tribute to Etheridge Knight, "Brother of My Heart," Kinnell asks him to

sing, even if you cry; the bravery
of the crying turns it into the true song; soul brother
in heaven, on earth
broken heart brother, sing to us
here, in this place that loses its brothers,
in this emptiness only the singing sometimes almost fills.

And in another poem, "The Still Time," Kinnell assures us it is
never too late "for those who can groan / to sing, / for those
who can sing to heal themselves."

"Wait" speaks to us most directly when every minute is bur-
dened by the absence of someone, when an hour looms inter-
minable and empty, when our only desire is to revive the past,
and, failing that, to die. The second stanza begins,

> Wait.
> Don't go too early.
> You're tired. But everyone's tired.
> But no one is tired enough.
> Only wait a little and listen

The persona calmly asserts that life, the song of life in its sor-
rowful and even suicidal passages, is beautiful and valuable. The
persona asks us to "be there to hear it, it will be the only time."
He asks us to accept time—which *appears* to be the enemy—
with humility and courage: "trust the hours. Haven't they //
carried you everywhere, up to now?" In this brief poem, Kinnell
challenges us to exhaust the whole of the experience, the finality
of loss and the renewal of hope.

TESS GALLAGHER

# From "The Poem as a Reservoir for Grief"

*On "Goodbye"*

As more and more of contemporary life is forced into the present moment, there seem to be fewer mechanisms which allow the past to be fully absorbed and lived once it has happened. It has become harder to experience grief since it is a retroactive emotion which requires subsequent returns to the loss over a period of time. Only through such returns may one hope for the very real gain of transforming losses of various kinds into meaningful contributions to our own becoming.

It is not simply release from sufferings we need, but understanding of loss and, beyond understanding, the need to feel, as in the word *mourning,* the ongoing accumulation of bodily and psychic communication which loss initiates in us. Here I am speaking not only of the loss one experiences in the death of a loved one, but also of those diminishments of being which become known gradually, as when child or parent or lover discovers piecemeal the signs of neglect and lost trust. Poems have long been a place where one could count on being allowed to feel, in a bodily sense, our connection to loss. I say *bodily* to emphasize the way poems act not only upon the mind and spirit, but also upon the emotions which then release the bodily signs of feeling—so that we weep, laugh, are brought to anger, feel loneliness or the comfort of companionship.

What often happens early on with a death or other incalculable loss is that one has a feeling of shock which brings about an

From *American Poetry Review* 13 (July/August 1984). Reprinted by permission of Tess Gallagher. The complete essay also contains discussions of William Heyen's "The Berries" and Michael Burkard's "Islands of Feeling."

absence of feeling. We are cut off from our bodily entrance to the loss. We stand outside the loss and are pulled along into new experiences before we have had the chance to ask, "What can this mean?" We may feel a kind of guilt because *we have not felt enough*. This can cause even more avoidance of the grieving process, so that the integrative steps that might be taken to bring the loss into some meaningful consequence in our lives are never attempted.

In this time of mass communication, there is the opposite cause of an inability to grieve—that one is asked to feel too much: we are asked to witness disasters claiming thousands of lives, numerous political atrocities, domestic brutalities, massacres in distant countries, and the rape around the corner. It is no wonder that a certain emotional unavailability has become a part of the modern temperament.

In such a world, poems allow a strictly private access to the grief-handling process, or, on another level, poems may bring one's loss into communion with other deaths and mythic elements which enlarge the view of the solitary death. It is as if the poem acted as a live-in church, and one might open the book of poems in order to arrive, through experiencing loss, at an approach to one's particular grief, and thereby transform that grief.

The failure of professional counseling, including psychiatry, to provide a lasting solace and a spiritual resource for those who need to grieve reflects a failure of American societal attitudes in general. America is, perhaps, a country *almost* ready for grief, for the serious considerations and admissions, recognitions and healings of grief. I see the public and private reassessments of the Vietnam War as one of the recent signs of this new willingness and capacity. The building of the Vietnam War memorial restored, in a symbolic way, the memory of those Americans who died in that war. At present, there is the growing awareness of the possibility of nuclear holocaust, so that whole days are viciously intersected by fears of such proportion that we have few ways of addressing them. It is as if we have been propelled into a kind of before-the-fact mourning for the earth and life in general because our fears are so stupifying. It is a productive mourning, however, in that it has provided the energy to motivate many sectors of the country to take action against this threat.

The ramifications of an entire society's inability to grieve might be more central to our problems than we have yet been able to recognize. For instance, one might consider the high divorce rate and its possible relationship to various kinds of unexpressed grief. The rise in other types of violence, especially against women and children, seems inextricably linked to a particularly male dilemma in which men, for various cultural and societal reasons, have been cut off and have cut themselves off from the grieving process.

The divorce rate relates perhaps more particularly to the grieving of an entire sex, the grieving of women, who have come to value themselves in new ways, and who, in many cases, must eschew entire lives lived in the dominions of choices made by others. As a stopgap measure for these ruptures in domestic matters, counseling and being counseled have become practically a national pastime, a place for assessment and making changes. But counseling has not answered this deeper need of the individual to grieve because its motives are too future-oriented in the short-term sense.

I am reminded of my own disappointment with marriage counseling when my second marriage was in a state of collapse. The counselor was sympathetic when I cried in the first session, but when I cried in the second and third sessions, she reverted to a very businesslike disapproval. I was not making "progress." I was not "forgetting" the attachments of the relationship quickly enough. I should have been able, within the space of three weeks, to leave grief behind and plunge ahead into "my own life." But my life had been so intricately defined in terms of the "other" that the grieving could not be accelerated as she would have liked. Counseling is often aimed at the practical: getting one to function *as though* the loss has been accommodated. And, of course, we do this . . . we act *as if we could* move on, and we do. But counseling or other "self-help" methods for handling grief often belong to what J. T. Fraser, in *Of Time, Passion, and Knowledge,* has aptly named "the business present."

The business present, he says, "pays only lip service to past and future; its essence is the removal of tension associated with future and past, in sharp contrast to the tragic present with its wealth of temporal conflicts."[1] Fraser explains that the tragic present, which I associate with poetry, "involves continuities and hidden necessities," while "the business present is informed only of discontinuities, that is, of chance" (416). When things happen to us only by chance we are not encouraged to search for meaning. Chance becomes its own meaning.

Self-help books exist to help the seeker package the problem and thereby allow a quick solution. They are the hamburger stands of the soul. We are all familiar with the questions, warnings, and promises of their titles: "Who Do You Think You Are?" "The Hazards of Being Male," "How to Win Over Depression," and "How Not to Make Love"!

Mass communication, unlike poetry, is aimed at the shrinking attention span. Its messages, according to Fraser, are engineered "to make the material digestible with minimal effort and with no effect other, or deeper, than the one desired by the financial sponsor" (426). This describes how the business present wants to act upon language and consequently upon our lives. It wants to drive out the ambiguity of language which is the lifeblood of grief feeling and of poem making and poem reading. Fraser quotes Picasso:

A green parrot is also a green salad *and* a green parrot.
He who makes it only a parrot diminishes its reality.

When our experience is negotiated without ambiguity, we become target-oriented and unaware of nuance, of the very subtleties that trigger how and why we act as we do. What most often promotes ambiguity is an access to our past through which we may relive it in some fullness, so that the past is not lost or left behind as dross, but is incorporated into the present.

What the business present encourages, as Fraser sees so acutely, is "the flight of the masses from the terror and *responsibility* of knowing time" (426, my italics). When we are told to settle a loss account quickly, efficiently, this often involves placing the experience in the old business file. We do this by relegating that experience to the past—the dead past. It was briefly relevant, but we must move on like good soldiers.

Poems, through ambiguity and the enrichments of images and metaphor, invite our returns. Poems partake of the tragic and recreated present, while the business present continues to focus entirely on the "now." The time of the poem is multi-directional: it reaches richly into the past and forms linkages with the present and with other isolated pasts. The poem searches into the future. It reminds us of longings.

Poems restore our need to *become,* a capacity the modern self is in danger of losing. Fraser recognizes the tragic poet as "the free, time-roaming ambassador" (420) who assists in our becoming. The poem does not package or merely deliver the message. Its knowledge evolves. Its very ambiguities point to the individualistic character of the artistic expression itself. This ambiguity permits the spectator to insert details of his or her own, niches of perception left undetermined or open by the artist.

Poems often remake the grief-causing experience in terms of myth or analogy so that the unconscious and the conscious experiences of the speaker and the reader are enabled to meet. Myth mediates between the conscious and the unconscious minds. It moves from ego release to psychic and spiritual embrace.

There are many poems one might turn to as examples of what I've been talking about—the elegies of Milton, Gray, Thomas, Yeats, Dickinson, Auden, the entire work of Rainier Maria Rilke, and poems by Akhmatova and Tsvetayeva and countless contemporary American women, some of whose voices are almost entirely elegiac in tone: Bogan, Plath, Glück, and Gregg. With so much to choose from, I don't introduce the poems I've selected with any sense of them as definitive except in their appeal to me at this writing for their particular ways of handling grief.

The first poem, by Galway Kinnell, typifies the power of many poets to move through the separations of grief into a state of embrace. His poem "Goodbye" begins with the death of his mother. Kinnell told me a fact outside the knowledge which the poem gives that might be useful: much to his sorrow, he could not be at his mother's deathbed. The poem was written in order to absorb regret: "I swallow down the goodbyes I won't get to use." There is also the suggestion that there was unresolved anguish between mother and son in the line "whatever we are, she and I, we're nearly cured," as though the mother's death were some closing of that case. The act of writing the goodbye is perhaps what will afford the speaker the wholeness of cure.

GOODBYE

1

My mother, poor woman, lies tonight
in her last bed. It's snowing, for her, in her darkness.
I swallow down the goodbyes I won't get to use,
tasteless, with wretched mouth-water;
whatever we are, she and I, we're nearly cured.

The night years ago when I walked away
from that final class of junior high school students
in Pittsburgh, the youngest of them ran
after me down the dark street. "Goodbye!" she called,
snow swirling across her face, tears falling.

2

Tears have kept on falling. History
has taught them its slanted understanding
of the human face. At each last embrace the dying give,
the snow brings down its disintegrating curtain.
The mind shreds the present, once the past is over.

In the Derry graveyard where only her longings sleep
and armfuls of flowers go out in the drizzle
the bodies not yet risen must lie nearly forever . . .
"Sprouting good Irish grass," the graveskeeper blarneys,
he can't help it, "a sprig of shamrock, if they were young."

3

In Pittsburgh tonight, those who were young
will be less young, those who were old, more old, or more
    likely
no more; and the streets where Syllest,
fleetest of my darlings, caught up with me
and hugged me and said goodbye, will be empty. Well,

one day the streets all over the world will be empty—
already in heaven, listen, the golden cobblestones have fallen
   still—
everyone's arms will be empty, everyone's mouth, the Derry
   earth.
It is written in our hearts, the emptiness is all.
That is how we have learned, the embrace is all.

The time sense of the poem is wonderfully agile in making a new arena for reexamining the loss of the mother. In the second stanza the poem suddenly shifts to "years ago" and the impulsive act of a student who runs after the poet in order to call out a furtive "goodbye." Her weeping and her calling after him enact the speaker's own wish for himself as regards his dying mother—that he could rush after, or to her, to say goodbye. The impassioned necessity and simple beauty of that act are impressed upon us through the superimposition of the past moment onto the present.

Part 2 of the poem moves the voice out of the personal realm into "history." The mother becomes "the dying." The snow in the poem is an emblem of separation, of "disintegrating," of loss of connection. But paradoxically, goodbye in the poem is given *in order to restore* the connection. The mind is seen to *need* the past, to wish to continue and complete it until the present is no longer needed. The present exists not for itself, as we often assume, but as the place to resolve the past. This means that the currency of the present is not as powerful as we often assume. It exists merely to facilitate the reliving of the past and, as Kinnell indicates, is "shredded" once the past is "over" or resolved. The present undergoes a reversal of importance here in accord with contemporary mandates to kill the past in order to live in the "now." But ironically, once the past is dead, the "now" suffers a loss of consequence and is not fulfilled.

As Kinnell approaches in imagination the Derry graveyard where his mother is buried, it is her longings he addresses first, linking her to a future embodied as "armfuls of flowers" that "go out in the drizzle," as if they were candles whose light had been extinguished by the gradual and natural element of the weather—not downpour, but "drizzle" so the hiss is almost audible as the flames go out, each with its little radius of silence. The mother's body lies with "the bodies not yet risen," so the act of the poem is the raising of the mother (her death) into the human embrace. Her body is seen to return to the elements—in the graveskeeper's words, "sprouting good Irish grass." This physical actuality coexists with the "nearly forever" which at this point brings together the temporal and atemporal.

Then we return with the speaker to Pittsburgh, the scene of the young student's goodbye. But now the time span, the aging of the speaker and the student and those in the world at large, is acknowledged: "those who were young / will be less young, those who were old, more old, or more likely / no more." The absence of that one caller who is now named tenderly "Syllest, fleetest of my darlings" is experienced as streets which "will be" empty. It is an imaginative living of those streets since the speaker is not there except as he recalls the moment of Syllest's catching up to him in streets where she no longer appears, as he also does not appear. Now the poet brings us physically closer to Syllest by allowing her to hug the speaker. We are moving closer to the longing for total embrace which impels the poem forward. Next, the speaker leaps from the emptying of particular and remembered streets to future streets: "One day the streets all over the world will be empty." The word "empty" moves us from the streets to the emptiness of arms, and now "everyone" begins to include the speaker of the past *and* the present. "Everyone's arms will be empty, everyone's mouth, the Derry earth." So at last, even the earth *will be* empty. The future exists as longing, but takes on a new palpability in the verbalization of it in the poem.

The end of the poem carries us into "our hearts," which includes the reader, uniting the word "emptiness" with the word "all" so the loss becomes enlarged. "All" has become the hinge which brings emptiness and embrace into conjunction. The last lines embrace but also release. Emptiness has somehow been carried into a fullness which *allows* release by virtue of the embrace.

> It is written in our hearts, the emptiness is all.
> That is how we have learned, the embrace is all.

This completion is the speaker's acknowledgement of the loss, having been able to bring together emptiness and embrace. Had Kinnell ended the poem on "the emptiness is all" we would have had an entirely different feeling, but by ending it as he does, we are gathered back *into* the all, enclosed. The necessity of the embrace has been reinstated. This perhaps allows the speaker to return that embrace Syllest gives him in the past and enables him to give the ungiven embrace to his dying mother, and finally to the "everyone" the poem admits at its close.

So it is the past which nourishes the present, which allows the resolution, the grieving for the death the speaker could not attend. There is an undercurrent too in the poem of the speaker's own self-embrace. It is as though he also has had to say goodbye to that part of himself which died with his mother. He enters the "all" which is the union with others and with the earth and with the spirit of the lost one the poem has been seeking. A symbolic accompanying of the mother's death does then finally occur. . . .

Poems engage our imaginations and emotions in a way that is particularly needed now, if we are, in our national and personal identities, to move from the state of being *almost* ready for the serious work of grieving to a true state of readiness. For it is the experiencing of grief which allows us to value fully those events, those people who are irreplaceable, so that, as Burkard says, we "love them as no other."

It is important that we be strengthened by the wisdoms of our grievings. The scientists may tinker, the politicians may instruct us in the various ploys of unconsciousness, the physicians may delay death awhile with yet another cure, but, until each individual maintains a responsible relationship to his or her own losses and changes, there will be no such thing as a hopeful future. For, as in the Taoist description of the wheel in terms of the strong, empty spaces *between* the spokes, one's future depends not only on the visible spokes of the present, but also on those invisible elements from the past, those things we are missing, are grieving for, have forgotten and left behind, so that they may be recovered.

It seems important that grieving not be separated from other aspects of living. It belongs there within the fabric of psychic, spiritual, intellectual, emotional, and intuitional perceptions through which we move. Because poems, as in no other way we use language, are able to carry the destiny of such a complex synthesis, they are the best and oldest forms we have for attending and absolving grief, for bringing it into a useful relationship to those things we are about to do toward a future.

## NOTE

1. J. T. Fraser, *Of Time, Passion, and Knowledge: Reflections on the Strategy of Existence* (New York: George Braziller, 1975), 416. Further references appear in parentheses in the text.

TED SOLOTAROFF

# Knowing and Not Knowing

I know nothing about how Galway Kinnell wrote this amazing poem ["The Fundamental Project of Technology," in *The Past*], but I imagine that he came to it in the common way, drawing upon an image and a feeling that the nuclear age fosters in most of us. The image is that of the white light that I sometimes envision when I walk to work in the morning in Manhattan, the last thing I've been told I'll see before all these buildings and people and I disappear. The feeling is the one I have sometimes when I see one of my children in full relief and think of the precariousness of his future. These items of shared experience recur through the poem's patterns of observation, vision, and prophecy: the homing devices, as it were, by which Kinnell stays on his course through the dark imponderables of his subject.

I

The poem begins with a series of objects that one of the two atom bombs we exploded in Japan has turned into images and omens. By these we can begin to imagine and foresee. The poet begins pretty much where the reader is at, standing before some material objects, taking them in. The objects have certain things in common. (1) They are in a display case in a museum; they are relics: i.e., pieces of history as well as of matter. (2) They are human relics, most of them household items, or otherwise—like the eyeglasses or the skullbone inside the helmet—made for human use. (3) They are more or less global in nature; there is

From *Singular Voices: American Poetry Today,* edited by Stephen Berg (New York: Avon, 1985). Reprinted by permission of Ted Solotaroff and Stephen Berg.

nothing particularly Japanese about these relics, nothing that trips the little protective device in our minds that distinguishes between them and us. (4) They are, with one exception, objects that are made by one or another heat process—cooking, forging, smelting—and hence have a high degree of heat resistance. This is also true of the exception, the relic of the once-animate object, the person whose skullbone was one of his most heat-resistant parts. Thus, if we are fully heeding the opening stanza, we must begin to imagine for ourselves a heat that transforms, melts, or otherwise alters glass, wire, helmet metal, human bone. (5) The items are unified in their meaning, semantically fused, as it were. The skullbone and the eyeglasses frame are of no more or less significance than the wires become iron lumps. In this glass case lies a small world of objects with only one common meaning which levels the distinctions between them— between glass, metal, and bone; between a thing and a person. Not even the relics of Pompeii are so tenaciously held in the grip of their event and so implacably signed by it.

The poet's voice in the first stanza is as neutral a medium as the glass through which one sees these objects, as impassive as the objects themselves. Just as they require our imagination to turn into deep images of an instant holocaust, so the tone is emotionally uninflected until we begin to read the lines with our own fear and pity. In these ways Kinnell counteracts the banality of another poem about the Bomb and also the underlying wariness, evasiveness, and dimness most of us bring to it. The objects speak for themselves; the poet appears at our side rather than on a platform. Part of the poem's power to move is in its sense of sharing rather than telling.

The structure of the first stanza, like that of the poem as a whole, is masterfully ordered and timed. It moves not only from the inanimate to the human images, that is from a lesser to a greater degree of identification (in both senses of the word), but also from a lesser to a greater degree of emotional implosion. For example, note the sequence of verbs, which grow more expressive as significances begin to hit home. This is accompanied by the slowly rising rhythm that thrusts aloft the final three verbs—"taken off," "vanished," and "sparkled"—leaving them to brood over the latent desolation and terror of what has come before and to anticipate what is to follow. That is to say, the wholeness of the poetry creates a rising movement from objectivity through pathos and into mystery. This is a traditional movement of prophecy, which the rest of the poem will follow.

## II

The figures of the next two stanzas, the old man in the museum, the schoolchildren outside, carry the pathos forward, connected as they are by the scorched school uniform, the crushed lunch box. But the poem is also moving quietly toward prophecy, and these figures are placed in an unfolding visionary field that distinguishes between them. In his recent book *The Gift*, Lewis Hyde develops the distinction between the two Greek words for life—*bios* and *zöe*. The former "is limited life, characterized life, life that dies." The latter is "the life that endures; it is the thread that runs through bios-life and is not broken when the particular perishes." The old man is seen mainly under the aspect of bios-life: subject to its accidents, he was elsewhere when the white flash sparkled; subject to its fate, he will soon die. However, as a human being he bears the imprint of generic, possibly genetic, feeling: as naturally as he might gaze into a fire, he sighs over the memento of a schoolchild who died that day. The schoolchildren of stanza 3 are seen mainly under the aspect of zöe-life: they are as animated and collectivized as a flock of birds, they evoke the ongoing revitalization of life from generation to generation; vivid creatures of the here and now, they also fade into their counterparts in the preceding generation, those of the scorched school uniforms and crushed lunch boxes. With them and, to some extent, with the old man, Kinnell's sight is turned into vision, passes into the zöe-life and its eternal present—or rather what used to be before the word "future" first learned, in a white flash, to jerk tears.

The zöe-life is often invoked in Kinnell's poetry: the perdurable moment that resonates through time, the incandescent image that illuminates a universal: a boy sighting a pond for the first time from a high tree from which he is about to fall; four older men struggling to keep their doubles game going as night and winter settle over the court. By such images we can imagine the wider, mysterious context of our lives, can move outside the "small ego," as Hyde calls it, into the collective consciousness and experience, the solidarity we share as human beings. Such images also function decisively in the circuitry of the poem. The images of stanzas 2 and 3 work like a relay network, gathering up the meaning and feeling previously fused in stanza 1 and shunting it on ahead to the vision of unprecedented horror that unfolds. The relics are omens from the white flash, flashing from past to future as the poet's eye and imagination, seeing together, begin to foresee and envision, his consciousness to join the collective one of the race itself in its terrible new disjunctions. Or, more concretely, the life in the old man about to pass into the unknown and the schoolboy relics lead to the sudden appearance of the schoolchildren—creatures of renewal, but who are associated instead with the dead schoolchildren of Hiroshima. From this disjunction of the zöe-life in the poet's mind is engendered the prophetic question about an unprecedented sound on earth.

In the deep circuitry of the collective mind into which the poet has now tapped and through which the sense of the white flash obsessively flows, the brain-empacted helmet presages a whole city's population of faceless skulls; the earthly sounds of the old man's sigh, the children's goodbyes presage the sound of an ultimate final lamentation beyond any previous obsequies of the wind or of the human voice, even "the infra-screams" made at Hiroshima and Nagasaki. Thus stanza 4 mingles the bios- and zöe-life at the split moment of extinction of the human mentality. From this expanded and intensified network of images, layer upon layer, comes its prophetic meaning: the elimination of the creaturely terror of death by means of technology, the answer "*pseudologica fantastica*" offers to religion, humankind's previous way of coping with this foreknowledge and fear.

I noted earlier that one of the other conduits of the poem's manifold power is the movement of its tone from objectivity to pathos; in stanza 5, the irony that has delicately limned the tone—the old man smoking his way to death, the animation of the schoolchildren in *their* black uniforms, the "flash-pop" of the cameras—now moves front and center to present the berserk rationalism of the nuclear weaponry. Objectivity, pathos, and irony, playing effectively off each other, have particularly potent synergy: the eyes, the heart, and the wit working together under difficult circumstances, harnessing oppositions, modulating incongruities, making them resonate in the mind in a complete way. What is happening in the poet's consciousness he makes happen in ours, passes on the impact of his vision as well as its burden. The tone of the poem is again finely tuned from moment to moment; its development is cunningly timed to deliver the abstract proposition of stanza 5 as an appalling vision, on the one hand, and to dramatically contrast with and test the emotionality of what has gone before on the other. Or to put it another way, objectivity and pathos are fused and triggered by wit, producing that laconic/tragic note of which Shakespeare was the master and his Hamlet the ultimate spokesman, particularly when he is at the pitch of his vision. It is what Robert Penn Warren speaks of as putting the feeling of the work through the fire which proves it.

## III

A third source of the poem's power lies in the development of its thought, the progressive widening of the consciousness in which its core image and feeling are held. Among the Herman Kahns and Albert Wohlstetters who think about the unthinkable, the trick is to narrow and reify the subject of nuclear war until writer and reader alike are sedated by statistics and terminology, not to mention ideology. Before we can blow up most of the earth and the human race, we must first shrink and numb our consciousness of them, beginning with that of death.

The tone of stanza 6 modulates out most of the previous irony to expand the context into a religious one, the widest one there is for contemplating the earth and mankind and our relation to them. Like the Japanese trees, the reader is "enticed down toward world-eternity" by the quiet contemplativeness in the language of this stanza, built by its sounds and slow cadences to produce a hush, as it were, in its mood. At the same time, the movement of consciousness is very rapid: the pseudologica fantastica of technology is whisked away and replaced by the ancient pantheism of the shinto and Zen's paradoxical ways of enlightenment, of knowing and not knowing, into which the poem's concerns are gathered.

Or so it seems to me. I know little about Japanese religion, but the poem instructs me well enough to grasp how Zen Buddhism too is a repository of the eternal present, invoked like a wise and ancient sage to minister to our disjunctions and apprehensions. Like the other world religions, Zen is a repository of the zöe-life from which we come and into which we return. Following the course of its cycle, the two generations of school-children, the one killed, the other imperiled, merge as they go away by nature and by memory, ghostly surrogates of the children we hold gratefully in our arms and release helplessly to the future of the white flash and the end of both the bios- and the zöe-life.

It is very difficult to write about Hiroshima and about the ten thousand Hiroshimas that are poised to happen. The subject is at once banal, incommensurable, and heavily defended against. We truly know and do not know. But the pathos and terror of this poem make the awareness of our ignorance permanently more difficult to evade or dismiss.

PART FIVE *A Reminiscence*

ANNE WRIGHT

# Sitting on Top of the Sunlight

One spring evening in 1967, shortly after our marriage, I came
home from teaching to find my husband James in excellent
spirits.

"Galway and Inés are in town," he announced. "I've invited
them for dinner tomorrow."

I wasn't sure who Galway and Inés were. At that point in my
life I had much to learn about contemporary poetry and poets. I
was pleased, however, to meet James's friends and show off our
home.

The next evening Galway and Inés joined a few other friends
for dinner. I was struck by the physical beauty of the Kinnells
and their spirit of warmth and intelligence, which radiated
throughout our small apartment.

Galway and James talked quietly in a corner for some time,
then joined the general conversation. The Kinnells were full of
stories about life at Reed College, where Galway had just
finished teaching, and their baby daughter Maud. Galway gal-
lantly offered to carve the leg of lamb and hacked it into great
pieces in his enthusiasm. Someone made a comment about
razor-thin slices but we ate the lamb happily enough.

A few days later we walked over to the apartment on Eighty-
third Street where Demetrio and Mercedes de Torres, the par-
ents of Inés, lived and where Galway and Inés were staying.
Maud was presented for our admiration. Galway had a new
camera and kept snapping pictures of James holding Maud on
his lap. In one pose he caught Maud poking James's cheek with
her tiny finger.

We stayed for dinner and ate at a long table set next to a big
window that overlooked the top branches of several trees. De-

Printed by permission of Anne Wright.

metrio talked of evenings he had spent long ago, before the Spanish Civil War, in Madrid cafés with some of the Spanish poets. They had read their work aloud in between conversations and arguments that lasted far into the night.

"That's what poetry is all about," James commented. "I wish it could be that way here." He and Galway went into a long discussion of the poetry world in the United States.

Galway came in and out of New York during the next few years. We might see him at a reading or with other friends but generally we met at the Eighty-third Street apartment. Sometimes Maud came with him. We watched her crawl, then walk. Fergus was born. The Kinnells went to California, Spain, Colorado, Iowa. Always, unexpectedly, would come a phone call and James would exclaim, "Galway's in town again! We're going to see him tonight."

When Maud was three, the Kinnells moved to New York City. She came to the West Side Community Nursery School where I was educational director. When I came into her classroom to talk with her, she hid in her cubby, then pulled on my clothes if I tried to walk away.

The nursery school, always in need of funds, recruited James, Mark Strand, and Galway to give a benefit reading. Galway was on a dozen poetry tours that year and didn't arrive back in New York until the day of the reading. He was pale, obviously exhausted, but ready to read.

People sat on the edge of their hard wooden chairs that evening when Galway recited from *Body Rags* and *The Book of Nightmares*. He held his body away from the podium at a slight angle, dangled a copy of the book from his hands but rarely glanced at it. He spoke slowly and carefully in a deep, melodious voice with passion and force. I don't think anyone moved, even to shift positions on those uncomfortable seats.

For the next eight years the Kinnells lived in New York; first at Westbeth, then in a railroad flat on Eighty-first Street. I remember a series of tall wardrobes built by Galway to partition off the huge loft room at Westbeth and an enormous round wooden table he made, which somehow fit into the tiny dining room on Eighty-first Street.

There were many gatherings at the Kinnells'. Poets and students would be there as well as old friends such as Saul Galin, Betty Kray, and Mary Kaplan. The conversation was exciting, the food and drink delicious. Someone might read a new poem or recite a translation. It didn't seem too different from the evenings in Spain described by Demetrio.

At one party so many of us were seated at the big round table Saul Galin had to use an upright suitcase for a chair. It was a diverse group that evening. The discussion grew loud and fierce. Galway and Inés exchanged amused looks over the heads of their guests. Finally Galway interrupted and made a long, involved comment in his soothing voice.

"I don't know what everyone was arguing about," said James on our way home. "I'm not even sure what Galway was talking about, but he certainly calmed everyone down."

In July 1975 Galway and James attended a writer's conference in Michigan. They read and conducted a series of lectures together. James returned from the conference filled with enthusiasm for Galway's scholarship and administrative ability.

"No one gives Galway credit for anything except writing poetry. He's wonderful at organization. They should give him a chance."

They met Etheridge Knight, the black poet, in Michigan. Whenever Etheridge was in New York he stayed with us or the Kinnells and we would all get together. One winter Etheridge came to read at the Ninety-second Street Y with Michael Harper. Galway was to introduce them. We planned to meet for dinner with Etheridge and the Kinnell family before the reading at Szechuan Taste East, a neighborhood place. There was a heavy snowfall that day. We plodded through unshoveled snow to the restaurant and saw Maud and Fergus playing on the sidewalk in front. They greeted us with snowballs and showed off their skill at sliding on the icy pavement. Inés was sitting inside at a big, empty table. We asked where Galway and Etheridge were.

"The one who is to read decided this was the perfect time to get a six-pack and the one who is to introduce is in the shower."

Soon Etheridge and the six-pack appeared and then Galway,

in a fresh white shirt, his hair still damp. We ate enormous portions of lobster with Szechuan sauce and found a taxi to take us to the reading on time.

It is useless now to regret we saw so little of each other when we lived so close. It is enough that the times we did meet were so memorable: afternoons and mornings of good talk and intimacy.

In 1976 we spent an October weekend with the Kinnells at their place in Vermont. It had been a warm autumn and the brilliant foliage I expected to see was almost gone. Galway and the children met us at the airport. We drove past small villages and tracts of forest while Maud and Fergus discussed the outstanding traits of each family member.

"Galway is the best table-maker, Inés the best artist, and Maud the best reader."

And you Fergus are the best swearer!"

Fergus grinned in agreement but was too modest to put Maud's claim to proof.

Galway slowed down at a group of mailboxes on the highway, reached into one for his mail, and turned down a dirt road next to the mailboxes. We went past a house, some fields, a grove of fir trees, and a long stretch of woods. There was a deep bend in the road, then a large, open pasture, a few apple trees, and Galway's dark red wooden farmhouse. A wicker chair and table stood under a maple tree on the lawn in front of the house.

Galway cooked steaks for us that night in the fireplace and concocted a special dressing for the salad.

"I forgot," said Maud, "Galway makes the best salad dressing in the world too."

Inés arrived by bus after dinner and had coffee with us by the fire. Galway went up with the children when they were ready for bed. After he came downstairs, he explained he read to them every evening and saved that time for special talks. Maud, now that she was older, was less open about discussing problems, but Fergus still told him everything. The conversations weren't always about troubles. Sometimes they talked about baseball or school or what he'd done during the day.

We woke up Saturday morning feeling very cold and huddled under a down quilt until the sound of sawing drove me out of bed and over to the window. During the night it had snowed and a big maple tree had blown down. It lay across the white lawn, the last few red leaves crushed in the snow. Galway was sawing off the branches. We had slept so soundly we hadn't heard the wind blow or the tree fall.

We ate breakfast in front of the fire and Galway told me about the huge granite hearthstone.

"You see those holes in back of the stone? In the winter the stonecutters used to drill lines of holes in the rock and fill the holes with water. When the water froze the ice expanded and split the rock."

He pointed to the front of the stone where a piece had chipped off. "This gash came from a fire. The rock used to be outside. Before I fixed up the house I slept outdoors and built campfires against the rock. One night there was a small explosion. The heat of the fire had broken off that piece of rock."

He pointed again, this time to a small indentation in the stone. "See this hole? That part of the rock was directly under the spout of the gutter pipe. Every time it rained the water dripped on that place. Over the years it wore away the rock and made that little hole."

He went on to tell how he found his house. He had saved up a certain amount of money and wanted to use it to buy a place in Vermont.

"I started to look in the south but land was too expensive, so I drifted further and further north until I came here. The farm had just been abandoned and the price was the exact amount that I had saved."

After breakfast we borrowed scarves and heavy jackets and took a long walk. Galway showed us a little cabin in the trees where he worked one winter.

"When I wanted water I scooped snow and heated it on the potbellied stove. It was pretty cold though."

He and James went up the road for a walk of their own. I went back to read by the fire and help Inés. She was cooking a turkey because Rosemary and Hayden Carruth were driving over from their place for dinner.

James had never met Hayden, although they corresponded. Both he and Galway admired Hayden's work and, because he did not make public appearances at that time, Galway had arranged to give several readings of Hayden's work himself.

The fragrance of roast turkey filled the house by the time the Carruths arrived. Inés and I set the table in the dining room but the children decided it would be fun to eat in front of the fire so we balanced plates of food on our laps, talked, and laughed by the burning logs. Despite a two-hour drive back to "Crow's Nest," their home, Hayden was reluctant to leave. I sensed the three men felt a deep closeness to one another. It didn't matter that James and Hayden had never met before, that opportunities for the three to see each other would be rare.

The Kinnells left New York City in the autumn of 1978. Galway had a teaching Fulbright in France at the University of Nice during the fall semester. From there he would go to Hawaii and, eventually, the entire family would move from New York to Honolulu.

James and I would be in France too, on a year's leave of absence. We planned to be in Nice for two weeks, at the beginning of 1979, while the Kinnells were still there. Years earlier, at one of our impromptu meetings, Galway prophesied that sometime we would all meet for a long, delicious meal together somewhere in France. That dream not only came true but exceeded our highest expectations.

The Kinnells rented a small villa in Vence, high above the sea. Their terrace overlooked the water and, across a valley of orchards, cultivated fields, and scrubby trees, the stone face of a huge mountain.

We met frequently during those two weeks and had a series of long, sumptuous banquets in beautiful places. Galway would pick us up at our hotel when his classes were over and we would go to the villa for lunch on the terrace or dinner in front of the fireplace. One evening, because a French friend was coming for dinner too, we stopped first in the village of Vence to market. Galway led the way down a narrow, tunnel-like street to the shops, whose lighted windows looked like oil paintings against a black wall. We trailed after him as he bought fish and vegetables, bread and croissants, cheese, fruit, wine, and pastries.

Maud painted placecards for everyone and Fergus built a huge fire. The French woman talked about literature and, after the children had gone to bed, the merits of harsh discipline for her sons. The four of us exchanged looks of horror as she insisted, "It's good for them to be hit! They do well after a beating."

As we drove to Antibes the next day, we spoke of her unpleasant method of child rearing. Maud and Fergus seemed proof to us all of the rich harvest reaped by wise, loving, and gentle discipline.

We walked through the open market in Antibes. Galway and Inés bought four large white porcelain coffee bowls and an assortment of small painted terra-cotta figures used in Provençal crèches. They chose replicas of village people: a peddler and an old woman carrying a bundle of sticks on her back. Then we drove along the coast to find a place to eat.

Restaurant Neptune, with tables set out under umbrellas on a terrace next to a shingle beach, seemed a perfect choice. Our table was a few feet from the sea. The water swirled the pebbles about and added a soft, grinding noise to the sound of breaking waves. We had fish soup, steaks, French fried potatoes, salad, cherry tarts, and wine. Galway and James rolled up their shirt sleeves in the warm January sun. The children ran along the beach, returning from time to time to pile pebbles on a corner of the table. Galway tried to slip the stones to the ground but Fergus saw him.

"We need them. We're going to take them back to New York."

"We're going to take most of France back to New York!" Galway rolled his eyes in mock dismay and ordered coffee.

We stayed at the villa one weekend. A professor from the university invited us all for dinner on Saturday night. After a long, pleasant evening we drove back to Vence under a full moon. It illuminated the sandy road. We stood out on the terrace for a short time looking across the silent valley to the mountain, which glowed in the moonlight.

James got up very early Sunday morning, sat on the terrace, and watched the sun come up. I was up next and tiptoed around the kitchen making coffee and cutting slices of bread. We were going with Galway to Mass at the Matisse Chapel.

"Good morning Annie." Galway's voice from the other room sounded so cheerful.

"There's no milk. Use crème fraîche." Inés's voice from the other room sounded so sleepy.

We ate quickly and drove to the chapel. An old man with white hair sat in front of us. Sun shone through the famous green and purple windows. After the service Galway asked if we had noticed the old man. "I watched his hair turn green and then purple."

The last evening we invited all four Kinnells for bouillabaisse at our favorite restaurant in Nice, La Petite Biche. The huge, steaming pot filled with various fish, vegetables, crabs, shrimp, and strange, unknown shellfish seemed impossible to empty but, after several hours of eating, laughing, and talking, there was nothing left but bones and shells. The red-headed waitress who never smiled not only smiled but laughed and dashed about to fill the breadbaskets and wine glasses. We lingered over parfaits and coffee, the last people to leave.

The Kinnells stood outside their car until we came onto the balcony off our room. We waved and waved. It seemed quite cold, all of a sudden, when the rear lights of their car disappeared up the street.

A year later the Kinnells were in Hawaii and James was at Mount Sinai Hospital with cancer. Galway was coming to New York in March to read at the Guggenheim and Sarah Lawrence College. When it seemed that March might be too late for him to see James, Jane Cooper arranged for the Sarah Lawrence reading to be held in February.

Galway came straight from the airport to the hospital. As soon as he saw James he leaned over his bed and hugged him, tubes and all. James couldn't talk but he wrote notes to Galway on a yellow-lined pad. During that visit James was alert, a little bit stronger, well aware his friend was there.

Galway returned in March. When he came to the hospital I had a photocopy of James's manuscript, *This Journey,* for him. Galway had always gone over manuscripts with James and, sick as he was, James urged me to have his latest one ready for Galway. Galway took the copy and James wrote on his pad, "I think the book is more or less done."

In the summer of 1980, after James's death, the Kinnells invited me to spend a little time with them in Vermont. After I arrived, Galway showed me his study, a huge room over the garage. Long shelves filled with books and magazines were under the eaves. His big desk was covered with papers, a typewriter, mail, and more books and magazines. About twenty-five cardboard cartons filled with papers were in the middle of the floor. The Lilly Library at the University of Indiana had just bought his papers and he was in the midst of organizing them. He showed me his system. Drafts of poems, individual manuscripts, and correspondence were all in separate boxes according to year. There were boxes of manuscripts from other poets labeled: "poets known" and "poets-not-yet-known." He kept one container solely for letters dealing with the business of publishing.

"This might help you when you go over James's papers," which, in fact, it did.

As we started downstairs, I noticed a photograph on the windowsill next to the steps. It was a picture of James and me walking down Eighty-third Street, taken, I suspect, after one of those long afternoons with Galway at the de Torres home.

The visit was quiet and healing. Galway worked in his study and played tennis during the day. He had no telephone then so endless trips were made to neighbors and pay phone booths in the nearby towns to set up each match.

We picked berries. Galway chopped wood and Inés made mounds of pesto sauce from fresh basil in the garden. We all took walks. Marion and Ted Hoagland came over for dinner one night. Galen Williams and Frank Russell stopped over for a few days. We had delicious dinners and spent the evenings sitting at the table drinking wine and talking.

Fergus was convinced he heard coyotes under his windows at night. He scolded us for talking and laughing so loudly we didn't hear them. Galway found books about coyotes and surviving in the wilderness and read them with Fergus. When Fergus showed the books to his friend Zeke, they discovered a diagram of a coyote trap and set about to make one, using fishing line and a three-pronged hook. They hung the trap from the branch of a tree at the end of the meadow next to the woods behind the house and baited it with chunks of cooked duck.

Zeke was invited to spend the night. The boys were convinced a coyote would be attracted to the bait and get caught. They planned to go out then and shoot it with their bows and arrows. At dinner, as it began to get dark, their voices grew shrill. They seemed to doubt the strength of the fishing line until Galway offered to go with them when they visited the trap.

"As soon as it's dark enough to see their glowing eyes we'll go."

Inés and I watched them walk across the field in the dim glow of Galway's flashlight. The boys stayed very close to Galway and limply carried their bows and arrows. Soon they were all back.

"No glowing eyes," stated Galway. His expression was serious but his eyes sparkled and, when the boys were upstairs and out of hearing, he exploded with laughter.

Donald Hall and his wife Jane Kenyon came over from New Hampshire on my last day to pick me up. Before I left, we had a long discussion about James's manuscript, *This Journey*. It was Galway's suggestion to complete *This Journey* with the poem "A Winter Daybreak Above Vence."

In March, 1981, Robert Bly and Galway took part in a memorial reading for James. Galway read the later poems and spoke in particular of the morning we had gone to Mass at the Matisse Chapel.

"I got up early to turn on the motor for hot water and saw James sitting on the terrace looking out at the sea. I didn't think he noticed me, but I see from this poem he did."

He went on to read "A Winter Daybreak Above Vence." I have heard Galway read James's work since that evening. It is always a strange and precious experience. His voice and tone are different from James's but he evokes in me similar emotions. It wouldn't surprise me to hear James's voice whisper in my ear, "Why, Galway is Ohioan too."

When I see Galway at different gatherings or readings we find a chance to talk together. I hear how Maud is doing at Princeton and Fergus at boarding school. Sometimes we talk about Vermont or Galway's trips to Japan, or Australia, or China. Then we are quiet for a moment and remember.

Life for us both is very different now but nothing can take away or change those brief, wonderful days when we were all together "sitting here strangely on top of the sunlight."

# Bibliography

Part I is organized chronologically within the categories. Part II is organized alphabetically.

## I. Works by Kinnell

POETRY

*What a Kingdom It Was.* Boston: Houghton Mifflin, 1960.
*Flower Herding on Mount Monadnock.* Boston: Houghton Mifflin, 1964.
*Body Rags.* Boston: Houghton Mifflin, 1968.
*First Poems 1946–1954.* Mt. Horeb, Wis.: Perishable Press, 1970.
*The Book of Nightmares.* Boston: Houghton Mifflin, 1971.
*The Shoes of Wandering.* Mt. Horeb, Wis.: Perishable Press, 1971.
*The Avenue Bearing the Initial of Christ into the New World: Poems 1946–1964.* Boston: Houghton Mifflin, 1974.
*Three Poems.* New York: Phoenix Book Shop, 1976.
*Mortal Acts, Mortal Words.* Boston: Houghton Mifflin, 1980.
*Selected Poems.* Boston: Houghton Mifflin, 1982.
*The Past.* Boston: Houghton Mifflin, 1985.

TRANSLATIONS

*Bitter Victory,* by Rene Hardy. New York: Doubleday, 1956. Novel.
*The Poems of François Villon.* New York: New American Library, 1965. Rev. ed. Boston: Houghton Mifflin, 1977.
*On the Motion and Immobility of Douve,* by Yves Bonnefoy. Athens, Ohio: Ohio University Press, 1968. Poems.
*Lackawanna Elegy,* by Yvan Goll. Fremont, Mich.: Sumac, 1970. Poems.

PROSE

"Only Meaning Is Truly Interesting." *Beloit Poetry Journal* 4 (Fall 1953):1–3.

Review of *Songs for a New America,* by Charles G. Bell. *Beloit Poetry Journal* 5 (Summer 1955):29–32.

*Black Light.* Boston: Houghton Mifflin, 1966. Rev. ed. San Francisco: North Point Press, 1981. Novel.

Note on "The Supper After the Last." In *Poet's Choice.* Edited by Paul Engle and Joseph Langland, 257. New York: Delta, 1966.

"Poetry, Personality, and Death." *Field,* no. 4 (Spring 1971):56–75. Reprinted in *A Field Guide to Contemporary Poetry and Poetics,* edited by Stuart Friebert and David Young, 203–23. New York: Longman, 1980.

"The Poetics of the Physical World." *Iowa Review* 2 (Summer 1971):113–26. Reprinted in part in *The New Naked Poetry,* edited by Stephen Berg and Robert Mezey, 133–36. Indianapolis: Bobbs-Merrill, 1976.

"Last of the Big-Time Amateurs." *Sports Illustrated,* 25 June 1973, 30–32, 37–40.

"Whitman's Indicative Words." *American Poetry Review* 2 (March/April 1973):9–11. Revised version reprinted in *Walt Whitman: The Measure of His Song,* edited by Jim Perlman, Ed Folsom, and Dan Campion, 215–27. Minneapolis: Holy Cow! Press, 1981.

*Walking Down the Stairs: Selections from Interviews.* Ann Arbor: University of Michigan Press, 1978.

*How the Alligator Missed Breakfast.* Boston: Houghton Mifflin, 1982. Children's book.

"Poets Against the End of the World." *Poetry East,* no. 9/10 (Winter 1982/Spring 1983):16–23. Introduction with interview.

Foreword to *The Selected Poetry of Hayden Carruth.* New York: Collier/MacMillan, 1985.

Postscript to *Eternity's Woods,* by Paul Zweig. Middletown, Conn.: Wesleyan University Press, 1985.

ILLUSTRATIONS

*The Snow Rabbitt,* by Pati Hill. Boston: Houghton Mifflin, 1962. Poems.

AUDIO-VISUAL

*Galway Kinnell: Interviews and Readings.* Brockport, N.Y.: Brockport Writers Forum, State University of New York, 1972. Videotape.

*The Poetry of Galway Kinnell.* Jeffery Norton Publishers/McGraw-Hill, 1965. Audio-cassette.

*Galway Kinnell.* San Francisco: American Poetry Archive and Resource Center, San Francisco State University, 1975. Videotape.

*The Poetry and Voice of Galway Kinnell.* Caedmon, TC 1502, 1975. Sound recording.

*Galway Kinnell.* Washington, D.C.: Watershed Foundation, 1986. C-217. Audio-cassette.


## II. Secondary sources

*An asterisk indicates publication for the first time in this book; annotations refer to shortened titles of Kinnell's works.*

Alexander, Floyce M. "Map of the Innards." *Kayak,* no. 17 (1969):68–71. Review of *Body Rags.*

Altieri, Charles. *Self and Sensibility in Contemporary American Poetry.* New York: Cambridge University Press, 1984.

Atlas, James. "Autobiography of the Present." *Poetry* 125 (February 1975):301–2. Review of *Avenue.*

Beaver, Harold. "Refuge in the Library, on the Farm, and in Memories." *New York Times Book Review,* 2 March 1986, 14–15. Review of *The Past.*

Beckman, Madeline. "Galway Kinnell Searches for Innocence." *Saturday Review,* September/October 1983, 14–16.

Bell, Charles G. "Galway Kinnell." In *Contemporary Poets,* 3d ed., edited by James Vinson, 835–37. New York: St. Martin's Press, 1980.

Bell, DeWitt. "Wonders of the Inner Eye." *New York Times Book Review,* 5 July 1964, 4–5. Review of *Flower Herding.*

Bellamy, Joe David, ed. *American Poetry Observed: Poets on Their Work.* Urbana: University of Illinois Press, 1984.

Benedikt, Michael. "The Apotheosis of Darkness vs. Bardic Privilege." *Poetry* 121 (November 1972):105–7. Review of *Nightmares.*

———. "The Shapes of Nature." *Poetry* 113 (December 1968):188–91. Review of *Body Rags.*

Bergonzi, Bernard. "Private Fortunes." *New York Review of Books,* 28 April 1966, 23–24. Review of *Black Light.*

Berke, Roberta. *Bounds Out of Bounds.* New York: Oxford University Press, 1981.

Bloom, Harold. "Straight Forth Out of Self." *New York Times Book Review,* 22 June 1980, 13. Review of *Mortal Acts.*

Bly, Robert. "Galway Kinnell and the Old Farmer."*

Boening, J. Review of *Walking Down the Stairs. World Literature Today* 53 (Summer 1979):512.

Bogan, Louise. "Verse." *New Yorker,* 1 April 1961, 130. Review of

*Kingdom*. Reprinted in *A Poet's Alphabet,* edited by Robert Phelps and Ruth Limmer. New York: McGraw-Hill, 1970.

Brinnin, John Malcolm. "Plath, Jarrell, Kinnell, Smith." *Partisan Review* 34 (Winter 1967):156–60. Review of *Flower Herding.*

Brownjohn, Alan. "Dark Forces." *New Statesman,* 12 September 1969, 346–47. Review of *Body Rags.*

Bruchac, Joseph. "I Have Come to Myself Empty: Galway Kinnell's Bear and Porcupine."*

Burns, Gerald. "Poets and Anthologies." *Southwest Review* 53 (Summer 1968):332. Review of *Body Rags.*

Cambon, Glauco. *Recent American Poetry*. Minneapolis: University of Minnesota Press, 1962.

————. "Dante on Galway Kinnell's 'Last River.'" In *Dante's Influence on American Writers 1776–1976,* edited by Anne Paolucci, 31–39. New York: Griffon House, 1976.

Carruth, Hayden. "Making It New." *Hudson Review* 21 (Summer 1968):403–4. Review of *Body Rags.*

Comito, Terry. "Slogging Toward the Absolute." *Modern Poetry Studies* 6 (1975):189–92. Review of *Avenue.*

Davie, Donald. "Slogging for the Absolute." *Parnassus* 3 (Fall/Winter 1974):9–22. Reprinted in *The Poet in the Imaginary Museum,* by Donald Davie. New York: Persea Books, 1979.

Davis, William Virgil. "'The Wasted Breath': Galway Kinnell's *The Book of Nightmares.*" *Montana Review* 3 (1982):57–64.

Davison, Peter. "Three Visionary Poets." *Atlantic,* February 1972, 104–5. Review of *Nightmares.*

Deen, Rosemary F. Review of *The Book of Nightmares. Commonweal,* 24 December 1971, 308–9.

Dickey, James. *Babel to Byzantium: Poets and Poetry Now*. New York: Farrar, Straus and Giroux, 1961, 1968.

Dickstein, Morris. "Intact and Triumphant." *New York Times Book Review,* 19 September 1982, 12, 33. Review of *Selected Poems.*

Edelman, Sandra Prewitt. "The Poet as Healer." *Southwest Review* 66 (Spring 1981):215–19. Review of *Mortal Acts.*

Flint, R. W. "At Home in the Seventies." *Parnassus* 8 (January 1980):51–62. Review of *Mortal Acts.*

Funsten, Kenneth. "To Accept Death as an Appreciation of Life." *Los Angeles Times Book Review,* 6 February 1983, 2. *Review of Selected Poems.*

Gallagher, Tess. "The Poem as a Reservoir for Grief." *American Poetry Review* 13 (July/August 1984):7–11. Reprinted in *A Concert of Tenses.* Ann Arbor: University of Michigan Press, 1986.

Goldman, Michael. "Joyful in the Dark." *New York Times Book Review,* 18 February 1968, 12. Review of *Body Rags.*

Guillory, Daniel L. Review of *The Past. Library Journal,* 15 November 1985, 100.

Guimond, James. *Seeing and Healing: A Study of the Poetry of Galway Kinnell.* Port Washington, N.Y.: Associated Faculty Press, 1984.

Hall, Donald. "A Luminous Receptiveness." *Nation,* 18 October 1971, 377–78. Review of *Nightmares.*

————. "Text as Test: Notes on and around Carruth and Kinnell." *American Poetry Review* 12 (November/December 1983):27–32.

Hamilton, Ian. "Declarations of Despair." *London Observer,* 21 September 1969, 34. Review of *Body Rags.*

Harmon, William. "Kumin and Kinnell (and Kilmer)." *Poetry* 142 (April 1983):50–52. Review of *Selected Poems.*

Hass, Robert. Review of *Selected Poems. Book World,* 5 September 1982, 6.

Hazo, Samuel. Review of *Body Rags. Commonweal,* 8 November 1968, 227–28.

Hilberry, Conrad. "The Structure of Galway Kinnell's *The Book of Nightmares.*" *Field* 12 (Spring 1975):28–46.

Hobbs, John. "Galway Kinnell's 'The Bear': Dream and Technique." *Modern Poetry Studies* 5 (1974):237–50.

Hoffman, Daniel, ed. *Harvard Guide to Contemporary American Writing.* Cambridge, Mass.: Harvard University Press, Belknap Press, 1979.

Howard, Richard. "Changes." *Partisan Review* 38 (Winter 1971–72):484–90. Review of *Nightmares.*

————. *Alone with America.* New York: Atheneum, 1969.

Hudgins, Andrew. "One and Zero Walk Off Together: Dualism in Galway Kinnell's *The Book of Nightmares.*" *American Poetry* 3 (Fall 1985):56–71.

Hudson, Berkley. "Poet Puts Human Experience into Words." *Los Angeles Times,* 16 June 1983, I-D14.

Hurt, James R. "Kinnell's 'First Song.'" *Explicator* 20 (November 1961):23.

Jerome, Judson. "Uncommitted Voices." *Saturday Review,* 1 June 1968, 32. Review of *Body Rags.*

Keane, Patrick. Review of *The Avenue Bearing the Initial of Christ into the New World. New Republic,* 27 July 1974, 30–31.

Koretz, Gene H. "Kinnell's 'First Song.'" *Explicator* 15 (April 1957):43.

LaFollette, Melvin Walker. "Kinnell's 'First Song.'" *Explicator* 14 (April 1956):48.

Langbaum, Robert. "Galway Kinnell's *The Book of Nightmares*." *American Poetry Review* 8 (March/April 1979):30–31.

Lask, Thomas. "The Makers and Their Works." *New York Times*, 1 September 1971, 35. Review of *Nightmares*.

Lattimore, Richmond. "Poetry Chronicle." *Hudson Review* 24 (Fall 1971):501–2. Review of *Nightmares*.

Lazer, Hank. "That Backward-Spreading Brightness." *Ironwood* 16 (Fall 1980):92–100. Review of *Mortal Acts*.

Ledbetter, J. T. "Galway Kinnell's 'The Bear.'" *Explicator* 33 (April 1975):63.

Lieberman, Laurence. "New Poetry in Review." *Yale Review* 58 (October 1968):137–39. Review of *Body Rags*.

Logan, John. "The Bear in the Poet in the Bear." *Nation*, 16 September 1968, 244–45. Review of *Body Rags*.

————. "Fine First Book." *Commonweal*, 4 November 1960, 154–56. Review of *Kingdom*.

McDonnell, Jane Taylor. Review of *The Book of Nightmares*. *Carlton Miscellany* 12 (Spring 1972):153–56.

McGann, Jerome. "Points of Departure in Recent Poetry." *Chicago Review* 27 (1975):161–64. Review of *Avenue*.

Malkoff, Karl. *Crowell's Handbook of Contemporary American Poetry*. New York: Thomas Y. Crowell, 1973.

Mariani, Paul. "Kinnell's Legacy: On "The Avenue Bearing the Initial of Christ into the New World."*

Marusiak, Joe. "Where We Might Meet Each Other: An Appreciation of Galway Kinnell and William Everson." *Literary Review* 24 (Spring 1981):355–70.

Matthews, William. "On the Tennis Court at Night."*

Mazzaro, Jerome. "Poetry Chronicle." *Hudson Review* 33 (Autumn 1980):457–59. Review of *Mortal Acts*.

Medwick, Cathleen. "Poetry in Motion." *Vogue*, November 1985, 280–81.

Mills, Ralph J. *Cry of the Human*. Urbana: University of Illinois Press, 1975.

Molesworth, Charles. *The Fierce Embrace*. Columbia, Mo.: University of Missouri Press, 1979.

————. "An Almost Unshakable Hold." *Commonweal*, 11 March 1983, 157–59. Review of *Selected Poems*.

Murray, Michele. "The New Style Is Rough and Hardly Pretty." *National Observer*, 31 May 1971, 19. Review of *Nightmares*.

Nelson, Cary. *Our Last First Poets: Vision and History in Contemporary American Poetry*. Urbana: University of Illinois Press, Illini Books, 1984.

Nelson, Howard. Review of *Mortal Acts, Mortal Words*. *Hawaii Review* 12 (Fall 1981):113–16.

———. "The Weight of Words, the Road from Here to There."*

Pack, Robert. "The Muse Is Always Gay." *Saturday Review*, 14 November 1964, 60–62. Review of *Flower Herding*.

Parris, Peggy. "Rags of His Body: Thoreau in Galway Kinnell's 'The Last River.'" *Thoreau Society Bulletin* 161 (Fall 1982):4–6.

Perloff, Marjorie. "Poetry Chronicle." *Contemporary Literature* 14 (Winter 1973):123–25. Review of *Nightmares*.

Peters, Robert. *The Great American Poetry Bake-Off*. Metuchen, N.J.: Scarecrow Press, 1979.

Pettingell, Phoebe. "Sane and Sacred Death." *New Leader*, 20 September 1982, 16–17. Review of *Selected Poems*.

———. "Songs of Science." *New Leader*, 16–30 December 1985, 19–20. Review of *The Past*.

Pollitt, Katha. "Two Poets: Run-on Lines." *Nation*, 5 July 1980, 26–27. Review of *Mortal Acts*.

Ransom, W. M. Review of *The Book of Nightmares*. *Chicago Review* 25 (1973):189–93.

Rich, Adrienne. "Poetry, Personality and Wholeness." *Field*, no. 7 (Fall 1972):11–18. Reprinted in *A Field Guide to Contemporary Poetry*, edited by Stuart Friebert and David Young, 224–31. New York: Longman, 1980.

Ricks, Christopher. "In the Direct Line of Whitman, the Indirect Line of Eliot." *New York Times Book Review*, 12 January 1975, 2. Review of *Avenue*.

Robertson, Nan. "An Upsurge in Readings by Writers." *New York Times*, 3 December 1984, 20.

Rodman, Selden. "A Quartet of Younger Singers." *New York Times Book Review*, 18 September 1960, 50. Review of *Kingdom*.

Rosenberg, Liz. "A Poet with the Flame of Greatness." *Philadelphia Inquirer*, 13 February 1983, R-06. Review of *Selected Poems*.

Rosenthal, M. L. "Under the Freeway, in the Hotel of Lost Light." *New York Times Book Review*, 24 November 1971, 77. Review of *Nightmares*.

Rosenthal, M. L., and Sally M. Gall. *The Modern Poetic Sequence*. New York: Oxford University Press, 1983.

Rowland, Stanley J., Jr. Review of *What a Kingdom It Was*. *Christian Century*, 22 February 1961, 248.

———. "Octet." *Christian Century*, 22 July 1964, 939. Review of *Flower Herding*.

Serchuk, Peter. "Confessions of Travelers and Pilgrims." *Sewanee Review* 89 (April 1981):271–78. Review of *Mortal Acts*.

Shaw, Robert B. "Utensils Down the Dream." *Nation,* 8 November 1980, 477. Review of *Mortal Acts.*

Shetley, Vernon. "Take But Degree Away." *Poetry* 137 (February 1981):298–99. Review of *Mortal Acts.*

Solotaroff, Ted. "Knowing and Not Knowing." In *Singular Voices,* edited by Stephen Berg, 137–42. New York: Avon, 1985.

Stitt, Peter. "Dimensions of Reality." *Georgia Review* 34 (Winter 1980):890–92. Review of *Mortal Acts.*

————. "Stages of Reality: The Mind/Body Problem in Contemporary Poetry." *Georgia Review* 37 (Spring 1983):205–8. Review of *Selected Poems.*

Taylor, Andrew. "The Poetry of Galway Kinnell." *Meanjin* 36 (July 1977):228–39.

Thompson, John. "An Alphabet of Poets." *New York Review of Books,* 1 August 1968, 33–36. Review of *Body Rags.*

Thompson, William E. "Synergy in the Poetry of Galway Kinnell." *Gypsy Scholar* 1, no. 2:52–69.

Thurley, Geoffrey. *The American Moment.* New York: St. Martin's Press, 1977.

Tillinghast, Richard. Review of *Selected Poems. Boston Review* 8 (February 1983):36.

Trodd, Kenith. "Hell for Mum." *New Statesman,* 1 September 1967, 261–62. Review of *Black Light.*

Unterecker, John. "Of Father, of Son: On 'Fergus Falling,' 'After Making Love We Hear Footsteps,' and 'Angling, a Day.'"*

Van Duyn, Mona. "The Poet as Novelist." *Poetry* 109 (February 1967):337–38. Review of *Black Light.*

————. "Vision, Celebration, and Testimony." *Poetry* 105 (January 1965):264–66. Review of *Flower Herding.*

Wagner, Linda. "Spindrift: The World in a Seashell." *Concerning Poetry* 8 (Spring 1975):5–9.

Weston, Susan B. "Galway Kinnell's *Walking Down the Stairs.*" *Iowa Review* 10, no. 1 (1979):95–98.

White, Marsha Peterson. "Trusting the Hours: On 'Wait.'"*

Whitehead, James. "Leaping Ghazals and Inside Jokes Concealed in Tropes." *Saturday Review,* 18 December 1971, 37. Review of *Nightmares.*

Williamson, Alan. *Introspection and Contemporary Poetry.* Cambridge, Mass.: Harvard University Press, 1984.

Wright, Anne. "Sitting on Top of the Sunlight."*

Yenser, Stephen. "Recent Poetry: Five Poets." *Yale Review* 70 (Autumn 1980):123–28. Review of *Mortal Acts.*

Young, David. "Galway Kinnell." In *The Longman Anthology of Contemporary American Poetry 1950–80,* edited by David Young and Stuart Friebert, 241–44. New York: Longman, 1983.

Young, Vernon. "Poetry Chronicle: Sappho to Smith." *Hudson Review* 27 (Winter 1974–75):598–600. Review of *Avenue.*

## POETS ON POETRY  Donald Hall, General Editor

Poets on Poetry collects critical books by contemporary poets, gathering together the articles, interviews, and book reviews by which they have articulated the poetics of a new generation.

**Goatfoot Milktongue Twinbird**
Donald Hall

**Walking Down the Stairs**
Galway Kinnell

**Writing the Australian Crawl**
William Stafford

**Trying to Explain**
Donald Davie

**To Make a Prairie**
Maxine Kumin

**Toward a New Poetry**
Diane Wakoski

**Talking All Morning**
Robert Bly

**Pot Shots at Poetry**
Robert Francis

**Open Between Us**
David Ignatow

**The Old Poetries and the New**
Richard Kostelanetz

**A Company of Poets**
Louis Simpson

**Don't Ask**
Philip Levine

**Living Off the Country**
John Haines

**Parti-Colored Blocks for a Quilt**
Marge Piercy

**The Weather for Poetry**
Donald Hall

**Collected Prose**
James Wright

**Old Snow Just Melting**
Marvin Bell

**Writing Like a Woman**
Alicia Ostriker

**A Ballet for the Ear**
John Logan

**Effluences from the Sacred Caves**
Hayden Carruth

**Collected Prose**
Robert Hayden

**Platonic Scripts**
Donald Justice

**A Local Habitation**
John Frederick Nims

**No Evil Star**
Anne Sexton

**The Uncertain Certainty**
Charles Simic

**You Must Revise Your Life**
William Stafford

**A Concert of Tenses**
Tess Gallagher